HAMILTON

THE
REVOLUTION

HAMILTON

THE
REVOLUTION

—

BEING THE COMPLETE LIBRETTO

of the

BROADWAY MUSICAL,

WITH A TRUE ACCOUNT OF

ITS CREATION,

AND CONCISE REMARKS ON

HIP-HOP, THE POWER *of* STORIES,
and THE NEW AMERICA

—

by LIN-MANUEL MIRANDA *and* JEREMY McCARTER

GRAND CENTRAL PUBLISHING | MELCHER MEDIA

GRAND CENTRAL PUBLISHING

Hachette Book Group
1290 Avenue of the Americas • New York, NY 10104
grandcentralpublishing.com • twitter.com/grandcentralpub

First Edition: April 2016

Grand Central Publishing is a division of Hachette Book Group, Inc.
The Grand Central Publishing name and logo is a trademark
of
HACHETTE BOOK GROUP, INC.

The publisher is not responsible for websites (or their content)
that are not owned by the publisher.

The Hachette Speakers Bureau provides a wide range of authors for speaking events.
To find out more, go to www.hachettespeakersbureau.com or call (866) 376-6591.

———

This book was produced
by
MELCHER MEDIA.

———

PCN: 2015957946
ISBNs: 978-1-4555-3974-1 (hardcover), 978-1-4555-6753-9 (ebook)

Printed in China

10 9 8 7 6 5 4 3 2 1

This book is dedicated to

SEBASTIAN *AND* SLOANE,

who will come of age with our young nation.

— L.M.M. & J.M.

TABLE *of* CONTENTS

ACT II

INTRODUCTION

OR PLAN OF THE WORK

ATE ON A HAZY NIGHT IN 2008, Lin-Manuel Miranda told me he wanted to write a hip-hop concept album about the life of Alexander Hamilton. For a second I thought we were sharing a drunken joke. We were probably drunk, but he wasn't joking.

We had bonded a year earlier over a shared love of hip-hop and theater, though that evening was the first time we were meeting. When Lin's first show, *In the Heights*, had its Off-Broadway premiere in 2007, I was the drama critic at *New York* magazine, where I had repeatedly argued for the enormous but neglected possibilities of hip-hop in the theater. ("Hip-hop can save the theater"; began one of those essays, "I am not kidding.") Rap, it seemed to me, wasn't like rock or jazz or any other kind of pop music: The lyrical density and storytelling ingenuity I heard on my headphones seemed closer to the verbal

energy of the great plays of the past than almost anything I saw onstage. This enthusiasm wasn't widely shared. "Don't hang back among the brutes," one of my senior colleagues advised me after reading one such essay, offering an erudite but demoralizing quotation from *A Streetcar Named Desire*.

After many disappointments and false alarms, *Heights* had made me sit up in my aisle seat: *Here's the guy*. Lin's show about immigrants in Upper Manhattan fused salsa, hip-hop, and traditional Broadway ballads to make something old and new, familiar and surprising. Best of all, he made the leap that virtually nobody else had made,

using hip-hop to tell a story that had nothing to do with hip-hop—using it as form, not content. Lin thought my review grasped what he had been trying to do. The show's publicist fixed us up. Hence the late-night drinks and the long talk about which of our favorite MCs should play Thomas Jefferson.

In the summer of 2011, after I'd left the magazine business and joined the artistic staff of the Public Theater, my boss, Oskar Eustis, asked me to propose some artists and projects. The first artist who came to mind was Lin, and the first project was his Hamilton idea. Lin and Oskar agreed to meet; Lin sent us demos; we went to Lin's concerts. Two years later, Oskar and Jeffrey Seller—the lead producer of what had by now ceased to be an album and had turned into a stage musical—agreed to develop the show at the Public. The opening night party there—another late, hazy conversation—is when Lin proposed that I write this book.

It tells the stories of two revolutions. There's the American Revolution of the 18th century, which flares to life in Lin's libretto, the complete text of which is published here, with his annotations. There's also the revolution of the show itself: a musical that changes the way that Broadway sounds, that alters who gets to tell the story of our founding, that lets us glimpse the new, more diverse America rushing our way. The fact that Lin wrote the show largely in sequence means that this book can trace the two revolutions in tandem. The story of the show's creation begins at the White House on May 12, 2009, when he performed the first song for the first time. It ends with opening night on Broadway, August 6, 2015, just after he completed the final scenes of the show.

The account of what happened in the intervening six years is based on what I saw in script meetings, set meetings, presentations, workshops, dressing-room hangouts, and at some excellent parties. It also draws on interviews with more than 40 people close to the show and on timely glimpses into their notebooks, inboxes, and Twitter feeds—Lin's in particular. All of the listening and watching and talking yielded three large surprises.

The first is that while *Hamilton* looks seamless and effortless and inevitable, it was none of those things. It could have been—and, at several points, almost was—a very different show. Thousands of choices and a fair bit of luck shaped the result. The same can be said of the 18th century revolution: inevitable in retrospect, but unprecedented and all but impossible to imagine ahead of time.

Second, the narrative of the show's creation amplifies the show's themes, like the one about how stories harden into history. A few hours before the opening night performance on Broadway, sitting in his dressing room, Lin and I realized that the tale we'd been telling about the show's origins—the already mythic account of how the idea came to him poolside in Mexico—wasn't entirely right. Lin got the idea from reading Ron Chernow's biography of Alexander Hamilton, and he read the book in Mexico—that much is true. But our late-night conversation about a hip-hop version of Hamilton's life happened a week *before* he started that trip. After much baffled poring over emails, we realized he must have read a few chapters as soon as he bought the book, and that that was enough for him to come up with the idea, and even with a title, which was already in place by the first night we met: *The Hamilton Mixtape*. If we can't keep our own histories straight, then the process of legacy formation that obsessed Hamilton and his contemporaries is even more fraught than we think, and the results more suspect.

Lastly, the secret history of *Hamilton*, if anything about the most heralded show in a generation can be regarded as secret, is that Lin's uniquely singlehanded achievement (as composer, lyricist, librettist, and star) required the artistry of dozens of very gifted people to be realized. A bunch of people from a bunch of backgrounds had to come together to make it work, and they did this so well that an even bigger bunch of people from yet more backgrounds flocked to see it. Alexander Hamilton would have admired the unifying power of the show based on his life, and would have felt vindication. Henry Cabot Lodge, who edited a collection of Hamilton's papers, wrote, "The dominant purpose of Hamilton's life was the creation of a national sentiment, and thereby the making of a great and powerful nation from the discordant elements furnished by thirteen jarring States." The widely acclaimed musical that draws from the breadth of America's culture and shows its audience what we share doesn't just dramatize Hamilton's revolution: It continues it.

> *"The widely acclaimed musical that draws from the breadth of America's culture and shows its audience WHAT WE SHARE DOESN'T JUST DRAMATIZE HAMILTON'S REVOLUTION: IT CONTINUES IT."*

The comparison might strike you as farfetched. What (you might be asking) can a Broadway musical possibly add to the legacy of a Founding Father—a giant of our national life, a war hero, a scholar, a statesman? What's one little play, or even one very big play, next to all that? But there is more than one way to change the world. To secure their freedom, the polyglot American colonists had to come together, and stick together, in the face of enormous adversity. To live in a new way, they first had to think and feel in a new way. It took guns and ships to win the American Revolution, but it also required pamphlets and speeches—and at least one play.

In the desolate winter of 1777-'78, General George Washington led the freezing, starving remnants of his army to Valley Forge. During that bleak encampment, when the prospects for American independence were as feeble as they would ever be, what did he do to strengthen his troops' resolve to defeat tyranny and secure their freedom? He arranged a production of his favorite play, Joseph Addison's *Cato*, which is about a man who gave his life to do just that. —JM

ACT I

———•———

"I am a stranger in this country. I have no
property here, no connexions."

—ALEXANDER HAMILTON, 1780

ON THE
ORIGINS *of* REVOLUTION,
BOTH NATIONAL & MUSICAL,

with Reference to

OPENING NUMBERS
& WHITE HOUSE RAPS

IN COULD SEE PRESIDENT OBAMA, but President Obama couldn't see Lin.

Standing at the back of the East Room, the 29-year-old actor/rapper/writer gazed at some of the most celebrated figures in American culture. James Earl Jones was there, and the musician Esperanza Spalding, and the novelist Michael Chabon. Some of them had performed in the program that night, "An Evening of Poetry, Music, and the Spoken Word," others were honored guests, sitting around the tables that filled the White House's ceremonial ballroom. It was May

12, 2009, one of the first cultural events of the Obama administration, and an early fulfillment of the new president's promise to celebrate America's artists.

"I'm actually working on a hip-hop album—a concept album—about THE LIFE OF SOMEONE WHO EMBODIES HIP-HOP . . . TREASURY SECRETARY ALEXANDER HAMILTON."

Lin had been asked to close the program. That was an honor, but it also meant that he had to wait all night to take the stage. Except for going on a tour a few years earlier, that night was his first experience of the White House—his first look at the East Room, where Abigail Adams had hung her laundry, where James Madison had held cabinet meetings, where Abraham Lincoln had lain in state.

At last he got his cue. He walked through the crowd, passed by the president, the first lady, and their daughters, and climbed to the stage.

"I'm thrilled the White House called me tonight," he said. He was also terrified.

The event's producers had asked him to perform a song from his musical *In the Heights*, which was still running on Broadway, and which reflected themes that the new administration wanted to celebrate: family, the importance of home, the vibrancy of the Latino community. Lin had a different idea. Instead of one of the well-tested songs that was drawing applause eight times a week, in a show that had won four Tony Awards, he wanted to try something new: a song that he had never performed in public, and hardly ever in private.

Lin gripped his mic and prepared the crowd for what they were about to hear. "I'm actually working on a hip-hop album—a concept album—about the life of someone who embodies hip-hop," he said. "Treasury Secretary Alexander Hamilton."

You can see what happened next on YouTube, where video of the performance has been viewed more than one million times. As Lin began to rap, the first lady took up his invitation to snap along. President Obama didn't snap: He watched, smiling. When the song ended, he was the first one on his feet.

The ovation owed a lot to the showbiz virtues on display: the vibrant writing, Lin's dynamic rapping, the skillful piano accompaniment from his friend Alex Lacamoire. But something else was in the air, something that would become clearer in the years to come. Sometimes the right person tells the right story at the right moment, and through a combination of luck and design, a creative expression gains new force. Spark, tinder, breeze.

That night, Lin reintroduced people to the poor kid from the Caribbean who made the country rich and strong, an immigrant who came here to build a life for himself and ended up helping to build the nation. He is the prototype for millions of men and women who followed him, and continue to arrive today. You can look up facts and figures that demonstrate the vast and growing importance of immigrants to our national life: that 13 percent of the population is foreign-born, which is near an all-time high; that one day soon, there will no longer be majority and minority races, only a vibrant mix of colors. Or you could just look around the East Room that night, and listen to the performance, and consider what made it possible.

> "*. . . 13 percent of the population is foreign-born, which is near an all-time high; that ONE DAY SOON, THERE WILL NO LONGER BE MAJORITY AND MINORITY RACES, ONLY A VIBRANT MIX OF COLORS.*"

In 1959, a young man came to the United States from Kenya, fell in love with a Kansas girl, and fathered a son who grew up to fulfill the American promise that any kid, however unlikely, can be president.

In 1973, another young man came here from Puerto Rico, learned English, started a family, and, one night in 2009, watched his son receive a standing ovation from the president of the United States.

In 1967, yet another young man came here with a fierce gift for rhythm, a knack for powerful sound systems, and countless warm memories of how music drew people together back home in Jamaica. He started throwing parties in his new Bronx neighborhood, creating a sound that would one day give Luis Miranda's son a way to perform for Barack Obama Sr.'s son at the White House. Like immigrants before and since, Clive Campbell reinvented himself when he came to America, which is why it is as DJ Kool Herc that a grateful nation honors him today as the first of the founding fathers of hip-hop.

ALEXANDER HAMILTON[1]

———◆———

Lights up on Aaron Burr & the company.[2]

AARON BURR: How does a bastard, orphan, son of a whore and a
Scotsman, dropped in the middle of a forgotten
Spot in the Caribbean by providence, impover-
ished, in squalor,
Grow up to be a hero and a scholar?

JOHN LAURENS: The ten-dollar Founding
Father without a father[3]
Got a lot farther by working a lot harder
By being a lot smarter
By being a self-starter
By fourteen, they placed him in charge of a
trading charter.

THOMAS JEFFERSON: And every day while
slaves were being slaughtered and carted
Away across the waves, he struggled and kept
his guard up.[4]
Inside, he was longing for something to be a
part of,
The brother was ready to beg, steal, borrow
or barter.

JAMES MADISON: Then a hurricane came,
and devastation reigned,
Our man saw his future drip, dripping down
the drain,
Put a pencil to his temple, connected it to
his brain,
And he wrote his first refrain, a testament to
his pain.[5]

BURR: Well the word got around, they said,
"This kid is insane, man"
Took up a collection just to send him to the
mainland.
"Get your education, don't forget from whence
you came, and
The world's gonna know your name. What's
your name, man?"

ALEXANDER HAMILTON: Alexander
Hamilton.[6]
My name is Alexander Hamilton.
And there's a million things I haven't
done
But just you wait, just you wait . . .

ELIZA HAMILTON: When he was
ten his father split, full of it,
debt-ridden,
Two years later, see Alex and his
mother bed-ridden,
Half-dead sittin' in their own sick,
The scent thick,

**FULL COMPANY (EXCEPT HAMIL-
TON) (WHISPERING):** And Alex got
better but his mother went quick.

GEORGE WASHINGTON: Moved
in with a cousin, the cousin
committed suicide.
Left him with nothin' but ruined
pride, something new inside,
a voice saying,
"You gotta fend for   **COMPANY:**
yourself."   "Alex,
He started retreatin'   You gotta
and readin' every   fend for
treatise on the shelf.   yourself."

BURR: There would have been nothin' left to do[7]
For someone less astute,
He woulda been dead or destitute
Without a cent or restitution,
Started workin'—clerkin' for his late mother's
    landlord,
Tradin' sugar cane and rum and all the things
    he can't afford

Scammin' for every book he can get his hands on	**COMPANY:** Scammin'
Plannin' for the future see him now as he stands on	Plannin' Ooohh . . .
The bow of a ship headed for a new land.	
In New York you can be a new man.	

COMPANY:	**HAMILTON:**
In New York you can be a new man—	Just you wait!
In New York you can be a new man—	Just you wait!

COMPANY: In New York you can be a
new man—

WOMEN: In New York—

MEN: New York—

HAMILTON: Just you wait!

COMPANY:
Alexander Hamilton

	COMPANY: Alexander Hamilton
We are waiting in the wings for you.	Waiting in the wings for you.

You could
Never back down.

You never learned to take your time!	You never learned to take your time!
Oh, Alexander Hamilton	Oh, Alexander Hamilton
When America sings for you	Alexander Hamilton
Will they know what you overcame?	America sings for you
Will they know you rewrote the game?	Will they know what you overcame,
The world will never be the same, oh.	Will they know you rewrote the game,[8]
	The world will never be the same, oh.

BURR:
The ship is in the
harbor now, see if you
can spot him.
Another immigrant,
comin' up from the
bottom.

His enemies destroyed his rep	**MEN:** Just you wait.
America forgot him.	**COMPANY:** Just you wait.

MULLIGAN, LAFAYETTE: We fought
with him.[9]

LAURENS: Me? I died for him.

WASHINGTON: Me? I trusted him.

ELIZA, ANGELICA, MARIA REYNOLDS:
Me? I loved him.

BURR: And me? I'm the damn fool that
shot him.

COMPANY: There's a million things I
    haven't done,
But just you wait!

BURR: What's your name, man?

COMPANY: Alexander Hamilton!

[6] From the very beginning, this was how I sang his name. It's an absurdly musical name.

[7] We double the tempo here because Hamilton's found his way out: He's going to double down on his education, and make himself undeniable. The image in my head is of Harry Potter finding out he's a wizard. Everything suddenly makes sense.

[8] Those who have seen my White House performance will note that these lyrics used to be "In our cowardice and our shame, we will try to destroy your name." Over the course of the show's development, we realized that the story would be told not only by his enemies but by his friends and loved ones. Friend or foe, they're in awe of him.

[9] Of course, the actors who play Mulligan and Lafayette fight with him as friends in Act One and fight *with* him as his enemies, Madison and Jefferson, in Act Two. It's also true of Laurens/Philip, who "dies for him" in both acts. I was very proud of myself for the double meanings in this section, hence this note.

IN WHICH

TOMMY KAIL

IS INTRODUCED

and

HIS ADVENTURES *with* LIN

SURVEYED

FOR TWO YEARS, NOBODY HEARD anything new about *The Hamilton Mixtape*, because there was nothing new to hear.

Lin got absorbed in other pursuits. With Tom Kitt and Amanda Green, he wrote the score to the stage adaptation of *Bring It On*, directed by his *Heights* choreographer Andy Blankenbuehler. He did Spanish translations of the Sharks' lyrics for a Broadway revival of *West Side Story*. He wrote a rap during the Tony Awards telecast that the host, Neil Patrick Harris, delivered to close the show. He married Vanessa Nadal, a scientist (now lawyer) he had met back in high school. (When they met again after college, they bonded over *Grand Theft Auto* and Jay Z. He calls her the smartest person he knows.) He turned 30, then he turned 31.

One constant in these years was Freestyle Love Supreme, an improv hip-hop group that must be seen to be believed. Taking suggestions from the audience—a word, a story—Lin and three or four other rappers create routines on the spot: inventive, hilarious, and often moving. In June 2011, the founders of Ars Nova, an adventurous theater on Manhattan's West Side, asked the group to take part in their annual benefit. Instead of doing their usual rap-by-the-seat-of-their-pants improvisation, the group's members decided to perform songs they had written ahead of time, for projects they'd been working on separately.

Lin wavered between two options. In what would turn out to be an exceptionally lucky break for musical theater, he decided against "Baked to a Crisp," his song about adolescent pot use, inspired by a Junot Diaz story. Instead he chose to premiere the second song from *The Hamilton Mixtape*.

"My Shot" is, in the lingo of musical theater, an "I want" song. These are the numbers that appear early in a show, when the hero steps downstage and tells the audience about the fierce desire that will propel the plot. Think of *West Side Story*, when Tony sings "Something's Coming," or *My Fair Lady*, when Eliza sings "Wouldn't It Be Loverly?" Without a song like this, you wouldn't get very far in a musical: A character needs to want something pretty badly to sing about it for two and a half hours. And you wouldn't get anywhere at all in hip-hop. For all of its variety of style and subject, rap is, at bottom, the music of ambition, the soundtrack of defiance, whether the force that must be defied is poverty, cops, racism, rival rappers, or all of the above. Think of Nas's "The World Is Yours," 2Pac's "Picture Me Rollin'," or Eminem's "8 Mile."

Like the rappers who performed those songs, Alexander Hamilton lived hard, wrote fast, and hustled his ass off. "For to confess my weakness, Ned," he wrote to a friend at age 14, "my Ambition is prevalent." This man was born to perform an "I want" song. Which is not to say that "My Shot" was easy to write. As Lin moved from project to project after his White House performance, the song lurked, semi-finished, in his notebooks. He wrote and rewrote, trying to capture Hamilton's sprawling ambition in beats and rhymes. It took more than a year to get it right. When the time came to perform it—when Lin stepped forward as Alexander Hamilton himself for the first time—he learned that writing it had been the easy part.

At Ars Nova that night, Lin took the stage with Chris "Shockwave" Sullivan, another member of Freestyle Love Supreme. Chris began to beatbox. Lin began to rhyme. He managed only a few bars before he got tangled in his words. He had gone way, way too fast.

Lin waved Chris off. He told the crowd that he needed to start over. They loved it, which didn't make him feel any less horrible.

Chris started beatboxing again. Lin took it from the top, but slower. He nailed it: three dense minutes of rapping about Hamilton's plans for his ascent, and the country's. The crowd loved it even more.

Out there in the dark, cheering with the rest, sat Tommy Kail. the director of Freestyle Love Supreme and *In the Heights*. Lin had been telling him about Hamilton for three years at that point, beginning with the g-chat mes-sages he had sent from Mexico while reading Chernow's book. Tommy could tell that "My Shot" left the audience hungry to hear more of Hamilton's story; he certainly felt that way himself.

———————

LIN AND TOMMY'S FIRST *HAMILTON* EXCHANGE: A GOOGLE CHAT TRANSCRIPT, 8/1/08

———————

11:21 AM **LIN:** Meeejico
TOMMY: Ho ho ho!
How's things?!
LIN: is hot and full of booze
11:22 AM **TOMMY:** believe it.
is the place nice?
having fun?
LIN: I don't want to come home.
I like reading performance reports drunk on miami vices
TOMMY: Ah.
Stay.
You outta stay . . .
LIN: If I marry V, I don't know how I can top this place.
we have a private roof pool
I've literally never seen the people who clean our rooms, they're ninjas
11:23 AM **TOMMY:** Wow. 2 Dreams came true.
LIN: How's STC doing?
TOMMY: I sent you a sesame email a few minutes ago—before you chatted me . . . just so you have it! I am not trying to have you work!
11:24 AM **LIN:** don't worry I won't
Lots of ping pong Mad Men season 1 backgammon and Hamilton reading
TOMMY: I went Tues.

———————

When the performance ended that night, everybody trooped upstairs to drink and mingle. Tommy found Lin, and told him that he should get serious about developing the Hamilton project. They both should.

What does a theater director have to do with a hip-hop album? Plenty. Tommy wasn't just the guy who staged Lin's material. He had become a close friend and something like an artistic confidant. Tommy had started a theater company after graduating from Wesleyan. A friend from school suggested that he consider producing a show by Lin, who had been a freshman when Tommy was a senior. (They'd never met, and their closest brush hadn't gone well: Tommy was annoyed that people kept showing up at the theater where he was working to take lights and other gear for the sake of some freshman's musical.) In June 2002, they had their first meeting to talk about the show that would become *In the Heights*. Somehow, in the course of that conversation, one of them started quoting a

grabbing the mic at family functions, imagining himself onstage whenever his parents could take him to a Broadway show, giving free rein to a creative impulse that was inexhaustible, omnidirectional, sometimes counterproductive. (He and some friends got arrested once for busking on a subway platform. A well-placed friend of his father got him out.)

Growing up in Alexandria, Virginia, Tommy cared a lot more about sports than theater. He excelled at soccer and baseball, and thrived in the middle of the action. But in high school, his understanding began to outpace his ability. "I could see what was supposed to happen on the field, but just wasn't able to do it," he says. "I realized my role needed to shift." That precocious insight, to recognize the talents of the people around him, and position himself accordingly, was a superb start to a directorial career. It put him in the ideal frame of mind to cross paths with a young writer who literally had more ideas than he knew what to do with.

At the Ars Nova reception, Tommy proposed that Lin start sending him Hamilton material on a regular basis. In fact, he thought they should aim to present a concert version of Hamilton songs in six months' time. The room could be small, the stakes could be low—that didn't matter. What mattered was setting a routine of writing and feedback. Lin agreed.

Then, a few days later, the profile became very high indeed: Lincoln Center invited Lin to perform in the American Songbook concert series. Tommy thought it could be an excellent way to try out Hamilton songs, even though it put pressure on Lin to write and polish enough material to suit such a prestigious occasion.

Still, how they could pass up this chance? Or, as Lin had put it for the first time that night at Ars Nova, how could they throw away their shot? Lincoln Center had offered them the Allen Room on the night of January 11—Alexander Hamilton's birthday.

> **"[HIP-HOP] IS, AT BOTTOM, THE MUSIC OF AMBITION, THE SOUNDTRACK OF DEFIANCE,** *whether the force that must be defied is poverty, cops, racism, rival rappers, or all of the above."*

legendary verse by Big Pun—"Dead in the middle of Little Italy little did we know / That we riddled some middlemen who didn't do diddly,"—and the other finished it.

"We cocked our heads at each other in recognition," Tommy recalls. "It was like two dogs in the park going, 'Oh, you live in this neighborhood, too?'"

The shared love of theater and hip-hop led them to collaborate on *Heights*, and that collaboration revealed something far more important: The talents of each complemented the talents of the other. Growing up in New York, Lin had developed an instinct for the spotlight:

ABOVE:
Rehearsal for the national tour of In the Heights.

AARON BURR, SIR

The lights change. Aaron Burr[1] emerges. He is approached by Hamilton.

COMPANY *(EXCEPT HAMILTON)*: Seventeen seventy-six. New York City.

HAMILTON: Pardon me. Are you Aaron Burr, sir?

BURR: That depends. Who's asking?

HAMILTON: Oh, well, sure, sir.
I'm Alexander Hamilton. I'm at your service, sir.
I have been looking for you.[2]

BURR: I'm getting nervous.

HAMILTON: Sir . . .
I heard your name at Princeton. I was seeking an accelerated course of study when I got sort of out of sorts with a buddy of yours. I may have punched him. It's a blur, sir. He handles the financials?

BURR: You punched the bursar.[3]

HAMILTON: Yes!
I wanted to do what you did.
Graduate in two, then join the revolution. He looked at me like I was stupid, I'm not stupid.
So how'd you do it? How'd you graduate so fast?

BURR: It was my parents' dying wish before they passed.

HAMILTON: You're an orphan?
Of course! I'm an orphan.
God, I wish there was a war!

Then we could prove that we're worth more than anyone bargained for . . .

BURR: Can I buy you a drink?

HAMILTON: That would be nice.

BURR: While we're talking, let me offer you some free advice.

They enter Fraunces Tavern, where a rap circle comprised of Laurens, Lafayette & Mulligan is underway.[4]

[1] I know every word that rhymes with Burr. It's a long list. I tried to use all of them in this show. The "Rhymes with Hamilton" list is nonexistent, so.

[2] This is, of course, a fictional first meeting between Hamilton and Burr, and I centered it around a rather remarkable fact: Burr graduated from college *crazy* young and fast. What he's *not* telling Hamilton: His father was the president of the college; privilege plays a role. But Hamilton doesn't know that: What he knows is that Burr graduated fast, and Hamilton has no money and no time to waste.

[3] Chernow blanched a bit at this historical leap—Hamilton wasn't needlessly violent—but the rhyme was too good to pass up.

[4] Fraunces Tavern, of course, still exists. They've got great Hot Toddies in the winter.

[5] This whole section is basically Harry Potter meeting Draco Malfoy before meeting his real friends. Just Hamilton's luck to meet his temperamental opposite.

[6] An homage to the amazing subway breakdancers of NYC circa present day, who start their shows this way.

BURR: Talk less. [5]

HAMILTON: What?

BURR: Smile more.

HAMILTON: Ha.

BURR: Don't let them know what you're against or what you're for.

HAMILTON: You can't be serious.

BURR: You wanna get ahead?

HAMILTON: Yes.

BURR: Fools who run their mouths off wind up dead.

LAURENS: Yo yo yo yo yo! What time is it?

LAURENS, LAFAYETTE, MULLIGAN: Show time! [6]

BURR: . . . like I said . . .

LAURENS: Show time! Show time! Yo!
I'm John Laurens in the place to be![7]
Two pints o' Sam Adams, but I'm workin' on
    three, uh!
Those redcoats don't want it with me!
Cuz I will pop chick-a pop these cops 'til
    I'm free!

LAFAYETTE: Oui oui, mon ami, je m'appelle
    Lafayette!
The Lancelot of the revolutionary set![8]
I came from afar just to say "Bonsoir!"
Tell the King, "Casse toi!" Who's the best?
    C'est moi!

MULLIGAN: Brrrah brraaah! I am Hercules
    Mulligan,
Up in it, lovin' it, yes I heard ya mother said
    "come again?"
Lock up ya daughters and horses, of course
It's hard to have intercourse over four sets
    of corsets . . .[9]

LAURENS: No more sex, pour me another
    brew, son!
 Let's raise a couple more . . .

LAURENS, LAFAYETTE, MULLIGAN:
To the revolution!

LAURENS: Well, if it ain't the prodigy of
Princeton college!

MULLIGAN: Aaron Burr!

LAURENS: Give us a verse, drop some knowledge!

BURR: Good luck with that: You're takin' a stand.
You spit. I'm 'a sit. We'll see where we land.

LAFAYETTE, MULLIGAN: Boooo!

LAURENS: Burr, the revolution's imminent.
What do you stall for?

HAMILTON: If you stand for nothing, Burr,
what'll you fall for?[10]

[7] This is a love letter to old school hip-hop. "I'm ___ in the place to be" is so old-school, it was a staple of the first raps I ever wrote as a kid.

[8] "I think Lafayette wants to rap in French now. I have to go learn some French. Damnit, Lafayette." —me, tweeting in 2013

[9] Listen, Mulligan didn't grow up to be a statesman like Lafayette or Hamilton. But his name is just the best rapper moniker I ever heard in my life. So he gets the most fun punchlines. I don't know what his thing is with horses, but I thought it was funny.

[10] "Those who stand for nothing fall for anything." This is a paraphrase of a line often misattributed to Alexander Hamilton. It was said by a later Hamilton in the 20th century. But the sentiment is so perfect for this moment, and so well underscores the difference between Hamilton & Burr, I flipped it for the occasion.

MY SHOT

LAURENS: MULLIGAN: LAFAYETTE:
Ooh, Ooh, Ooh,
Who are you?

Who are you?

Who are you?

MULLIGAN, LAFAYETTE, LAURENS: Ooh, who is this kid? What's he gonna do?

HAMILTON: I am not throwing away my shot!
I am not throwing away my shot!
Hey yo, I'm just like my country,
I'm young, scrappy and hungry,
And I'm not throwing away my shot!
I'm 'a get a scholarship to King's College
I prob'ly shouldn't brag, but dag, I amaze and astonish.
The problem is I got a lot of brains but no polish
I gotta holler just to be heard.[1]
With every word, I drop knowledge!
I'm a diamond in the rough, a shiny piece of coal
Tryin' to reach my goal. My power of speech: unimpeachable.
Only nineteen but my mind is older.[2]
These New York City streets get colder, I shoulder
Ev'ry burden, ev'ry disadvantage
I have learned to manage, I don't have a gun to brandish.
I walk these streets famished.[3]
The plan is to fan this spark into a flame
But damn, it's getting dark, so let me spell out the name,
I am the—

HAMILTON, LAFAYETTE, MULLIGAN, LAURENS: A-L-E-X-A-N-D-E-R—we are— meant to be . . .[4]

HAMILTON: A colony that runs independently.
Meanwhile, Britain keeps shittin' on us endlessly.
Essentially, they tax us relentlessly,
Then King George turns around, runs a spending spree.[5]
He ain't ever gonna set his descendants free,
So there will be a revolution in this century.
Enter me!

LAFAYETTE, MULLIGAN, LAURENS:
(He says in parentheses.)[6]

HAMILTON: Don't be shocked when your hist'ry book mentions me.
I will lay down my life if it sets us free.
Eventually, you'll see my ascendancy,

HAMILTON:
And I am not throwing away my shot. LAURENS:
My shot!
I am not throwing away my shot. My shot!
Hey yo, I'm just like my country,
I'm young, scrappy and hungry

And I'm not throwing away my shot. And I'm not throwing away my shot.

HAMILTON, MULLIGAN, LAURENS, LAFAYETTE: I am not throwing away my shot.
I am not throwing away my shot.
Hey yo, I'm just like my country,
I'm young, scrappy and hungry
And I'm not throwing away my shot.

They drink.

[1] And Tupac responds, "Holla if ya hear me."

[2] Mobb Deep's greatest lyric, revisited here.

[3] This is the Big Pun effect: stacking internal rhymes into lyrics so densely and making them feel conversational.

[4] This cadence is used by The Notorious B.I.G. in "Going Back To Cali" when spelling his own name: I'm calling on all the East Coast rap gods in this verse.

[5] Some have pointed out that I also rhymed "spending spree" in *In The Heights*. Totally accidental, but true. What is it with me and spending sprees?

[6] Stage direction humor.

HAMILTON, MULLIGAN, LAURENS, LAFAYETTE: It's time to take a shot!

LAFAYETTE: I dream of life without a monarchy.[7]
The unrest in France will lead to 'onarchy?
'Onarchy? How you say, how you say, "anarchy?"
When I fight, I make the other side panicky.
With my—

HAMILTON, LAURENS, LAFAYETTE, MULLIGAN: Shot!

MULLIGAN: Yo, I'm a tailor's apprentice,
And I got y'all knuckleheads in loco parentis.[8]
I'm joining the rebellion cuz I know it's my chance
To socially advance, instead of sewin' some pants!
I'm gonna take a—

HAMILTON, LAURENS, LAFAYETTE, MULLIGAN: Shot!

LAURENS: But we'll never be truly free
Until those in bondage have the same rights
    as you and me.
You and I. Do or die. Wait till I sally in
On a stallion with the first black battalion.
Have another—

HAMILTON, LAURENS, LAFAYETTE, MULLIGAN: Shot!

BURR: Geniuses, lower your voices.
You keep out of trouble and you double
    your choices.
I'm with you, but the situation is fraught.
You've got to be carefully taught:[9]
If you talk, you're gonna get shot!

HAMILTON: Burr, check what we got.[10]
Mr. Lafayette, hard rock like Lancelot,
I think your pants look hot,
Laurens, I like you a lot
Let's hatch a plot blacker than the kettle callin'
    the pot . . .
What are the odds the gods would put us all in
    one spot,

Poppin' a squat on conventional wisdom,
    like it or not,
A bunch of revolutionary manumission
    abolitionists?
Give me a position, show me where the
    ammunition is!
Oh, am I talkin' too loud?
Sometimes I get overexcited, shoot off at
    the mouth.
I never had a group of friends before,
I promise that I'll make y'all proud.

LAURENS: Let's get this guy in front of
a crowd.

HAMILTON, LAURENS, LAFAYETTE, MULLIGAN, ENSEMBLE: I am not throwing
    away my shot.
I am not throwing away my shot.
Hey yo, I'm just like my country,
I'm young, scrappy and hungry
And I'm not throwing away my shot.

I am not throwing away my shot.
I am not throwing away my shot.
Hey yo, I'm just like my country,
I'm young, scrappy and hungry.
And I'm not throwing away my shot.

LAURENS:	**HAMILTON, LAFAYETTE, MULLIGAN:**
Ev'rybody sing:	
Whoa, whoa, whoa	Whoa! Whoa! Whoa!
Hey!	
Whoa!	Whoa!
Wooh!!	
Whoa!	Whoa!
Ay, let 'em hear ya!	
Let's go!	Yea!
	COMPANY:
	Whoa! Whoa! Whoa!
I said shout it to the rooftops!	Whoa!
Said to the rooftops!	Whoa!
Come on!	Yea!
Come on, let's go!	

[7] I love writing for Lafayette because it allows me to indulge something I have found to be true in my own life: Those for whom English is a second language are capable of fantastic, outside-the-box thinking with our language.

[8] Latin humor.

[9] This is a shout-out to "You've Got To Be Carefully Taught" from *South Pacific*, a Rodgers and Hammerstein classic about racism. As Laurens and the boys rap about equality, Burr comes in with some cold reality.

[10] And here's Hamilton, synthesizing everything his friends have said and going further. This song took *years* to write, and here's why: We have to systematically prove that Hamilton is the most fearsome intellect in the room, not just by saying so, but by demonstrating it.

[11] This lyric used to be Laurens yelling, "Don't this sh*t make my people wanna rise up?" A nod to Busta Rhymes's refrain in "Pass The Courvoisier." Once we learned that clearing this sample was fiscally prohibitive, I built the new lyric around Anthony Ramos's voice. He's a crooner at heart, and his bravado is unmatched. I'm really glad I got to suit it to his strengths.

[12] This verse took the better part of a year to write. It's the Rosetta Stone of Hamilton's brain, and the first line of it is the most autobiographical thing I've ever written. It's what I feel I have most in common with Hamilton: The ticking clock of mortality is loud in both our ears, and it sets us to work. In this verse he goes from nihilism to a list of what needs to be done to hope towards tomorrow, and he takes himself there through one uninterrupted train of thought.

LAURENS: Rise up!
When you're living on your knees,
You rise up. [11]
Tell your brother that he's gotta rise up.
Tell your sister that she's gotta rise up.

LAURENS AND ENSEMBLE:
When are these colonies gonna
Rise up?
When are these   Whoa! Whoa! Whoa!
colonies gonna rise up
When are these   Whoa!
colonies gonna rise up
When are these colonies   Whoa!
gonna rise up?

Rise up!   Rise up!

Hamilton alone.

HAMILTON: I imagine death so much it feels
     more like a memory [12]
When's it gonna get me?
In my sleep? Seven feet ahead of me?
If I see it comin' do I run or do I let it be?
Is it like a beat without a melody?
See, I never thought I'd live past twenty
Where I come from some get half as many.
Ask anybody why we livin' fast and we
Laugh, reach for a flask,
We have to make this moment last, that's plenty.

Hamilton joins the group, and we see that he is now speaking to a larger crowd.

HAMILTON: Scratch that,
This is not a moment, it's the movement
Where all the hungriest brothers with something
to prove went.
Foes oppose us, we take an honest stand,
We roll like Moses, claimin' our promised land.
And?[13] If we win our independence?
'Zat a guarantee of freedom for our
descendants?
Or will the blood we shed begin an
endless

Cycle of vengeance and death with no
defendants?
I know the action in the street is excitin',
But Jesus, between all the bleedin' 'n fightin' I've
been readin' 'n writin'.[14]
We need to handle our financial situation.
Are we a nation of states? What's the state of our
nation?
I'm past patiently waitin'. I'm passionately
smashin' every expectation,
Every action's an act of creation!
I'm laughin' in the face of casualties and sorrow,
For the first time, I'm thinkin' past tomorrow.

[13] Continuing the rhyme at the top of the next line—this is what Big Pun does *so* well. It knits all his rhymes together. I play with it a lot in this show, and this is my favorite one.

[14] And this is one of the Big Pun-est lines in the show—multiple five-syllable rhymes inside the line.

HAMILTON AND COMPANY: And I am not
    throwing away my shot
I am not throwing away my shot.
Hey yo, I'm just like my country,
I'm young, scrappy and hungry
And I'm not throwing away my shot.

**HAMILTON,
LAURENS, LAFAY-
ETTE, MULLIGAN:**   **ENSEMBLE:**
We're gonna rise up!   Not throwin' away
Time to take a shot!   My shot.

We're gonna rise up!   Not throwin' away
Time to take a shot!   My shot.
We're gonna   We're gonna
                          Rise up!
                          Rise up!

HAMILTON:
It's time to take a shot! [15]
                          Rise up!
**HAMILTON,
LAFAYETTE,
MULLIGAN,
LAURENS:**   Rise up!
It's time to take a shot!
                          Rise up!
Take a shot!   Rise up!
Shot!   Ri-ri-ri
Shot!
A-yo, it's
Time to take a shot!   Time to take a shot!
Time to take a shot!   Time to take a shot!
And I am—   And I am—

**HAMILTON, LAFAYETTE, MULLIGAN,
LAURENS:** Not throwin' away my—

COMPANY: Not throwin' away my shot!

*End of song. Hamilton, Laurens, Mulligan
& Lafayette are back in the tavern, after
several drinks.*

[15] So how do you build
an ending like this?
*Endless conversations with
Tommy, Alex Lacamoire,
and Andy Blankenbuehler.*
Seriously, so many
versions of different
counterpoints to build
to just the right finish.
In these meetings,
I find I'm more the
editor than the
writer—Alex will have
50 musical ideas, Andy
will have 50 staging
ideas, and Tommy and
I will sift them in the
middle. It's like this for
most of the buttons in
the show.

GIVING THE HISTORY OF

RON CHERNOW

Along with Remarks on

WHO MAY PLAY

A FOUNDING FATHER

WHAT DID HAMILTON DO WITH HIS hands? Did he smoke a pipe?

These were excellent questions, and Ron Chernow wished that he knew how to answer them. Soon after Lin returned from his vacation to Mexico (having folded down many page-corners in Chernow's book, having called out many ideas to Vanessa as they popped into his brain), he reached out to the author of the biography that had seized his imagination. A friend's father supplied Ron's email address, and Lin invited him to see *In the Heights*.

Onstage, after the show, on the spot, Lin asked him to be the historical consultant for the story he planned to tell.

"You mean you want me to tell you when there are errors?" asked Ron.

"I want historians to take this seriously."

"Yes," said Lin. "I want historians to take this seriously." And, to Ron's surprise, he meant it.

Even as Lin worked on other projects over the next few years, he kept checking in with Ron, asking questions. Would George Washington have seen Alexander Hamilton as a younger version of himself? (*Plausible*, Ron thought.) Other times, Lin tried to accrue what Ron called "the small change of everyday life," the quotidian human details that give a character texture and dimension. Ron loves including such details in his books, which is why they are both popular and esteemed: He won a Pulitzer Prize for a biography of Washington that followed his book on Hamilton. Unfortunately, those details are hard to find about people who lived in the 18th century.

"There's not a lot on the cutting room floor," Ron says. "Everything I got is in the book."

He told Lin that much of the detail that Lin wanted for the show—about smoking and a hundred other things—he would have to invent for himself.

More than mere fact-checking, the eminent historian, who was then 59 years old, gave Lin affirmation. "This was a risky and I'm sure scary thing to do, and I always thought it was important to provide encouragement," Ron says.

Ask Lin about Ron's value to the project, and "encouragement" is the first thing he mentions. Both of them recall a crucial day when Lin came to Ron's house in Brooklyn Heights to try out part of a song and make sure he was on the right track. As it happens, they have different memories of which song Lin performed—a discrepancy that delights him.

"That's this whole show," says Lin. "Ron tells you a story and he's the star of the story. I tell you a story and I'm the star of the story. History is entirely created by the person who tells the story."

Ron had been helping Lin to accrue this historical "small change" for a few years when he received an invitation to come hear actors sing through part of Act One. He walked into a rehearsal studio in the Garment District and was, by his own admission, "shocked" by what he saw. The men who were going to sing the roles of Washington, Hamilton, and the other Founding Fathers were black and Latino. Not being a rap listener, Ron hadn't given much thought to the fact that the people best able to perform the songs that Lin had been writing might look nothing like their historical counterparts.

Lin and Tommy saw no difficulty in making this imaginative leap. In fact, they raised it to a principle. As Tommy would state it again and again in the years that followed: "This is a story about America then, told by America now."

Within five minutes, Ron was carried away by what he heard. He became what he calls a "militant" defender of the idea that actors of any race could play the Founding

Fathers. After the reading ended, he sat on folding chairs with Lin, Tommy, and Jeffrey Seller, the show's lead producer, and gave a more conventional note, the kind of expert scrutiny that Lin had asked him to provide. The chorus tells the audience that the early songs are set in 1776, but, Ron pointed out, "The Story of Tonight" features two men Hamilton wouldn't meet until years later. Ron had noticed that unlike most playwrights and screenwriters, Lin "starts with the presumption that he'll use the historical facts and see if they work." He figured the note would stick.

This time, though, Lin defended the liberties he had taken. He explained that he needed a quartet of characters—Hamilton and three friends—that the audience could follow through Act One.

"Ron tells you a story and he's the star of the story. I tell you a story and I'm the star of the story. HISTORY IS ENTIRELY CREATED BY THE PERSON WHO TELLS THE STORY."

The astoundingly named Irish tailor Hercules Mulligan had to be one of them. So did John Laurens, Hamilton's closest friend and fellow opponent of slavery. And when the decisive battles of the revolution came, the Marquis de Lafayette would step to the fore. For the sake of dramatic coherence, he needed to roll these guys out early, and roll them out all at once.

Ron saw Lin's point, and withdrew the objection. He was coming to admire Lin's skill for compression just as much as his loyalty to the facts.

Lin, for his part, isn't sure how principled a stand for poetic license he was really making that day.

"Some of this is really smart dramaturgical work and some of this is like, I just forgot they hadn't met yet."

The
STORY OF TONIGHT

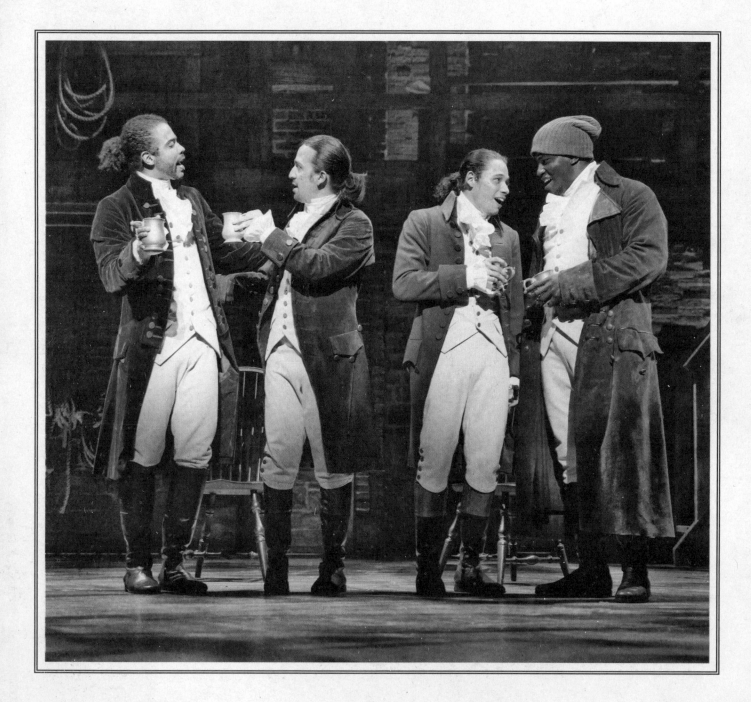

HAMILTON: I may not live to see our glory![2]

LAFAYETTE, MULLIGAN, LAURENS: I may not live to see our glory!

HAMILTON: But I will gladly join the fight!

LAFAYETTE, MULLIGAN, LAURENS: But I will gladly join the fight!

HAMILTON: And when our children tell our story . . .

LAFAYETTE, MULLIGAN, LAURENS: And when our children tell our story . . .

HAMILTON: They'll tell the story of tonight.

MULLIGAN: Let's have another round tonight.

LAFAYETTE: Let's have another round tonight.

HAMILTON: Let's have another round tonight.

LAURENS: Raise a glass to freedom,
Something they can never take away,
      no matter what they tell you.[3]
Raise a glass to the four of us.

LAURENS, MULLIGAN: Tomorrow there'll be more of us.

MULLIGAN, LAFAYETTE, LAURENS: Telling the story of tonight.

HAMILTON: They'll tell the story of tonight.

LAURENS, MULLIGAN, LAFAYETTE: Raise a glass to freedom,
Something they can never take away.

HAMILTON: No matter what they tell you.

MULLIGAN, LAFAYETTE: Let's have another round tonight.

LAURENS: Raise a glass to the four of us.

HAMILTON, LAURENS, MULLIGAN, LAFAYETTE: Tomorrow there'll be more of us.

HAMILTON, LAURENS: Telling the story of tonight.

MULLIGAN, LAFAYETTE: Let's have another round tonight.

HAMILTON, LAURENS, ENSEMBLE:
They'll tell the story of tonight.

MULLIGAN, LAFAYETTE, ENSEMBLE:
Raise a glass to freedom.

They'll tell the story of tonight.

Raise a glass to freedom.

They'll tell the story of tonight.

They'll tell the story of—

ENSEMBLE: Tonight.[4]

Scene shift. A city square. Burr enters.

[1] I wrote this melody when I was 16 years old. I had a doo-wop group with four other friends, and I'd written this song called "I've Got a Bridge to Sell You." When it came time to write this number for the show, that melody did everything I wanted this scene to do: It conveyed a yearning and innocence I felt in finding a group of friends to sing with me.

[2] Yes, these lyrics are foreshadowing, but they're no more dire than most pub drinking songs.

[3] I've got a bridge to sell you . . . (see note at top of scene.)

[4] Tommy and I discussed using this song as a theme that would keep coming back as we checked in with these young men. We took our cue from Sondheim's *Merrily We Roll Along*, where the core trio of friends repeatedly sings, "Here's to us. Who's like us? Damn few." This theme will mutate as time wears on and people fall away, but here it is in its first full blush.

THE PEN
&
THE PAD I

From Lin's Notebooks

———

TOP LEFT:
This is my outline of Act One. Everything in brackets refers to a song that does not yet exist, but can connect/ fill in what's there. "Ladies Musical Moment" became "The Schuyler Sisters." "Hamiltonia" was an idea for an actual moment when Hamilton came home to New York and was greeted as a hero. It was a nice historical moment, but we needed to keep moving.

TOP RIGHT:
These are my character notes for the Sons Of Liberty for the second verse of "My Shot."

BOTTOM:
I wrote this song on my honeymoon, without a piano, and it took a while for the melody to settle. This version is close to the final form. Even though the lyrics are different, you can see I've got my head around the existing melody.

Alexander Hamilton "My New Man"
-Boys-- my shot suite
My Shot [Burr-Hamilton song]
My shot act no [Ladies Musical Moment]
Heed Not The Rabble
Right Hand Man
-You'll Be Back

Tomcat
Helpless
Satisfied [Lee -Suite]
[Burr] Duel! Fight
[Ham-Wash Duel]
That wald be enough [Yorktown]
Dear Theodosia
[Hamiltonia]

Lafayette -- I came from France
to do something incredible
-freedom liberty equality
- came to fight
Laurens - Equality for all
not just whites

Mulligan -- I came to move up
apprenticed to a tailor
military glory own my own shop

Hamilton - synthesizes
- all argument
- Struggle for Universal equality
- work our way up.

Since we're now
miles apart
You may long to make a brand new start
well that would do
that's all u say
so I am sending an unstoppable army
to remind you where you belong

Dadadadadadaa

You'll be back

You say
the price of my love's not a price
that you're willing to pay
You cry
in your tea which you hurl in the sea
when you see me go by, why so sad?
Remember we made an arrangement
when you went away and now you're mad
Remember, despite our estrangement
I'm your man
You'll be back
Time will tell
You'll remember you were treated well
In my strong embrace
I'll you kill your friends you add your place
You may stray but never tell from grace

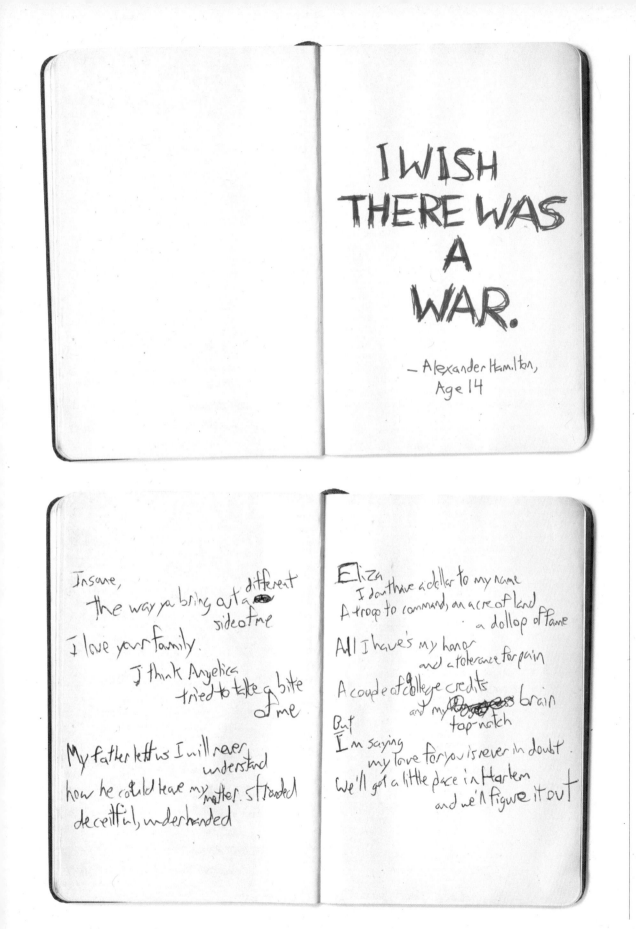

I WISH THERE WAS A WAR.

— Alexander Hamilton, Age 14

Insane,
   the way ya bring out a different
        side of me
I love your family.
      I think Angelica
        tried to take a bite
           of me

My father left us I will never
        understand
how he could leave my mother, stranded
deceitful, underhanded

Eliza
  I don't have a dollar to my name
A troop to command, an acre of land
         a dollop of fame
All I have's my honor
     and a tolerance for pain
A couple of college credits
    and my ~~~~ brain
       top-notch
But
I'm saying
   my love for you is never in doubt.
We'll get a little place in Harlem
     and we'll figure it out

BOTTOM:
Early draft of Hamilton's "Helpless" rap. Peggy hadn't arrived yet, but the pieces are all there and waiting to gel.

IV

IN WHICH THE CHARACTER OF

NEW YORK CITY

IS CONSIDERED IN ITS MUSICAL & SCENIC ASPECTS

BY REFERENCE TO DAVID KORINS

and a Curious Episode of

HISTORICAL VERTIGO

THE FOUNDERS TENDED TO BE COUNTRY boys. Washington, Jefferson, Adams, and many other key figures of the revolution hailed from, and frequently returned to, estates and farms out of town. But like most of us living in America today, Alexander Hamilton called a city home. New York City, to be exact.

Just as Hamilton is the prototype of the immigrant striver (hard-working, ambitious, desperate to prove himself), he is also the model New Yorker: opinionated, hyperverbal, always on the make. It's no wonder that John Adams, who despised Hamilton, also despised the town and its citizens: "They talk very loud, very fast, and all together," he complained before retreating to Massachusetts. Nor is it a surprise that hip-hop, which took root in Hamilton's city like an orchid in a swamp, suits his life so well.

Before a performance of *Hamilton* reaches its 15-minute mark, Lin has planted the show squarely in New York. "The Schuyler Sisters," his R&B ode to his hometown, arrived relatively late in the show's development. Tommy liked the songs that Lin had written for Eliza and Angelica Schuyler, and wondered if there might be a way to introduce them sooner. The result is what Lin calls "a New York anthem." It evokes the mixed blessings of living here: There are rich people and poor people, work is on everybody's minds, sex is in the air, and violence is a constant possibility—in this case, a looming war with Britain. (Also—an absolute necessity for a New York

anthem—it offers a fanfare of triumphalism. With the bluntness of a lifelong Manhattanite, Lin comes right out and calls it "the greatest city in the world.")

In other words, Lin wrote a song about Hamilton's New York that reveals it to be largely the same as our own New York. That poses a special challenge for a production of the show. Instead of helping theatergoers to make sense of a faraway historical land, they have to recognize the city that's right outside the door. By the time Lin wrote this song, *Hamilton* was on its way to its world premiere production. It meant that Tommy had already found the collaborator who would work with him the most to crack this puzzle.

David Korins has a long string of Broadway credits, a handful of collaborations with the *Hamilton* creative team, and the experience of being Kanye West's creative director, but he still prepared like crazy for his interview with Tommy: He listened to Lin's demos obsessively, sketched ideas furiously, and even did a scene breakdown, something he normally does *after* he gets a job. He felt a fierce connection to the material: its ambition, its drive.

"We all have something to prove here," Korins told Tommy in his interview. "I am not going to throw away my shot." He got the job.

Listening to all of Lin's demos—his many, many demos—told Korins that he couldn't possibly depict all of the show's settings realistically. He would have to

suggest, evoke, imply. Plus, the action had to move almost instantly from one scene to the next. He had an early hunch that images of construction might help to unlock the visual world of the show. After all, the show was about builders—the men and women who created the nation. Korins imagined the Capitol dome being split in half, its beams and rafters exposed.

Research revealed that there was something special about carpenters in New York and other coastal towns in Alexander Hamilton's era: Many of them were shipbuilders. Oskar Eustis, the artistic director of the Public Theater, told Korins and Tommy that his house in Brooklyn had been built by 19th-century laborers using techniques they had learned on the docks. Korins began to imagine immi-

grants coming to the New World, landing on unfamiliar shores, and building cities out of their ships.

How do you evoke then and now? How can scenery be both general and specific? How can a set be substantial yet nimble? Korins struck these balances by creating an onstage world that might have looked familiar to those early American workers. There's lots of wood and masonry, all sorts of joists and beams. Part of it looks like scaffolding, part like the hull of a ship. There are burn marks on the wooden beams to mimic the effect of sawtooth friction. Coiled ropes are everywhere, along with details drawn from the corners of modern-day New York that remain truest to Hamilton's time. The set's chandeliers are inspired by the fixtures at Fraunces

Tavern, in Lower Manhattan, where George Washington bid farewell to his officers. Korins visited Morris-Jumel Mansion, which served as one of Washington's headquarters during the war, and remains miraculously preserved in what Lin calls "this weird Brigadoon in the middle of Washington Heights."

"The Schuyler Sisters," in its writing and its staging, lets us glimpse a nation being built. In a town square, as people disseminate ideas—pamphlets, flyers, arguments—we watch a city going up around them. Members of the ensemble sling planks and boards around Korins's set while they scope the Schuyler ladies, who scope them right back. There's motion, energy, and lots of people-watching—all facilitated by the balcony that

"It looked like New York City—not in 1776 or in 2015, but some idealized version of itself, independent of time, where PEOPLE OF MANY RACES AND BACKGROUNDS DANCE TOGETHER."

rings three sides of the stage. Squint your eyes just right, and thanks to all the period touches, you could be looking at a Brooklyn restaurant today.

Zigzagging back and forth through history this way can make you dizzy—you can get vertigo from moving through time as well as space—but it's a lovely disorientation. One day, as the show prepared for Broadway, the cast assembled onstage to sing "The Schuyler Sisters." Because they were only doing a soundcheck, it didn't matter how they moved, or if they moved at all, so everybody stood around. But as Lin's song took hold, they began to dance—separately or together, however they pleased. All at once, Korins's set stopped looking like the scenery of a Broadway musical and started to look like a club. It looked like *New York City*—not in 1776 or in 2015, but some idealized version of itself, independent of time, where people of many races and backgrounds dance together.

The actors didn't have an audience that day and didn't need one: They had been through a lot of ups and downs by that point. Twenty young New Yorkers sang Lin's words to—and for—each other: "Look around, look around, how lucky we are to be alive right now."

The
SCHUYLER SISTERS[1]

———◆———

BURR: There's nothing rich folks love more
Than going downtown and slummin' it with the poor.
They pull up in their carriages and gawk
At the students in The Common
Just to watch them talk.[2]
Take Philip Schuyler: The man is loaded.
Uh-oh, but little does he know that
His daughters: Peggy, Angelica, Eliza
Sneak into the city just to watch all the guys at—

The Schuyler Sisters—Angelica,
Eliza & Peggy—enter.

COMPANY: Work, work!

ANGELICA: Angelica!

COMPANY:
Work, work!

ELIZA: Eliza!

PEGGY: And Peggy![3]

COMPANY: Work, work!
The Schuyler sisters!

ANGELICA: Angelica!

PEGGY: Peggy!

ELIZA: Eliza!

COMPANY: Work!

PEGGY: Daddy said to be home
by sundown.

ANGELICA: Daddy doesn't
need to know.

[1] This is our "One Short Day in the Emerald City." It's a love letter to New York, and it lets us know who the Schuyler sisters are outside the context of Hamilton and his future affections.

[2] Union Square didn't exist in its current form yet, but I wanted that kind of feel—a place where you could find any type of New Yorker in the same place. Talking to Chernow got me to The Common, a square downtown.

[3] Poor Peggy—she doesn't stick around the story long enough to merit a musical motif. She married rich and died young, in case you're wondering where she is in Act Two.

PEGGY: Daddy said not to go downtown.

ELIZA: Like I said, you're free to go.

ANGELICA: But—look around, look around, the revolution's happening in New York.

ELIZA, PEGGY: New York.

COMPANY: Angelica,

SCHUYLER SISTERS AND COMPANY: Work!

PEGGY: It's bad enough Daddy wants to go to war.

ELIZA: People shouting in the square.

PEGGY: It's bad enough there'll be violence on our shore.

ANGELICA: New ideas in the air.

ANGELICA AND MALE ENSEMBLE: Look around, look around—

ELIZA: Angelica, remind me what we're looking for . . .

ALL MEN: She's lookin' for me!

[4] Our little Jay Z/ Pharrell homage.

[5] This is my wife's favorite line in the show.

[6] When this was still an album in my head, I really wanted the rapper Common Sense to read a selection of "Common Sense." I am nothing if not literal.

[7] She did, of course, meet Jefferson in Paris, and corresponded with him later in life. It kills me that I couldn't fit that detail in the show—so here it is in this book.

[8] I tell myself this every day. It was nice to give it to Eliza.

ANGELICA:
Eliza, I'm lookin' for
a mind at work.
I'm lookin' for a mind
at work!
I'm lookin' for a mind
at work!
Whooaaaaa!

COMPANY:

Work, work!

Work, work!

Work, work!

ELIZA, ANGELICA, PEGGY: Whooaaaaa!
Work!

Work!

BURR: Whoo! There's nothin' like summer in
the city.
Someone in a rush next to someone lookin' pretty.
Excuse me, miss, [4] I know it's not funny
But your perfume smells like your daddy's
got money.
Why you slummin' in the city in your fancy heels?
You searchin' for an urchin who can give you ideals?

ANGELICA: Burr, you disgust me.

BURR: Ah, so you've discussed me.
I'm a trust fund, baby, you can trust me! [5]

ANGELICA: I've been reading "Common Sense"
by Thomas Paine. [6]
So men say that I'm intense or I'm insane.
You want a revolution? I wanna revelation
So listen to my declaration:

ELIZA, ANGELICA, PEGGY: "We hold these
truths to be self-evident
That all men are created equal."

ANGELICA: And when I meet Thomas Jefferson,

COMPANY: Unh! [7]

ANGELICA: I'm 'a compel him to include
women in the sequel!

WOMEN: Work!

ELIZA: Look around, look around at how
Lucky we are to be alive right now! [8]

ELIZA, PEGGY: Look around,
look around at how
Lucky we are to be alive right now!

ELIZA, ANGELICA, PEGGY: History is
happening in Manhattan and we
Just happen to be in the greatest city in the world!

COMPANY *(EXCEPT WASHINGTON &*
HAMILTON): In the greatest city in the world!

ANGELICA:
Cuz I've been
reading
"Common
Sense" by
Thomas Paine.
So men say that
I'm intense or
I'm insane.

ELIZA, PEGGY:
Look around,
look around

The revolution's
happening in—

MEN:
Hey! Hey!
Hey! Hey!

MEN:
Hey! Hey!
Hey! Hey!

ANGELICA:
You want a
Revolution?
I wanna
revelation

So listen to my
Declaration

ELIZA, PEGGY:
New York!

in New York!

WOMEN:
Look around,
Look
around, the
Revolution's
Happening

ANGELICA, ELIZA, PEGGY:
We hold
these truths
to be self-evident
That all men are
created equal

FEMALE ENSEMBLE:
Look around!

Look around!

Hey! Hey!

Hey! Hey!

Whoo!

At how lucky
we are to be
alive right now!

Hey! Hey!

Hey! Hey!

COMPANY: Look around, look around at how
lucky we are to be alive right now!
History is happening in Manhattan and we just
happen to be

WOMEN: In the greatest city in the world.

MEN: In the greatest city—

COMPANY: In the greatest city in the world!

COMPANY: Work, work!

Work, work!

Work, work!

Work, work!

Work, work!

Work, work!

Work, work!

ANGELICA:
Angelica!

ELIZA: Eliza!
PEGGY: And Peggy!
ANGELICA, ELIZA, PEGGY:
The Schuyler sisters!

We're looking for a
mind at
work!
Hey!

Hey!

COMPANY:
Work, work!
Work, work!

Work, work!

ANGELICA:
Whoa!

In the greatest
city in the world

ELIZA, PEGGY: Hey!
Hey!
Hey! Hey!
Hey!

In the greatest
city in the world

COMPANY:
In the greatest city in the world!

V

STAKES IS HIGH;

OR,

WHAT HAPPENED AT LINCOLN CENTER

AND WHAT CAME AFTER,

Including Lunch with

JEFFREY SELLER

WHEN LIN ACCEPTED LINCOLN CENTER'S offer to perform an American Songbook concert, he and Tommy viewed it as a festive, freewheeling gig.

Tommy recalls thinking: "We can have a band, so we can orchestrate some of the songs. So let's get seven or eight of our friends, and let's just throw a party, and everybody else here is invited to that party." The surprise was who showed up: On January 11, 2012, all 450 seats in Lincoln Center's Allen Room were filled. Plenty of friends and collaborators were in the crowd, but so were members of the press and some heavyweights of New York theater. It was not the last time that the public's interest in *Hamilton* would catch its creators off-guard.

Lin opened the program with a set of songs that he called "the DNA of my brain." These were formative hits by some of his favorite rappers: The Notorious B.I.G., Talib Kweli, Eminem. Then he and his friends performed all the *Hamilton* songs he had produced so far, a catalog that had swelled rapidly in the half-year since the Ars Nova benefit, when he and Tommy had started working on them in earnest.

But what *were* those songs, exactly? Stephen Holden's review for *The New York Times* captured the audience's puzzlement—and its delight. "Is *The Hamilton Mixtape*, from which 12 numbers were performed, a future Broadway musical? A concept album? A multimedia extravaganza in search of a platform? Does it even matter? What it is, is hot."

To Jeffrey Seller, the answer was obvious. "It became crystal clear to everyone in the room that it was a Broad-

way show," he says. Lin had played a few of the songs for him before that night. The chance to hear them in order, with a rapt live audience, was a revelation. "I thought, *Here's the show. The musical has emerged. This makes dramatic sense, and is scintillating*," he recalls. "Even in a concert format, the story was taking shape."

CHAPTER V

A few weeks later, he took Lin to lunch. "If you want me to produce your show, I'd love to produce your show," he said. A few weeks after that, he sent an email to Lin and Tommy, offering to be a "passionate advocate, cheerleader, sounding board, constructive critic, and barker."

Some Broadway producers spend years mastering one of those tasks before stretching to do the others; Jeffrey had been doing them all since before he learned to shave. He grew up in Oak Park, a working-class suburb of Detroit: People called his neighborhood "Cardboard Village," because the houses had asphalt shingles instead of bricks. When he was in fourth grade, his synagogue strained the bounds of holy writ and copyright law to stage a Purim play that set Queen Esther's story to the score of *South Pacific*. ("Bali Ha'i may call you" became "Mordecai they called me.") Theater grabbed him and never let go. He went home and wrote a play of his own, *Adventureland*. Then he joined his community theater, thinking of being an actor. Pretty quickly after that, he discovered it would be more fun to choose the plays than to perform them—and to stage them, promote them, and raise money for them. He still wasn't old enough to drive.

He dreamed of New York, a city he lacked the money to visit, let alone call home. But after college he made the leap. In the mid-'90s, he teamed up with Kevin McCollum to produce a rock opera almost as daring as that Purim play: Jonathan Larson's *Rent*. Their follow-ups included the audacious puppet musical *Avenue Q* and the salsa/hip-hop breakthrough *In the Heights*. All three shows won the Tony Award for Best Musical.

When Lin and Tommy had their lunches and phone calls with Jeffrey after the Lincoln Center concert, they liked the way that he talked about the Hamilton project. "The things that he was saying about the show really lined up with what we had in mind," says Lin. They agreed that Jeffrey should produce the show. In summer 2012, he optioned *Hamilton* for the company that he had formed earlier that year to strike out on his own, as a solo lead producer: He called it Adventureland.

The American Songbook concert put *Hamilton* on the path to Broadway. It also offered the first glimpse of the show's ambitions, the way it would challenge audiences to think differently about Broadway. "Just as we continue to forget that immigrants are the backbone of

the country, we forget that musical theater is a mongrel art form," Lin says. Broadway absorbed jazz, then it absorbed rock, but it hadn't absorbed hip-hop, even though he saw the enormous potential of fusing those sounds. To make the connection explicit, he opened the Songbook program by combining two iconic songs about New York City: "Another Hundred People," from Stephen Sondheim's *Company*, and Jay Z and Alicia Keys's "Empire State of Mind."

That fusion of styles and traditions permeates all of *Hamilton*, but it appears in super-concentrated form early in Act One. Lin knew he would need a song to set up King George III's big number, "You'll Be Back." He also needed to depict the fiery brilliance of the young Alexander Hamilton. *We're going to demonstrate that he fights in the war, but how do we demonstrate that he's quick-witted and fighting in a war of ideas?* he wondered. He wrote the jauntiest tune he could imagine for a British loyalist to sing: drums, fifes, harpsichord—

"Just as we continue to forget that IMMIGRANTS ARE THE BACKBONE OF THE COUNTRY, we forget that MUSICAL THEATER IS A MONGREL ART FORM."

"getting my Bach on, essentially," in Lin's words. This was pretty much what an audience expected a musical about the nation's founding to sound like. But Lin added a hip-hop twist.

In the 1770s, the real-life Alexander Hamilton used a pair of pamphlets to eviscerate the real-life Samuel Seabury, a leading loyalist. The stage Hamilton would do it with a rap. Lin had been listening to an ingenious tribute that Joell Ortiz had recorded for the greatest Puerto Rican MC, Big Pun. Ortiz had kept all the rhyming syllables from a classic Pun song, but he incorporated them into new lyrics that paid homage to the late rapper. "It was a weirdly casually brilliant a way of doing a tribute," Lin says.

In "Farmer Refuted," Lin weaponized the idea, as he illustrates in the annotations on page 49. And, in an added display of virtuosity, Hamilton did it in Seabury's waltz tempo. Only rarely does a rapper depart from the usual 4/4 for another time signature. (Jay Z's "My 1st Song" is the rare track in 6/8.) If they dropped mics in 1776, Hamilton would drop one here.

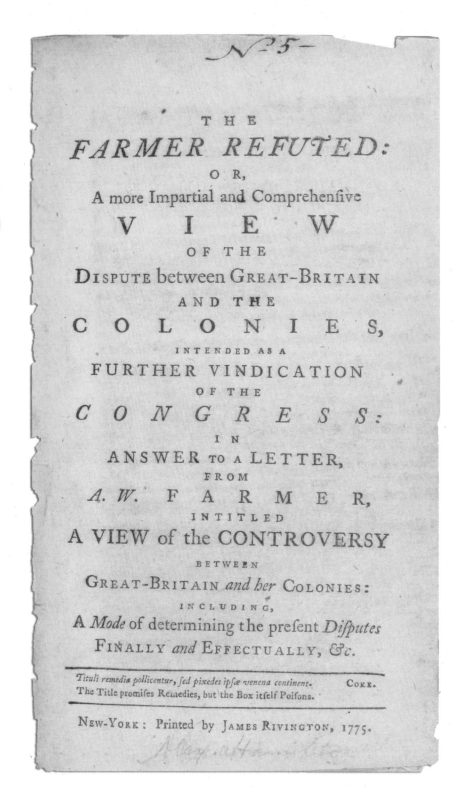

Alexander Hamilton's precociously brilliant response to the "Westchester Farmer," Samuel Seabury.

N° 5.

THE
FARMER REFUTED:
OR,
A more Impartial and Comprehensive
VIEW
OF THE
DISPUTE between GREAT-BRITAIN
AND THE
COLONIES,
INTENDED AS A
FURTHER VINDICATION
OF THE
CONGRESS:
IN
ANSWER TO A LETTER,
FROM
A. W. FARMER,
INTITLED
A VIEW of the CONTROVERSY
BETWEEN
GREAT-BRITAIN *and her* COLONIES:
INCLUDING,
A *Mode* of determining the prefent *Difputes*
FINALLY *and* EFFECTUALLY, *&c.*

Tituli remedia pollicentur, fed pixedes ipfæ venena continent.   COKE.
The Title promifes Remedies, but the Box itfelf Poifons.

NEW-YORK: Printed by JAMES RIVINGTON, 1775.

FARMER REFUTED

Samuel Seabury stands on a box. He reads.

SAMUEL SEABURY: Hear ye, hear ye!
My name is Samuel Seabury and I present:
"Free Thoughts On the Proceedings of the
Continental Congress!"
Heed not the rabble who scream revolution,
They have not your interests at heart.[1]

MULLIGAN: Oh my god. Tear this dude apart.

SEABURY: Chaos and bloodshed are not a solution.
Don't let them lead you astray.
This Congress does not speak for me.

BURR: Let him be.

SEABURY: They're playing a dangerous game.
I pray the King shows you his mercy.
For shame, for shame . . .

HAMILTON:	
Yo!	**SEABURY:**
He'd have you all	Heed not the rabble
unravel at the	
Sound of screams but the	Who scream
Revolution is comin'	Revolution, they
The	
Have-nots are gonna	Have not your
win this, it's	interests at
Hard to listen to you	heart.[2]
with a straight face.	
Chaos and bloodshed	Chaos and bloodshed
already haunt	are not
Us, honestly you	A solution
shouldn't even	
Talk and what about	Don't let them lead
Boston?	you
Look at the	
Cost, 'n all that we've	Astray.
lost 'n you talk	
About Congress?!	This Congress does
	not speak for
My dog speaks more	Me,

eloquently
than thee!

	They're playing a
	dangerous
But strangely, your	Game.
mange is the same.	
	I pray the King shows
	you his mercy
Is he in Jersey?[3]	
	For shame,
For the revolution!	
	For shame,
COMPANY:	
For the revolution!	

SEABURY: Heed—

HAMILTON: If you repeat yourself again
I'm gonna—

SEABURY, HAMILTON: Scream—

HAMILTON: Honestly, look at me, please
don't read!

SEABURY: Not your interests—

HAMILTON: Don't modulate the key then not
debate with me![4]
Why should a tiny island across the sea regulate
the price of tea?

BURR: Alexander, please!

HAMILTON: Burr, I'd rather be divisive than
indecisive, drop the niceties.

The King's heralds enter.

ENSEMBLE: Silence! A message from the King!
A message from the King!

FULL COMPANY: A message from the King!

(King George appears.)

---

[1] I began with the harpsichord progression and wrote this melody and lyrics rather quickly. None of this is in Seabury's writings.

[2] The fun (and laborious part) of this tune was having Hamilton dismantle Seabury using the same vowels and cadences and talking over him. Heed becomes He'd. Rabble/Unravel. Heart/*hard* to listen to you, etc. It felt like the kind of superpower Hamilton could deploy to impress his friends.

[3] I have a lot of family in Jersey. When I kid, it's with love.

[4] Meta joke. I love this joke. It just showed up.

VI

On *the* ORCHESTRATING TECHNIQUES *of*

ALEX LACAMOIRE

with Lively Appearances by

VAN HALEN, ELMO, AND

AN ACTUAL BEATLE

IF YOU WANT TO BE PICKY ABOUT Lin's songwriting process, he makes songs without actually writing them down. Like some of the best song-writers in the business—even the very best, such as Paul McCartney or Michael Jackson—he doesn't record the musical ideas that swirl in his brain by notating them on lined sheets of paper with keys and sharps and flats. He used the music-recording program Logic Pro to create demos of most of the songs in *Hamilton*. He played chords on a keyboard plugged into his laptop, and created a rudimentary arrangement with sounds drawn from the program's library of samples, adding vocals by singing or rapping into the little mic that's attached to his headphones. There is an endorsement deal in there someplace.

As Lin completed these songs, he shared them with Tommy and a few other close collaborators, but only one person was responsible for immediately turning them into something else: Alex Lacamoire. As the orchestra-tor, he translated the demos into notated music (the keys, the sharps, the flats) that would allow them to be played by a 10-person band. Did a certain moment call for a touch of violin? A drum fill? Loud, soft, fast, slow? Alex made those interpretive calls, then discussed them with Lin and Tommy. It's a very American pastime, this inter-preting and discussing. Our musical culture is built on standards, songs meant to be reworked endlessly, such as

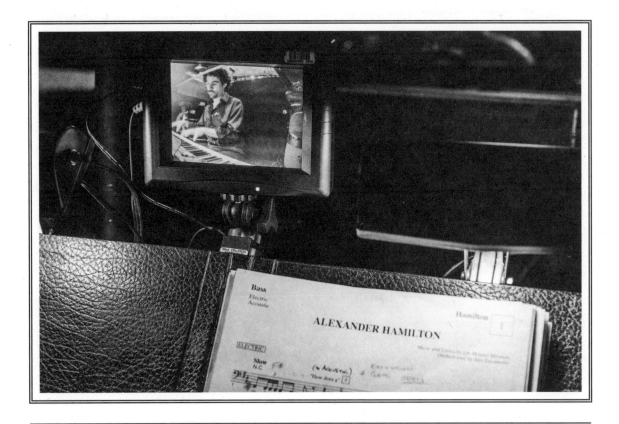

> **"LIN WILL HAVE AN AMAZING INSPIRATION and put it forward in a way that you know exactly where he's driving. ALEX WILL PAVE THE STREET."**

"Blue Skies" or "Summertime." And it's not just our music: Think of the blood we've spilled looking for the best expression of "All men are created equal" or "Congress shall make no law. . ."

This process of interpretation turns out to be as vital to *Hamilton* as it is anywhere else in the republic. Andy Blankenbuehler, the show's choreographer, says that Alex is the guy who makes everything happen. "Lin will have an amazing inspiration and put it forward in a way that you know exactly where he's driving. Alex will pave the street."

Like Tommy, Alex first came to know Lin through *In the Heights*. An actor involved in the show's development told Lin about a music director he knew: a Cuban-American kid from Miami, somebody that Lin might like. Unlike Lin's first meeting with Tommy, hip-hop didn't play much of a role when he got to know

Alex, whose tastes ran more to radio pop and classic rock. (They still do: Other members of the *Hamilton* staff might own banana-yellow Van Halen T-shirts, only Alex wears his to work.) But they bonded all the same. They were both Latino, they both talked fast, they thought faster.

Above all, they discovered that their talents harmonized. Lin percolates a million musical ideas, but he is, by his own admission, "a shitty piano player." He admires Alex's superior musicianship, the way that a song springs to life when he's in front of a keyboard. "Lac can make anything happen by playing it," says Lin. From the time Lac started playing piano, at age four, he wanted to capture not just the notes on the page but what he called "the whole picture" of a song. "I tried not to just play the piano part, I wanted to play the drums on the piano and the guitar licks on the piano."

Alex manages these musical feats despite a condition that you might think would derail a career in music. Around the time that he began learning how to make a piano sing, his family noticed he was having trouble hearing. Though he had always been fixated on music—while still a toddler, he would sit in front of the speakers, staring—he seemed to be missing things that people were saying to him. He was fitted for two hearing aids. Growing up, he sometimes wore only one of them, when his family couldn't afford the other. In high school, he stopped wearing them altogether because he didn't want to stand out. He kept playing, though. Today, he sometimes defers to his collaborators on how loud certain high-pitched tones ought to be, but prefers to think that his hearing deficiency might have aided his life in music. Maybe it trained him to listen harder. "Maybe I'm more attuned to certain things," he says.

He's also humble, in his upbeat way, about writing songs of his own. "Composing is very intimidating," he says. "Think about who my friends are. Lin-Manuel Miranda. Tom Kitt. These people are titans of what they

do. Why bother, since it's not going to be as good as what they do?" When Alex does compose music, it's for children's television. "*Sesame Street*, 90-second songs—that, I can handle," he says with a laugh. He's particularly proud of "First Second Third," which Elmo sings in a politics-themed episode of the show.

The final versions of the *Hamilton* songs resulted from the push/pull in the way that Lin and Lac interpret songs. "Lin's approach is to keep things simple, simple. I'm more complicated," says Lac. Lin has a different way of describing his friend's creativity: "It's not so much he likes it complicated, it's that he'll speed past one idea to the next one. And I'll say *no no no*, two ideas ago was the winner." Lac is not what you'd call a strict constructionist when it comes to orchestrating the songs, but then Lin doesn't want him to be. "Lin gives me freedom to put my stamp on certain things," he says.

Consider "You'll Be Back," the song in which King George warns the American colonists not to rebel. It was one of the first things Lin wrote for the show, back when he was sharing most of his ideas as lyric sheets

with chords. As Lac looked for ways to lift the song off the page, he thought about using a harpsichord, which would evoke the song's era and the royal stature of the person singing it. But the cheery music and romantic lyrics (it's a love song, even if it does threaten mass murder) also reminded him of the *other* British invasion, of the late 1960s.

"It just spoke to me, it was so Beatlesque," says Alex. "If we're gonna go there, let's really go there."

Listen closely to it now, and you'll hear a guitar homage to "Getting Better" and a vibraphone nod to "Penny Lane." There's even a synth shout-out to "Being for the Benefit of Mr. Kite." The contrast between those sunny

songs and the king's threats makes him sound even more sociopathic, and hilarious.

Alex was delighted to have a chance to evoke The Beatles, whom he regards with "mad respect, mad wonder. There's nothing better. That, to me, is the ultimate." It turns out the admiration flows both ways.

After an early performance of the show at the Public Theater, Lin and Alex walked into the green room to find *an actual Beatle* standing there. Sir Paul McCartney told them how much he liked their vocal harmonies. Somebody snapped the photo that appears on this page, the one that shows three resourceful musicians standing together: Lin grinning under Sir Paul's left arm, Alex beaming under his right.

YOU'LL BE BACK[1]

KING GEORGE: You say
The price of my love's not a price that you're
    willing to pay.
You cry
In your tea which you hurl in the sea when you
    see me go by.[2]
Why so sad?
Remember we made an arrangement when
    you went away.
Now you're making me mad.
Remember, despite our estrangement,
    I'm your man.
You'll be back.
Soon you'll see.
You'll remember you belong to me.
You'll be back.
Time will tell.
You'll remember that I served you well.
Oceans rise.
Empires fall.
We have seen each other through it all,
And when push
Comes to shove,
I will send a fully armed battalion
To remind you of my love!

Da da da dat da da dat da da da ya da[3]
Da da dat dat da ya da!
Da da da dat da dat da da da da ya da,
Da da dat dat da ya . . .

You say our love is draining and you can't go on.
You'll be the one complaining when I
    am gone . . .

And no don't change the subject,
Cuz you're my favorite subject,
My sweet, submissive subject,
My loyal, royal subject,[4]
Forever and ever and ever and ever and ever . . .

You'll be back,
Like before,
I will fight the fight and win the war
For your love,
For your praise,
And I'll love you till my dying days.
When you're gone
I'll go mad,[5]
So don't throw away this thing we had.
Cuz when push comes to shove
I will kill your friends and family to
    remind you of my love.

Da da da dat da da da da da ya
Da da dat dat da ya da!
Da da da dat da dat da da da
Da ya da da da dat dat-
Everybody!

ENSEMBLE:
Da da da dat da dat da da da ya da
Da da dat dat da ya da!
Da da da dat da dat da da da ya da
da da dat dat da ya da!

British soldiers in red coats emerge. One rebel is killed.

---

[1] I was having a drink with Hugh Laurie, with whom I'd worked on his series *House*, and I told him I wanted to write a breakup letter from King George to the colonies. Without blinking, he improv'd at me, "Awwww, you'll be back," wagging his finger. I laughed and filed it away. Thanks, Hugh Laurie.

[2] The Boston Tea Party reference. Blink and you miss it.

[3] I wrote this song on my honeymoon in the South Pacific. I'd already had the idea, but as my wife and I walked around these amazing islands, I started hearing King George and singing to myself. The whole tune was written without a piano. Just a melody in search of its moorings.

[4] I just love that King George has a clever turn of phrase on "subject" and beats it into the ground.

[5] He did.

VII

ON THE CHARACTER OF
GEORGE WASHINGTON

—

and the Character of
CHRIS JACKSON

GEORGE WASHINGTON WAS FIRST IN war, first in peace, and first in Lin's imagination. Even as he read Ron Chernow's book, he was beginning to think about who could fill the various roles, especially the Father of Our Country.

Lin had an early hunch that the leader of the Continental Army and first president would sing and rap in equal measure. He also knew that the performer would have to project greatness, an aura of command that surrounded Washington from his youth. And yet he couldn't be a bloodless superman: The first glimpse of Washington, in "Right Hand Man," shows him scrambling to stave off defeat, not coasting to glory.

Lin thought that someone like Common, the universally respected rapper from Chicago, might possess the stature and depth for the role. Another prospect was much nearer at hand.

One night, during a performance of *In the Heights*, Lin and his costar Chris Jackson were standing just off-stage, waiting for their cue.

"I got the next one," Lin said. Meaning he had come up with his next idea. "Want to play George Washington?"

Like Lin, Chris was a history buff. They were both reading *Team of Rivals*, about Abraham Lincoln's cabinet, around that time. (Lin was thinking of adapting the book until he heard that Steven Spielberg had gotten there first.) Chris was also a fan of the first president, whom he considers "*the* great American icon." And so he said: "Sure."

Still, Chris didn't know how seriously to take it. Lin has lots of ideas; they come and go. But a few days later, Tommy visited the *Heights* cast.

"Hey, G-Dubs," he said to Chris.

"All right," Chris replied. It was on.

Chris Jackson had the makings of a Washington for reasons that anybody can see and hear. He has a tall, athletic stature that suits the finest horseman in all Virginia, the man that bullets knew better than to mess with. He also has a powerful R&B baritone, honed while singing in church choirs back in Cairo, Illinois. When Lin met Chris, he was so impressed that he rewrote the character of Benny in *In the Heights* to suit him better. "Chris is so sure of his instrument and has this kind of moral authority onstage," says Lin. "He's just fucking majestic."

But there are other, better reasons why Lin, and only Lin, would look to Chris for the role. Washington was taller, older, quieter, more reserved, and more experienced than Hamilton. All of these things fit the relationship between Chris and Lin. By the time *Heights* came together, Chris had already spent four years in *The Lion King*, making him what he calls "a grizzled vet" of Broadway. Their friendship deepened when Chris joined Lin in Freestyle Love Supreme, which was a little like being in a band together and a little like sharing a foxhole.

"At this point there is not a situation Chris and I have not found ourselves in at a performative level," says Lin. "You know what someone is capable of when you're thrown in front of a hundred drunk strangers in Edinburgh."

Chris didn't coast on any of this, conscientiousness being another trait he shares with the father of our country. He did his homework, poring over Chernow's biography of George Washington, which he pronounces excellent. (Chernow returns the esteem: "That guy nailed

"Chris is so sure of his instrument and has this kind of moral authority onstage... HE'S JUST FUCKING MAJESTIC."

it," he told Lin after seeing Chris play Washington for the first time, marveling at his gravitas, his presence.) "The more I retain about the specifics of his life, it enriches my thought of the man," said Chris. Knowing how buried in paperwork General Washington was during the war, he asked David Korins to add more books and papers and things to his desk. He even visited Mt. Vernon, and laid a wreath on Washington's grave.

"It was unexpectedly heavy," he says. "It was the utmost reminder. He lived, and was here, and he died. And he's still here."

Like Washington, Chris seems to lead out of instinct, not some will to rule. In rehearsal, he would sometimes "shh" the cast when people got too loud, but look at the ceiling while he did it, so nobody knew who was doing the shushing, or was being shushed. Before every show, he's the one who rounds up his castmates and arranges them in a prayer circle beneath the stage. "Hey, every team has a huddle, right?" he says of his preshow rite. "Every good one."

Chris tells the actors, musicians, and backstage crew to hold hands and to breathe, and to breathe again. He then offers a little benediction: half locker-room pep talk, half petition to the Almighty.

"Let's be sure that no matter what happens out there, I've got you," he told the congregation one night. "Let's agree that for the next two and a half hours, this is the most important thing we'll do in our lives." He closes with the hope that everybody—in the audience, on the stage, and in the orchestra pit—will leave the theater a better person than they walked in.

If his friend wanted to be a pastor, Lin thinks, he'd have a megachurch. For now, Chris is an actor trying to get used to the entrance applause he gets at some performances. Up to a point, the *Hamilton* audience is cheering someone they've been watching for nearly 20 years. But when he makes that brisk, bold entrance—a black man striding straight downstage, slamming his sword into a scabbard—the thought crosses your mind: Is Chris somehow getting all of these people to cheer for *George Washington himself?*

RIGHT HAND MAN

The company sees a full armada, offstage.

COMPANY: British Admiral Howe's got troops
    on the water.
Thirty-two thousand troops in New York
    harbor.[1]

<table>
<tr><td>

ENSEMBLE 1:
Thirty-two thousand
troops in New York
harbor
When they surround
our troops!
They surround our
troops!
When they surround
our troops!
</td><td>

ENSEMBLE 2:
Thirty-two thousand
troops in New York
harbor

They surround our
troops!
They surround our
troops!
</td></tr>
</table>

HAMILTON: As a kid in the Caribbean I wished
    for a war.[2]
I knew that I was poor
I knew it was the only way to—

HAMILTON, BURR, LAURENS, MULLIGAN,
LAFAYETTE: Rise up!

HAMILTON: If they tell my story
I am either gonna die on the battlefield in
    glory or—[3]

HAMILTON, BURR, LAURENS, MULLIGAN,
LAFAYETTE: Rise up!

HAMILTON: I will fight for this land
But there's only one man
Who can give us a command so we can—

HAMILTON, BURR, LAURENS, MULLIGAN,
LAFAYETTE: Rise up!

HAMILTON: Understand? It's the only way to—

HAMILTON, BURR, LAURENS, MULLIGAN,
LAFAYETTE: Rise up! Rise up!

HAMILTON: Here he comes!

George Washington enters, heralded by soldiers.

ENSEMBLE: Here comes the general!

BURR: Ladies and gentlemen!

ENSEMBLE: Here comes the general!

BURR: The moment you've been waiting for!

ENSEMBLE: Here comes the general!

BURR: The pride of Mount Vernon!

ENSEMBLE: Here comes the general!

BURR: George Washington!

<table>
<tr><td>

WASHINGTON:
We are outgunned,
Outmanned,

Outnumbered,
outplanned.

We gotta make an all
out stand

Ayo, I'm gonna need a
right hand man.
</td><td>

ENSEMBLE:
What?
What? [4]

Buck, buck, buck,
buck, buck!

Buck, buck, buck,
buck, buck!
</td></tr>
</table>

[1] This section used to live in the middle of the song, but it's much more effective at the top: Imagine the waterways around New York surrounded by an armada so thick it chokes out the sky.

[2] He did. In a letter to his friend Ned Stevens at age 14, he writes "I wish there was a war."

[3] For many in this country, joining the armed services is still seen as a path to security. 'Twas ever thus.

[4] I wanted this to sound chaotic, and I often cited to Lacamoire the background vocals in Pharoahe Monch's "Simon Says": It sounds like a *million dudes in a basement*. I love that sound.

WASHINGTON: Check it—
Can I be real a second?
For just a millisecond?
Let down my guard and tell the people how
    I feel a second?
Now I'm the model of a modern major
    general,[5]
The venerated Virginian veteran whose men
    are all
Lining up, to put me up on a pedestal,
Writin' letters to relatives
Embellishin' my elegance and eloquence,
But the elephant is in the room.
The truth is in ya face when ya hear the
    British cannons go . . .

ENSEMBLE: Boom!

WASHINGTON: Any hope of success is fleeting,
How can I keep leading, when the people I'm
    leading keep retreating?
We put a stop to the bleeding as the British
    take Brooklyn,
Knight takes rook,[6] but look,

WASHINGTON:	ENSEMBLE:
We are outgunned,	What?
Outmanned,	What?
Outnumbered,	
outplanned.	
	Buck, buck, buck,
	buck, buck!
We gotta make an all	
out stand	
Ayo, I'm gonna need a	
right hand man.	Buck, buck, buck,
	buck, buck!
Incoming!	

HAMILTON: They're battering down the
    Battery
Check the damages.

MULLIGAN: Rah!

HAMILTON: We gotta stop 'em and rob 'em
Of their advantages.

MULLIGAN: Rah!

HAMILTON: Let's take a stand with the stamina
    God has granted us.
Hamilton won't abandon ship,
Yo, let's steal their cannons—[7]

MULLIGAN: Shh-	COMPANY:
boom!	Boom!

WASHINGTON: Goes the cannon, watch the
blood and the shit spray and . . .

COMPANY: Boom!

WASHINGTON: Goes the cannon, we're
abandonin' Kips Bay and . . .

COMPANY: Boom!

WASHINGTON: There's another ship and . . .

COMPANY: Boom!

WASHINGTON: We just lost the southern
tip and . . .

COMPANY: Boom!

WASHINGTON: We gotta run to Harlem quick,
    we can't afford another slip.
Guns and horses giddyup,
I decide to divvy up
My forces, they're skittish as the British cut the
    city up.
This close to giving up, facing mad scrutiny,
I scream in the face of this mass mutiny:
Are these the men with which I am to defend
    America?[8]
We ride at midnight, Manhattan in the distance.
I cannot be everywhere at once, people.
I'm in dire need of assistance . . .

[5] My first part in high school was as The Pirate King in *The Pirates of Penzance*. It was going to sneak in one way or another. I also think my rhyme for general is better than theirs, "mineral." All props to Gilbert & Sullivan, kings of light patter.

[6] My elementary school had mandatory chess class from K–4th grade. I'm still not very good at the game, but I know my way around a chess metaphor.

[7] Hamilton and Mulligan really did go on cannon-stealing adventures together.

[8] This is a direct quote from Washington, in a rare temper tantrum.

Washington's tent. Burr enters.

BURR: Your Excellency, sir!

WASHINGTON: Who are you?

BURR: Aaron Burr, sir?
Permission to state my case?

WASHINGTON: As you were.

BURR: Sir,
I was a captain under General Montgomery.
Until he caught a bullet in the neck in Quebec,
      and well, in summary [9]
I think that I could be of some assistance.
I admire how you keep firing on the British
      from a distance. [10]

[9] Burr showed valor as a soldier in his own right, and took part in expeditions against the British. He worked for Washington for a few weeks and that's about it. We don't know why they parted. So I made this scene up.

[10] My first draft of this line read,"I don't mean to brag, but my dad was the president of Princeton, soooo . . . " It was funny, but too snotty. I wanted Washington to not trust Burr on a chemical level, the way only really wise people, dogs, and kids can read people on first meeting.

WASHINGTON: Huh.

BURR: I have some questions, a couple of
      suggestions
On how to fight instead of fleeing west.

WASHINGTON: Yes?

BURR: Well—

HAMILTON: Your Excellency, you wanted to
see me?

WASHINGTON: Hamilton, come in, have you
met Burr?

HAMILTON: Yes, sir.

HAMILTON, BURR: We keep meeting.

BURR: As I was saying, sir, I look forward to seeing your strategy play out.

WASHINGTON: Burr?

BURR: Sir?

WASHINGTON: Close the door on your way out.

Burr exits.

HAMILTON: Have I done something wrong, sir?

WASHINGTON: On the contrary.
I called you here because our odds are
    beyond scary.
Your reputation precedes you, but I have
    to laugh.

HAMILTON: Sir?

WASHINGTON: Hamilton, how come no one can get you on their staff?

HAMILTON: Sir!

WASHINGTON: Don't get me wrong, you're
    a young man, of great renown.
I know you stole British cannons when we were
    still downtown.
Nathaniel Green and Henry Knox wanted to
    hire you . . .

HAMILTON: To be their secretary? I don't think so. [11]

WASHINGTON: Why're you upset?

HAMILTON: I'm not—

WASHINGTON: It's alright, you want to fight,
    you've got a hunger.
I was just like you when I was younger.
Head full of fantasies of dyin' like a martyr?

HAMILTON: Yes.

WASHINGTON: Dying is easy, young man.
Living is harder. [12]

HAMILTON: Why are you telling me this?

WASHINGTON: I'm being honest.
I'm working with a third of what our Congress
    has promised.
We are a powder keg about to explode,
I need someone like you to lighten the load. So?

COMPANY (EXCEPT HAMILTON): I am not
    throwin' away my shot!
I am not throwin' away my shot!
Ayo, I am just like my country, I'm young,
    scrappy and hungry!

HAMILTON: I am not throwing away my shot! [13]

WASHINGTON: Son,

WASHINGTON, COMPANY: We are outgunned,
outmanned!

HAMILTON: You need all the help you can get.
I have some friends. Laurens, Mulligan,
Marquis de Lafayette, okay, what else?

WASHINGTON AND COMPANY:
Outnumbered, outplanned!

HAMILTON: We'll need some spies on the inside,
Some king's men who might let some things
    slide—

HAMILTON:	COMPANY:	ELIZA, ANGELICA, PEGGY, WOMEN:
I'll write to Congress and tell 'em we need supplies, You rally the guys, master the element of surprise.	Boom!	Whoa, whoa, whoa . . .

[11] This used to read, "I came to be a soldier, not a secretary." The revision reflects Hamilton's inability to contain his anger. Papi, Washington's only trying to figure out what's wrong, be easy.

[12] Real talk from Washington. Nothing to add, except if present-day me could talk to adolescent me, this is probably what I'd say.

[13] I rewrote this line late in the process. Tommy and I wanted to pinpoint the moment when Hamilton puts away dreams of martyrdom to rise in a different way. (Not that he doesn't still harbor martyrdom fantasies. Keep reading.)

I'll rise above my station, organize your information 'til we rise to the occasion of our new nation. Sir!

Chicka-boom!

Whoa, whoa, whoa . . .

ELIZA, ANGELICA, PEGGY, WOMEN: Whoa, whoa, whoa . . .

ENSEMBLE: Here comes the general!

HAMILTON: Rise up!

LAURENS, LAFAY-ETTE, MULLIGAN: What?

ENSEMBLE: Here comes the general!

HAMILTON: Rise up!

SCHUYLER SISTERS, WOMEN: Rise up!

LAURENS, LAFAY-ETTE, MULLIGAN: What?

ENSEMBLE: Here comes the general!

HAMILTON: Rise up!

SCHUYLER SISTERS: Rise up!

LAURENS, LAFAY-ETTE, MULLIGAN: What?

COMPANY: Here comes the general!

HAMILTON: What?

WASHINGTON: And his right hand man!

COMPANY: Boom!

VIII

CONCERNING THE

LADY AND THE TRAMP,

IN OLDEN DAYS AND OUR OWN,

with Reference to

"HELPLESS"

AND MANY SONGS THAT FEATURE JA RULE

ONE COLD DAY IN FEBRUARY 1780, Elizabeth Schuyler arrived in Morristown, New Jersey, the winter headquarters of the raggedy American army. She was rich, well-born, lively, pretty—all the attributes of a princess, if the colonies needed a princess. Amid the social swirl of Morristown, she got to know Alexander Hamilton. He was poor, illegitimate, unpolished, unsophisticated—a hustling young officer who was trying, literally, to fight his way into respectability. They made for an odd combination. After barely a month, they were engaged.

The musical theater canon offers many ways to depict this courtship: sweeping waltzes, soaring ballads, the conventions of stage romance. Lin had a better idea. Having grown up on hip-hop and R&B, he saw that the story of Alexander and Eliza's relationship is hip-hop and R&B's *wheelhouse*.

From the early days of hip-hop, producers have seen the appeal of putting rappers on records with female pop stars: Melle Mel with Chaka Khan, Rakim with Jody Watley. In the '90s, when hip-hop was bounding toward the mainstream, these duets became a genre of their own. The breakthrough came when Mary J. Blige released a duet with Method Man, "I'll Be There for You/You're All I Need to Get By," that ruled the summer of '95. Here was a way for hardcore rappers to stay hard and R&B queens to stay regal, an arrangement that let two people from very different backgrounds bring their best selves together without losing what made them appealing in the first place. When Beyoncé (R&B star, veteran of church choirs) sang "Crazy in Love" with a guest verse from Jay Z (platinum rapper, former crack dealer), they didn't just achieve the perfect expression of

ABOVE:
The Schuyler mansion in Albany, where Alexander and Eliza wed.

the genre: They made one of the greatest pop songs of all time.

"Helpless," Lin's song about Alexander and Eliza, doesn't riff on this tradition—it *is* this tradition. Put "Helpless" next to "Crazy in Love": A sweet girl sings about the boy she loves, then the rough-around-the-edges boy pops up to rap his reply. (In both cases, he doesn't rap about her, he raps about himself.) Lin uses the conventions of a pop song to help a 21st-century audience understand 18th-century social distinctions. And he does it with the extreme concision that a theater song demands: A meeting, a courtship, and a wedding flit by in four minutes of stage time, in a song that still manages to reach back to the opening number (when the chorus sings "In New York, you can be a new man,") and to set up the finale (when Eliza introduces herself by singing, "I have never been the type to try and grab the spotlight.")

If you're a fan of these R&B/hip-hop duets, or were within earshot of a radio in the early years of the century,

you know that their all-time king is Ja Rule. Jennifer Lopez and Ashanti had huge hits thanks to his one-in-a-million voice (a bear roaring at the bottom of a well, approximately). One day, near the end of a very long *Hamilton* rehearsal, when everybody had gotten a little punchy, Lin delivered the last two lines of his "Helpless" rap in a Ja Rule growl. Anything to keep morale up on a

---

"She was rich, well-born, lively, pretty—ALL THE ATTRIBUTES OF A PRINCESS, if the colonies needed a princess."

---

long day, you might think. But a few weeks later, when Lin and his Eliza, played by Phillipa Soo, had begun to perform the song in actual shows for actual audiences, the distinctively gravelly growl was still there. Was it a tribute to the king of the hip-hop/R&B hybrid?

No, Lin said. "I do it because it makes Pippa laugh."

And he was right. When Alexander rumbled through his last couple of lines, Eliza did indeed let out a pretty peal of laughter as he whirled her into their wedding.

ANSWER TO THE INQUIRY

WHY I SIGHED

Before no mortal ever knew
A love like mine so tender, true,
Completely wretched——you away,
And but half blessed e'en while you stay.

If present love [illegible] face
Deny you to my fond embrace
No joy unmixed my bosom warms
But when my angel's in my arms.

A. Hamilton

ABOVE:
Alexander Hamilton's love poem for Eliza Schuyler, who wore it in a necklace for the rest of her life.

A WINTER'S BALL

BURR: How does the bastard orphan son of a
   whore go on and on,
Grow into more of a phenomenon?
Watch this obnoxious arrogant loudmouth
   bother
Be seated at the right hand of the father.[1]
Washington hires Hamilton right on sight.
But Hamilton still wants to
   fight, not write.
Now Hamilton's skill with a
   quill is undeniable
But what do we have in common?
   We're reliable with the

ALL MEN: Ladies!

BURR: There are so many to deflower.

ALL MEN: Ladies!

BURR: Looks! Proximity to power.

ALL MEN: Ladies!

BURR: They delighted and distracted him.
Martha Washington named her
   feral tomcat after him![2]

HAMILTON: That's true.

*The scene gradually shifts. We are at a winter
soldiers' ball.*

COMPANY: Seventeen eighty.

BURR: A winter's ball
And the Schuyler sisters are the envy of all.
Yo, if you could marry a sister, you're rich, son.

HAMILTON: Is it a question of if, Burr, or
   which one?[3]

Eliza, Angelica & Peggy enter.

[1] Religion is like chess for me—I grew up learning it, and it came in awfully handy as a shared reference for our characters.

[2] This is most likely a tale spread by John Adams later in life. But I like Hamilton owning it. At this point in the story he is at peak cockiness.

[3] Here's an example of internal assonance strengthening a punchline: We've got the rhyme at the end—"rich, son" with "which one"—but you're scarcely aware of the agreement between "sister" and "if, Burr" in the middle of the sentence.

HELPLESS[1]

— ❖ —

HAMILTON, BURR, LAURENS: Hey
Hey
Hey hey

HAMILTON, BURR, LAURENS, ALL WOMEN (EXCEPT ELIZA): Hey hey hey hey

ELIZA:	**FEMALE ENSEMBLE, ANGELICA, PEGGY:**
Ohh, I do I do I do I	Hey hey hey hey
Dooo! Hey!	Hey hey hey hey
Ohh, I do I do I do I	Hey hey hey hey
Dooo! Boy, you got me	Hey hey hey hey

ELIZA AND WOMEN: Helpless!
Look into your eyes, and the sky's the limit.
   I'm helpless!
Down for the count, and I'm drownin' in 'em.

ELIZA: I have never been the type to try and
   grab the spotlight.[2]
We were at a revel with some rebels on a hot night,
Laughin' at my sister as she's dazzling the room.
Then you walked in and my heart went "Boom!"
Tryin' to catch your eye from the side of
   the ballroom.
Everybody's dancin' and the band's top volume.

ELIZA, WOMEN: Grind to the rhythm as we
   wine and dine.

ELIZA: Grab my sister, and whisper, "Yo, this
   one's mine."[3]

	WOMEN:
	Ooohh
ELIZA: My sister made her way across the room to you	Ooohh
And I got nervous, thinking "What's she gonna do?"	Ooohh

She grabbed you by the arm, I'm thinkin' "I'm through."	Ooohh
Then you look back at me and suddenly I'm helpless!	Helpless!
Oh, look at those eyes,[4]	
	Look into your eyes,
Oh!	And the sky's the limit
Yeah, I'm	I'm
Helpless, I know	Helpless!
	Down for the count,
	And I'm drownin' in 'em
I'm so into you I am so into you	I'm helpless!
	Look into your eyes, And the sky's the limit I'm helpless!
I know, I'm down for the count And I'm drownin' in 'em	
	Down for the count, And I'm drownin' in 'em

HAMILTON: Where are you taking me?[5]

ANGELICA: I'm about to change your life.

HAMILTON: Then by all means, lead the way.

ELIZA: Elizabeth Schuyler. It's a pleasure to meet you.

HAMILTON: Schuyler?

ANGELICA: My sister.

ELIZA: Thank you for all your service.

6 This is based on a
real letter Angelica sent
Eliza. She was being as
playful as she is here.

7 This is just a note to
say I wish you could
hear the insane things
Sydney Harcourt, who
originated the role of Pa
Schuyler, and I say to
each other upstage in
this scene.

Hamilton kisses Eliza's hand.

HAMILTON: If it takes fighting a war for us to
meet, it will have been worth it.

ANGELICA: I'll leave you to it.

ELIZA, WOMEN One week later

ELIZA: I'm writin' a letter nightly
Now my life gets better, every letter that you
    write me.
Laughin' at my sister, cuz she wants to form
    a harem.

ANGELICA: I'm just sayin', if you really loved
me, you would share him. 6

ELIZA:	WOMEN:
Ha!	Two weeks later,
Two weeks later,	
In the living room	
Stressin'	Stressin'
My father's stone-faced 7	
While you're asking for his	
Blessin'.	Blessin'.
I'm dying inside, as you	
wine	
And dine	
And I'm tryin' not to	
cry, 'cause	
There's nothing that	
your mind can't do.	Ooohh
My father makes his	
way across the room	
to you.	Ooohh
I panic for a second,	
thinking, "We're	
through."	Ooohh

But then he shakes
your hand and says,
"Be true."   Ooohh
And you turn back to
me, smiling, and I'm
Helpless!   Helpless!
                                    Look into your eyes,
                                    And the sky's the
                                    limit I'm
Helpless!   Helpless!
Hoo!   Down for the count,
                                    And I'm drownin' in
                                    'em I'm
                                    Helpless!
That boy is mine.
That boy is mine!

                                    Look into your eyes,
                                    And the sky's the limit
                                    I'm

Helpless! Helpless!   Helpless!
Down for the count,   Down for the count,
And I'm drownin' in 'em.   And I'm drownin' in 'em.
Helpless! Helpless!
Down for the count,
And I'm drownin' in 'em.

HAMILTON:
Eliza, I don't have a dollar to my name [8]
An acre of land, a troop to command,
     a dollop of fame.
All I have's my honor, a tolerance for pain,
A couple of college credits and my top-notch brain.
Insane, your family brings out a different
     side of me.
Peggy confides in me, Angelica tried to take a
     bite of me.
No stress, my love for you is never in doubt,
We'll get a little place in Harlem and we'll
     figure it out.

[8] And here comes Hamilton, anti-bragging. In reality, before their marriage, Hamilton wrote a heartbreaking letter trying to shatter any romantic notions Eliza might have about marrying a penniless man. At the same time, he's bragging about his top-notch brain. This swagger, built on a bedrock of total insecurity, is the contradiction that is our Hamilton.

I've been livin' without a family since I was a child.
My father left, my mother died, I grew up buckwild.
But I'll never forget my mother's face, that was real [9]
And long as I'm alive, Eliza, swear to God, you'll
            never feel so . . .

HAMILTON:
I do I do I do
Eliza   I dooo!

I do I do I do
I dooo!

I've never felt
so—

ELIZA:

Hey! Yeah,
yeah!

WOMEN:
Helpless!

Helpless!

Helpless!

Down for the
count
And I'm
drownin' in
'em

I'm
Down for the
count, I'm—

My life is gon'
be fine
Cuz Eliza's in it.

I look into
your eyes,
And the sky's
the limit
I'm

drownin' in
'em

Helpless!

Helpless!

Helpless!

Helpless!
Down for the
count, And
I'm drownin'
in 'em

Hamilton & Eliza's wedding. As Eliza & Alexander exchange rings, the guests sing.

WOMEN:
In New York, you can be a new man . . .
In New York, you can be a new man . . .
In New York, you can be a new man . . .

ELIZA: Helpless.

[9] And here's where we prove that my wife was right, and "This One's Mine" was *never* going to be right approach for this moment. By wrapping the song around the word "Helpless," we encapsulate several things: the giddy helplessness of falling in love, but also Hamilton's fear of helplessness, and his identification of helplessness in the first woman he ever knew, his mother. It's a weak point for him, it's Kryptonite. And it'll come back in the form of another character in Act Two. Stay tuned.

ON THE

PERFECT UNION

OF ACTOR AND ROLE

with Allusion to

RENÉE ELISE GOLDSBERRY

CASTING OFFICES CAN BE BAD FOR morale: Actors contort themselves to become something they're not; writers and directors pretend it's working. During a casting session for *Hamilton*, though, one audition left Lin, Tommy, and Oskar Eustis, the artistic director of the Public Theater, looking genuinely stunned, as if lightning had flashed through the room.

"She's—so—*fast*," said Lin, eyes wide.

Tommy agreed.

"It's from doing all that Shakespeare," Oskar explained.

"She" was Renée Elise Goldsberry, who had just auditioned for the role of Hamilton's sister-in-law and possible love interest, the headstrong and quick-thinking Angelica Schuyler. Renée had indeed performed Shakespearean roles as part of the Public Theater's Shakespeare in the Park seasons. She had also appeared on Broadway four times, sung in a top-40 band, and done some TV. It sounds like the kind of cross-training that might prepare somebody for a role in this intensely demanding show. Still, she came very close to not auditioning for it at all. *Twice.*

The first near-miss was because Renée and her husband had just adopted a baby girl from Ethiopia. Any job that she accepted, they believed, "had to be something that felt as monumental as what we were building in our family." Lin's joking-but-actually-pretty-accurate description of Angelica in the casting notice—that she was a combination of Nicki Minaj and Desiree Armfeldt—left Renée cold. Neither the raucous female rapper nor the heroine of *A Little Night Music* were her type. She decided to stick to her self-imposed maternity leave, and stay in Harlem with her son and baby girl.

But the casting agents at Telsey + Company persisted. They sent her the demo recording of Angelica's big first-act song. One listen to "Satisfied" convinced Renée that *Hamilton* might indeed be monumental—so monumental, in fact, that it led to another almost-miss.

"Satisfied" was the fastest and most brilliant theater song that she had ever heard. It retraces the ground covered in "Helpless," but from Angelica's perspective. (As staged by Tommy and the choreographer Andy Blankenbuehler, time itself seems to wind backwards, giving the show another chance to suggest that history looks very different depending on who's telling it.) She was dazzled by the song's intricacies, but was supposed to perform it for Lin and Tommy the very next day.

"I just remember thinking, *Oh no. This is the motherlode, and it's tomorrow. I can't learn it in a day.* In a night, actually." She showed up without any real hope of landing

"It was the first delivery of 'Satisfied' . . . that DIDN'T MAKE ME THINK FOR A SECOND ABOUT THE DELIVERY that was happening."

the part, but thought she might convince Lin and Tommy to take her money and let her invest in the show.

If Renée had stuck around after her audition, if she had seen the expression on Lin's face after she left the room, she would have known how right for the role she was, and not because of how she had crammed the night before.

"Renée was the first one who came in and made us say, 'Oh, she thinks exactly that fast,'" he recalls. Her whirring brain made Angelica come alive in a new way. "It was the first delivery of 'Satisfied' that didn't make me think for a second about the delivery that was happening." This was, he thought, the key to the song. He hadn't written a rapid-fire rap so an actor could show off, as in a Gilbert and Sullivan patter song. Her velocity expresses her brilliance, and her distress: "She's demonstrating that Angelica read Hamilton the moment she saw him, but it didn't stop her from falling in love with him, and didn't stop her calculating *in a moment* to yield to her sister's love for him."

Renée acknowledges that she does indeed think pretty fast—"too fast to have good handwriting." But the snug fit between singer and song is also due to the way Lin wrote it. "The way I memorize is, I memorize a thought process," she says. It's one reason why Oskar thought of her Shakespeare roles. His plays stick with us because his language—in fact, any verse, if it's written sharply enough—gives form to our formless thoughts. It's Hamlet debating suicide, "To be or not to be, that is the question," and it's Scarface having nightmares, "At night I can't sleep, I toss and turn, / Candlesticks in the dark, visions of bodies being burned," and it's Angelica Schuyler choosing her sister's happiness over her own.

"If a song is written well, you know what you have to say," says Renée. "Even in this instance, this woman is talking very fast, and making decisions in an instant, but she is extremely analytical. The path is very clear. The path is so intrinsic."

She insists that other actresses will have no trouble singing it in future productions. Lin can't wait to see them try.

"I want to fast forward to when high schools do Hamilton & the girl playing Angelica Schuyler gets to spit the HARDEST BARS IN THE SHOW," he tweeted during the run at the Public.

SATISFIED[1]

[1] This is the most ambitious tune in this show (and that's saying a lot). It was always a wedding toast, originally entitled, "Can I Say Something?" I made several starts and stops on this thing, never really satisfied (heh) with the musical feeling. The answer came in a song I'd already written.

About two years prior, I'd written some music for Karen Olivo for a project that never saw the light of day. She'd written some beautiful, unrequited-love lyrics, which I'd adapted into a pretty, haunting, and cool dance tune. It popped up in my shuffle and I, like Angelica upon meeting Hamilton, realized it was everything I ever wanted in that moment. I frantically called Karen and said, "Hey, remember that tune I wrote you? I kind of need it back. I won't use any of your lyrics, but I need that music, and you're not using it anyway, soooooooo please?"

There was a pause, and she said, "Yeah, dude. It's your music." So Angelica's haunting arpeggio in "Satisfied" owes a debt to Karen Olivo—she helped bring it into the world.

[2] There's no reason this should be funny, except Anthony Ramos says it all the time, so I just had him say it, and it is funny.

[3] "Satisfied," like "Helpless," allows us to twist several meanings from it. There is all manner of satisfaction—sexual, emotional, financial. It's also a code word used in dueling—"To demand satisfaction." It's also onomatopoetic—it feels like it sounds, satisfying to sing. We wring every last bit from it.

It is Alexander & Eliza's wedding night. Laurens is finishing up his speech.

LAURENS: Alright, alright. That's what I'm talkin' about![2] Now everyone, give it up for the maid of honor, Angelica Schuyler!

ANGELICA:
A toast to
the groom

ALL MEN:
To the groom!
To the groom!   **ALL WOMEN:**
To the groom!   To the groom!

To the bride.

                       To the bride!
To the bride!   To the bride!

From your
sister.   To the bride!
Angelica!
Angelica!   **ELIZA:**
Who is always   Angelica!   Angelica!
by your side.

By your side!   By your side!
To your union.

                       To the union!
To the union!   To the
                       revolution!
To the
revolution!
And the hope
that you provide.
You provide!
You provide!   You provide!
May you
always . . .   **HAMILTON:**
Always—   Always—
be satisfied.[3]

Rewind—   Rewind—

Rewind to the ballroom scene where Hamilton met Eliza.[4]

ANGELICA: I remember that night I just might Regret that night for the rest of my days

I remember those soldier boys
Tripping over themselves to win our praise

I remember that dreamlike candlelight
Like a dream that you can't quite place

But Alexander, I'll never forget
    the first
Time I saw your face
I have never been the same
Intelligent eyes in a hunger-pang frame
And when you said hi I forgot my dang name
Set my heart aflame, ev'ry part aflame,

FULL COMPANY: This is not a game . . .

HAMILTON: You strike me as a woman who has never been satisfied. 5

ANGELICA: I'm sure I don't know what you mean. You forget yourself.

HAMILTON: You're like me. I'm never satisfied.

ANGELICA: Is that right?

HAMILTON: I have never been satisfied.

Hamilton kisses Angelica's hand. The company gasps.

ANGELICA: My name is Angelica Schuyler.

HAMILTON: Alexander Hamilton.

ANGELICA: Where's your fam'ly from?

4 This is the genius of choreographer Andy Blankenbuehler, who did the math on how far back we'd have to rewind the scene. We don't just cover "Helpless"—by necessity, we rewind all the way to "A Winter's Ball," because Angelica meets Hamilton *first*, and Andy stages that in pantomime here. I'm getting a headache just thinking about planning it.

5 This exchange, like the six lines of dialogue, needs to carry everything in a super-compact amount of time. It's when the multiple meanings of "Satisfied" will come in the handiest. Hamilton goes full Jordan Catalano here.

HAMILTON: Unimportant. There's a million things I haven't done but
Just you wait, just you wait . . .

ANGELICA: So so so—[6]
So this is what it feels like to match wits
With someone at your level! What the hell is the catch? It's
The feeling of freedom, of seein' the light,
It's Ben Franklin with a key and a kite!
    You see it, right?
The conversation lasted two minutes, maybe three minutes,
Ev'rything we say in total agreement, it's
A dream and it's a bit of a dance,
A bit of a posture, it's a bit of a stance, he's a
Bit of a flirt, but I'm 'a give it a chance.
I asked about his fam'ly, did you see his answer?
His hands started fidgeting, he looked askance
He's penniless, he's flying by the seat of
    his pants
Handsome and boy does he know it!
Peach fuzz, and he can't even grow it!
I wanna take him far away from this place,
Then I turn and see my sister's face
    and she is . . .

ELIZA: Helpless . . .

ANGELICA: And I know she is . . .

ELIZA: Helpless . . .

ANGELICA: And her eyes are just . . .

ELIZA: Helpless . . .

ANGELICA: And I realize

ANGELICA AND COMPANY: Three fundamental truths at the exact same time . . . [7]

HAMILTON: Where are you taking me?

ANGELICA: I'm about to change your life.

HAMILTON: Then by all means, lead the way.[8]

COMPANY: Number one!

ANGELICA: I'm a girl in a world in which
My only job is to marry rich.

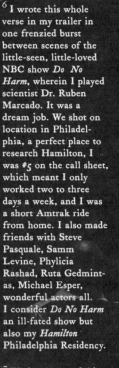

[6] I wrote this whole verse in my trailer in one frenzied burst between scenes of the little-seen, little-loved NBC show *Do No Harm*, wherein I played scientist Dr. Ruben Marcado. It was a dream job. We shot on location in Philadelphia, a perfect place to research Hamilton, I was #5 on the call sheet, which meant I only worked two to three days a week, and I was a short Amtrak ride from home. I also made friends with Steve Pasquale, Samm Levine, Phylicia Rashad, Ruta Gedminas, Michael Esper, wonderful actors all. I consider *Do No Harm* an ill-fated show but also my *Hamilton* Philadelphia Residency.

[7] The structure of this song is exactly the form of the Personal Literary Essay I learned in 8th grade English. Introduction, Statement of Thesis, Three Proofs, conclusion. Here come the three proofs.

[8] This scene, when broken up because of the rewind, now takes on more meaning. When the scene ends *here*, we see how into Angelica Hamilton is. *Lead the way!*

My father has no sons so I'm the one [9]
Who has to social climb for one,
'Cause I'm the oldest and the wittiest and
    the gossip in
New York City is insidious
Alexander is penniless,
Ha! That doesn't mean I want him any less.

ELIZA: Elizabeth Schuyler. It's a pleasure to
meet you.

HAMILTON: Schuyler?

ANGELICA: My sister.

COMPANY: Number two!

ANGELICA: He's after me cuz I'm a
    Schuyler sister.
That elevates his status, I'd
Have to be naïve to set that aside,

[9] Okay, so Philip Schuyler really had *loads* of sons. I conveniently forgot that while I was writing this in service of a larger point: Angelica is a world-class intellect in a world that does not allow her to flex it.

Maybe that is why I introduced him to Eliza.
Now that's his bride.
Nice going, Angelica, he was right,
You will never be satisfied.

ELIZA: Thank you for all your service.

Hamilton kisses Eliza's hand.

HAMILTON: If it takes fighting a war
for us to meet, it will have been worth it.

ANGELICA: I'll leave you to it.

COMPANY: Number three!

ANGELICA: I know my sister like I know
    my own mind,
You will never find anyone as trusting or as kind.
If I tell her that I love him she'd be silently
    resigned,
He'd be mine.
She would say, "I'm fine."

COMPANY: She'd be lying.

The scene dissolves, as Angelica continues.

ANGELICA: But when I fantasize
    at night
It's Alexander's eyes
As I romanticize what might
Have been if I hadn't sized him
Up so quickly.
At least my dear Eliza's
    his wife,
At least I keep his eyes
    in my life . . .[10]

Angelica pauses and raises a glass as the wedding reassembles around her.

ANGELICA:	COMPANY:	
To the groom!	To the groom!	
	To the groom!	WOMEN:
	To the groom!	To the groom!

ANGELICA		
To the bride!		
		To the bride!
	To the bride!	
	To the bride!	To the bride!
From your sister.		
	Angelica!	ELIZA:
	Angelica!	Angelica!
Who is always		
by your side.		
	By your side.	
		By your side.
To your union.		
	To the union!	To the union!
	To the	To the
	revolution!	revolution!
And the hope		
you provide.		
	You provide!	
	You provide!	You provide!
May you		
always	HAMILTON:	
	Always—	Always—
Be satisfied.		
	Be satisfied,	
		Be satisfied.
	Be satisfied,	
And I know	MEN:	
	Be satisfied.	WOMEN:
	Be satisfied.	Be satisfied.
	Be satisfied.	
She'll be	Be satisfied.	
happy as		
	Be satisfied.	
	Be satisfied.	
his bride.		
And I know	Be satisfied.	Be satisfied.
	Be satisfied.	
	Be satisfied.	
	Be satisfied.[11]	
		Be satisfied.

ANGELICA: He will never be satisfied.
I will never be satisfied.

10 Oof. Tryin' to out-Eponine Eponine up in this piece.

11 Funny thing about saying a word a lot: It starts to feel the opposite of what it means. With the world singing "be satisfied," without the first half of the sentence, it feels like a perverse, tragic mantra.

The
STORY OF TONIGHT
(REPRISE)

———◆———

Later in the night. Mulligan, Laurens & Lafayette enter, with goblets in hand, razzing Hamilton.

LAURENS: I may not live to see our glory!

MULLIGAN, LAFAYETTE: I may not live to see our glory!

LAURENS: But I've seen wonders great and small.

MULLIGAN, LAFAYETTE: I've seen wonders great and small.

LAURENS: Cuz if the tomcat can get married,

MULLIGAN, LAFAYETTE: If Alexander can get married—

LAURENS: There's hope for our ass, after all!

LAFAYETTE: Raise a glass to freedom.

LAURENS, MULLIGAN: Hey!
Something you will never see again! [1]

MULLIGAN: No matter what she tells you.

LAFAYETTE: Let's have another round tonight!

LAURENS: Raise a glass to the four of us!

LAFAYETTE, HAMILTON: Ho!

MULLIGAN: To the newly not poor of us!

HAMILTON, LAURENS, LAFAYETTE: Woo!

LAFAYETTE: We'll tell the story of tonight.

LAURENS: Let's have another round—

Burr enters.

HAMILTON: Well, if it isn't Aaron Burr.

BURR: Sir.

HAMILTON: I didn't think that you would make it.

BURR: To be sure.

MULLIGAN, LAFAYETTE: Burr!

BURR: I came to say congratulations.

MULLIGAN: Spit a verse, Burr!

BURR: I see the whole gang's here.

LAFAYETTE: You are the worst, Burr! [2]

HAMILTON: Ignore them. Congrats to you, Lt. Colonel.
I wish I had your command instead of manning George's journal.

BURR: No, you don't.

HAMILTON: Yes, I do.

BURR: Now, be sensible.

[1] I wanted to hear this tune again: This is the tune of brotherhood among these friends, but it can also encapsulate rowdiness and the lewd roast that occurs.

[2] Tommy Kail and I always described this scene as "When your hometown friends are at the party with your college friends."

From what I hear, you've made yourself
  indispensable.

LAURENS: Well, well, I heard
You've got a special someone on the side, Burr.

HAMILTON: Is that so?

LAURENS: What are you tryin' to hide, Burr?

BURR: I should go.

HAMILTON: No, these guys should go.

LAFAYETTE: What?

LAURENS: No!

HAMILTON: Leave us alone.

MULLIGAN: Man . . .

Mulligan, Laurens & Lafayette slink off.

HAMILTON: It's alright, Burr. I wish you'd
brought this girl with you tonight, Burr.

BURR: You're very kind, but I'm afraid it's
unlawful, sir.

HAMILTON: What do you mean?

BURR: She's married.

HAMILTON: I see.

BURR: She's married to a British officer. [3]

HAMILTON: Oh shit . . .

BURR: Congrats again, Alexander. Smile more.
I'll see you on the other side of the war.

HAMILTON: I will never understand you.
If you love this woman, go get her! What are
  you waiting for?

BURR: I'll see you on the other side of the war.

HAMILTON: I'll see you on the other side of
the war.

[3] *This* was the way into Burr. I knew he and Hamilton circled each other all their lives, I knew they went from friends to frenemies to foes, but it wasn't til I read this detail online—that Theodosia was married to a British officer when Aaron Burr met her, and he waited until she was available—that the character of Burr came free in my imagination. Imagine Hamilton waiting—for anything. That's when I realized our task was to dramatize not two ideological opposites, but a fundamental difference in temperament. No easy task. But that was the task.

THE SAME SUBJECT CONTINUED,

with Allusion to

LESLIE ODOM, JR.

Plus Remarks on the

VIRTUES AND MERITS OF UNION

LOOKING BACK NOW, SUCCESS SEEMS foreordained. It wasn't. No colonists in the history of the world had defeated their mother country on the battlefield to win their independence. Few republics had managed—or even attempted—to govern an area bigger than a city-state. Somehow, in defiance of all precedent, Washington, Hamilton, and the other founders pulled off both.

Their deliriously unlikely success—first as soldiers, then as statesmen—tends to obscure the true lessons of the American Revolution. The past places no absolute limit on the future. Even the unlikeliest changes can occur. But change requires hope—in the case of both of those unlikely victories, the hope that the American people could defy all expectation to overcome their differences and set each other free.

In the summer of 1788, Alexander Hamilton carried this message to Poughkeepsie, where he pleaded with New York's leaders to trust in the possibilities of union, and vote to ratify the new federal Constitution. Yes, he conceded, the 13 newborn states included many different kinds of people. But this did not mean that the government was bound to fail. It took an immigrant to fully understand the new nation, and to declare a fundamental hope of the American experiment: Under wise government, these diverse men and women "will be constantly assimilating, till they embrace each other, and assume the same complexion."

Two hundred twenty-five years later, and about two miles up the road from where Hamilton gave that speech, Lin, Tommy, Lac, and a group of actors assembled to make a crucial step in their own bold experiment. They had been invited to Poughkeepsie to take part in the New York Stage and Film series of developmental workshops at Vassar College. For a week, they would live together in Vassar dorms, refining Lin's songs. Beyond providing time to work, the program gave them blessed isolation, a chance to get away from other projects for a while. Tommy exaggerates only slightly when he says that Lin would wake up in the morning and find him sitting next to the bed, primed with another idea.

They had made an important break with precedent before they arrived—the most important, maybe, in the entire development of the show. When they decided that *The Hamilton Mixtape* was going to be a stage musical and not an album, they assumed that they would need spoken dialogue to connect the songs. *Song-scene-song-scene* has been the standard structure of the modern Broadway musical since Rodgers and Hammerstein perfected the form in the 1940s. Tommy asked a playwright they both respected enormously to write a libretto. But a single reading with a few scenes of spoken dialogue, in January 2013, convinced them that through no fault of the script, everyday speech couldn't sustain the energy of the rapped lyrics.

CHAPTER X

That meant that all of the writing duties would fall to Lin. Every textual problem was now his to solve. Tommy and Jeffrey pep-talked him: He was more skilled now than during *In the Heights*, they told him. Anyway, nobody else would be able to catch up to him at this point. Fortunately, Lin was already feeling "just super preggo," by which he meant: "Well it's coming out one way or the other, and nobody else is going to deliver it."

At the end of that week in Poughkeepsie, on a hot Saturday afternoon, 150 friends of the production and Broadway professionals crowded into Vassar's Powerhouse Theater to see what Lin had birthed. There was no scenery and no blocking. The only accompaniment came from Lac, who played an upright piano, and Scott Wasserman, who supplied loops created on Ableton, the potent musical-production software. Still the audience got to hear something remarkably close to the final version of Act One. When it ended, Lin treated the crowd to a couple of songs from Act Two. That was as far as he had written.

Sitting in the last row of the audience, more than a little amazed, was Leslie Odom, Jr. The young actor was in Poughkeepsie that day to watch his wife, Nicolette Robinson, take part in another reading at New York Stage and Film. When the audience erupted at the end of the encore, Leslie was on his feet too. He sent Lin a text afterwards to say that he would be the show's biggest cheerleader when it got staged.

Lin and Tommy didn't want him to cheer—they wanted him to *act*. As they took stock after the week at Vassar, they realized that the actors who had played Burr so far had been too similar to Lin. "What was great about Leslie is that in every way he's a contrast to me," says Lin.

"What was great about Leslie is that in every way he's a contrast to me . . . HE IS COOL, HIS BLOOD RUNS COOL, HE IS ELEGANT."

"He is cool, his blood runs cool, he is elegant. It sounds like I'm reverse-describing myself as feral monster. Anyway he's my opposite." Or, as Lin said of Leslie around that time: "Dude makes me look *scruffy*."

Lin and Tommy had approached Leslie about taking part in an early workshop of *Hamilton*, but his schedule had prevented him. That fall, they tried again, inviting him to read Burr the next time they gathered some actors to test new material. He said yes and immediately got to work. A lot of work.

"How do you let people know what you want?" Leslie asks. "You let them know through preparation. You *show* them." By the time the reading came around, he had memorized the role. For a brief workshop with no audience, learning a part as big as Aaron Burr is a preposterous display of dedication. The role seemed to be his.

But once again something that seems inevitable in retrospect almost didn't happen at all. Like most young actors, Leslie had operated on the theory that the road to

lugged a two-volume biography of Burr—a gift from Oskar—back and forth from his apartment in Brooklyn to rehearsals all over Manhattan. It requires some imagination to think of Leslie straining under a heavy bag. Besides being the best-dressed person in almost every room he enters, he exudes an easy grace that makes it hard to imagine him being weighed down by anything.

After a long day and night of rehearsal, Leslie still lights up when he talks about playing Aaron Burr. "Lin is asking you to bring your complete and total self to the stage—all your joy, all your rage, all your pain, your capacity for fun." Burr, he says, is "arguably the best role for a male actor of color in the musical theater canon."

"Ever?"

"*Ev-er*. You get to show all your colors. *Nobody* asks us to do that."

It's true that there's something new and potent about Burr. We've seen the nemesis-as-narrator before: Think of Judas in *Jesus Christ Superstar*. But even in the songs that Leslie first heard at Vassar, there are depths and complexities to Burr that make him the equal of the title character. One song in particular captivated Leslie

> *"Lin is asking you to BRING YOUR COMPLETE AND TOTAL SELF TO THE STAGE—all your joy, all your rage, all your pain, your capacity for fun."*

stage success lay through television. As he puts it, "You get the cover of *EW*, then you come back to Broadway." After 10 years of struggling, a guest role on *Smash* had finally paved the way for a lead role on a new network drama, *State of Affairs*. This posed a dilemma: move to Los Angeles for his shot at TV success, or stay in New York to play Burr? It was a choice, he says, "between my *Grey's Anatomy* and my childhood dream." Going to Los Angeles, he knew, was the smart thing to do—the adult thing to do. "I want to buy my mama a house too."

Even if he chose to stay in New York, his fate wasn't entirely up to him. He had already signed a network contract. What was he supposed to do, go to war with NBC? After some sleepless nights, he got on an airplane. He went to Los Angeles and sought out his patrons in the TV business. He explained his situation. They let him go. And nobody else has gotten near the role of Aaron Burr since.

So there is no house in the Hills for Leslie just yet. Instead he spent a lot of 2014 working on Burr's songs with Lac. ("He gets in the sandbox with you," says Leslie. "He helped me so much.") He also hit the books. He

that day. He didn't catch its name—he only knew it had something to do with "waiting," and that whoever got to sing it would be one lucky actor.

Now Leslie is the one who gets to sing "Wait for It," Burr's musical declaration of his code. When he talks about the song, he sounds like a mountain climber just returned from a treacherous peak, or a bullfighter back from the ring. "You don't have to put anything on 'Wait For It,'" he says. "Just sing it with honesty, and as much vulnerability as you can. Don't get ahead of it"—which is a very Burr-like thing to say.

"I love it. God, I love it," he says of the song. "I'll sing it for the rest of my life." And every time he does, it'll be a little different from the times he sang it before. Leslie says that it is vital to sing the song *to* the audience: "They're my confidants." That means the song changes as the crowd changes—its size, its composition, the way it emits a million little signals that a first-rate actor can detect from the stage. In other words—to state the revolutionary lesson one more time—what happened yesterday never guarantees what'll happen tonight.

WAIT FOR IT

— ✦ —

BURR: Theodosia writes me a letter ev'ry day.
I'm keeping her bed warm while her husband
    is away.
He's on the British side in Georgia.
He's tryin' to keep the colonies in line.
But he can keep all of Georgia.
Theodosia, she's mine.

Love doesn't discriminate
Between the sinners
And the saints.
It takes and it takes and it takes
And we keep loving anyway.
We laugh and we cry
And we break
And we make our mistakes.
And if there's a reason I'm by her side
When so many have tried
Then I'm willing to wait for it.
I'm willing to wait for it.

BURR:
My
grandfather
was a fire and
brimstone
preacher,[1]

| | MEN: |
| Preacher, |
| preacher, |
| preacher |

But these are
things that
the homilies
and hymns
won't teach
ya.[2]   Teach ya,
    teach ya,
    teach ya

My mother   WOMEN:
was a genius,   Genius
My father
commanded   Respect,
respect.   respect

BURR: When they died they left no instructions.
Just a legacy to protect.

BURR, ENSEMBLE:
Death doesn't discriminate[3]
Between the sinners and the saints,
It takes, and it takes, and it takes
And we keep living anyway.
We rise and we fall
And we break,
And we make our mistakes.
And if there's a reason I'm still alive
When ev'ryone who loves me has died
I'm willing to wait for it.
I'm willing to wait for it.

Wait for it.

ENSEMBLE:
Wait for it.
Wait for it.
Wait for it.

BURR:
I am the one thing in life I can control.

ENSEMBLE:
Wait for it.
Wait for it.
Wait for it.
Wait for it.

BURR:
I am inimitable,
I am an original.

ENSEMBLE:
Wait for it.
Wait for it.
Wait for it.
Wait for it.

[1] Jonathan Edwards, writer of "Sinners in the Hands of an Angry God."

[2] Just a note to say that I love how *"hymns won't teach ya"* agrees with *"brimstone preacha."* Super subliminal but effective. I actually wrote this verse first and swapped it with the Theodosia verse after taking a step back.

[3] I often write loops.
  I'll make eight or 16 bars of music I think I like, and I sing over it until it feels true. This is how "Wait For It" was born.
  At this point in my life, I was carrying around both an iPod and a phone. I'm grateful for this in retrospect because the entire chorus came in one ridiculous rush, as I listened to the music on a loop on a crowded A train to a friend's birthday party in Williamsburg.
  I lived at the top of the A train at the time, so that meant taking the A from 207th street to 14th street, then the L into Brooklyn. I don't know how to describe the feeling. It did not exist one moment and then there it was, coursing through my head: "Death doesn't discriminate . . ." I got out of the train in Williamsburg and began singing into the voice memo function in my iPod from the loop I was listening to in my phone. (This is why I was glad I had them both.) I said hi to my friend, wished him happy birthday, had exactly half a beer, and turned around for another hour-and-a-half train ride home, during which I worked out the other verse variations. Music doesn't discriminate when it arrives either. It'll get you on the A train if you're open to it.

BURR:
I am not falling behind or running late

ENSEMBLE:
Wait for it.
Wait for it.
Wait for it.
Wait for it.

BURR:
I am not standing still,
I am lying in wait.

ENSEMBLE:
Wait
Wait
Wait

BURR:
Hamilton faces an endless uphill climb.

ENSEMBLE:
Climb
Climb
Climb

BURR:
He has something to prove
He has nothing to lose.

ENSEMBLE:
Lose
Lose
Lose
Lose

BURR:
Hamilton's pace is relentless, he wastes no time.

ENSEMBLE:
Time
Time
Time

BURR: What is it like in his shoes?
Hamilton doesn't hesitate.

He exhibits no restraint.
He takes and he takes and he takes
And he keeps winning anyway.
He changes the game.
He plays and he raises the stakes.
And if there's a reason
He seems to thrive when so few survive,
     then goddamnit—

BURR: I'm willing to wait for it.	**COMPANY:** I'm willing to wait for it.
	Wait for it,
	Wait for—
I'm willing to wait for it . . .	
Life doesn't discriminate	Life doesn't discriminate
Between the sinners and the saints.	Between the sinners and the saints.
It takes and it takes and it takes	It takes and it takes and it takes
We rise	And we keep living anyway
We fall	We rise and we fall and we break
	And we make our mistakes
And if there's a reason	And if there's a reason
I'm still alive	I'm still alive
When so many have died	When so many have died
Then I'm willin' to—	Then I' willin' to—

BURR:
Wait for it . . . [4]

        WOMEN:
          Wait for it . . .   **MEN:**
Wait for it . . .   Wait for it . . .
            Wait for it . . .
                    Wait for it . . .
            Wait for it . . .
                    Wait for it . . .
            Wait for it . . .
                    Wait for it . . .
            Wait for it . . .
                    Wait . . .

[4] How do you dramatize stasis (waiting for it)? You give the audience a glimpse of the immense self-control that makes it possible. I make you wait even for the *words* "wait for it."

XI

WHEREIN

MOBB DEEP

IS SAMPLED

AND THE IMMORTAL

BIGGIE SMALLS

IS REVIVED

"**I** WANT TO ADD A SAMPLE," LIN SAID. He had come to the theater early one morning to listen to Alex Lacamoire's soundcheck with the band. He was a little bleary-eyed and was standing at the front of the nearly empty theater wearing his "REHEARSAL IS THE BEST PART" hoodie.

"We cleared it," he told Lac. "Let's use it."

He propped his laptop on the edge of the stage, and played the song that he had cleared—that is, that he had gotten permission to quote in the show: "Shook Ones, Pt. II" by Mobb Deep, one of the grimy classics of '90s New York hip-hop. He had incorporated one of the song's best-known lyrics in "My Shot." Now he wanted to evoke the distinctive siren effect that opens the track: a sharp rising squeal, a sound of trouble on the way.

Lac cocked an ear toward Lin's laptop, staring into the middle distance. If he had heard this song before, he didn't say so.

"That's cool," he said after listening a few times. He wondered if they should use a snippet from the actual record.

Lin said he would rather not. Before making *Hamilton*, he co-wrote a new musical version of the movie *Bring It On*, which Lac music-directed. The experience taught them how tricky it can be to blend prerecorded samples and live instruments in a theater. They ended up using Ableton to supply some of the sounds in *Hamilton*: record scratches, the rewind sound effect in "Satisfied," some of the drum loops, etc. But wherever possible, they tried to generate every sound from within the 10-person band. Lin thought there might be a way to evoke the Mobb Deep squeal that way. "Steampunk sampling," he calls it.

Alex explored up and down his keyboard, trying to find the note.

"Let's do it with a violin," Lin suggested. "With crazy vibrato."

Alex described to the four-person string section what he was looking for. A violinist began to scrape away, looking for the right tone.

"It's subtle," said Lin, "but Mobb Deep fans will love it."

Alex decided he was ready to try it. The band tore into "My Shot," with Lin rapping along. When he got to the Mobb Deep line—"I'm only 19 but my mind is older"—one of the violins unleashed a shrill, dissonant tone that slid higher as it went. The hip-hop fans in the room laughed in recognition. Lin beamed, and threw a couple of triumphant middle fingers in the air.

Hamilton is laced with these shout-outs to the traditions that birthed it, both hip-hop (DMX, Grandmaster Flash and the Furious Five) and musical theater (*South Pacific*, *The Last Five Years*). These serve, in part, as invitations, a signal to people from diverse backgrounds that the show is meant for them. When Lin rapped, in the opening number of *In the Heights*, that "It's gotten too darn hot, like my man Cole Porter said," he was creating

"...AMERICAN HISTORY CAN BE TOLD AND RETOLD, CLAIMED AND RECLAIMED, *even by people who don't look like George Washington and Betsy Ross.*"

a crossroads for himself, where much of his subsequent work has appeared, *Hamilton* very much included.

In this show, though, the shout-outs have a subtle second meaning. They're another way of saying that American history can be told and retold, claimed and reclaimed, even by people who don't look like George Washington and Betsy Ross. Alexander Hamilton, who spent his life trying to live down his lowly origins, knew better than the other founders that even something as unprecedented and revolutionary as the United States would carry traces of many tangled traditions—the same way that "My Shot" carries the DNA of "Shook Ones," which in turn sampled Quincy Jones and Herbie Hancock, who had their own constellations of riffs, quotes, inspirations.

The predecessor who gets sampled the most in *Hamilton* is the Notorious B.I.G., a.k.a. Biggie Smalls, a.k.a. the King of New York, the greatest rapper of all time. Lin's annotations throughout this book reveal the many subtle ways that Biggie influenced the show. In one song, "Ten Duel Commandments," the influence couldn't be more direct or profound.

Lin and Tommy wanted to explain the rules of the *code duello* in the first act. That way, when the show rose to its second-act climax, the Hamilton-Burr confrontation, they could skip the mechanics of dueling, and focus on the question that has tortured historians for two centuries: What happened on that cliff in Weehawken? What were Hamilton and Burr *doing* up there?

Biggie's song "Ten Crack Commandments" gave Lin the template he needed. The rules of dueling slip neatly into spots originally occupied by the rules of selling crack. The enormous shadow of Biggie himself proved useful too, as his story helps to collapse the distance between the revolutionary era and our own time.

How, you think, could someone with the brilliance and the survival instincts of Alexander Hamilton find himself looking down the barrel of a gun, giving his friend-turned-nemesis a chance to put a .54-caliber bullet in his spine? It's not so hard to imagine. Christopher Wallace (a.k.a. The Notorious B.I.G., etc., etc.) was a lyrical genius, a master storyteller, an inspiration to millions, and nobody's fool. He was shot and killed at 24. The murder still hasn't been solved.

STAY ALIVE

Hamilton is seated. He is writing letters.

ELIZA: Stay alive . . .

ELIZA, ANGELICA, ENSEMBLE WOMEN:
Stay alive . . .

HAMILTON: I have never seen the general
 so despondent.
I have taken over writing all his correspondence.
Congress writes, "George, attack the
 British forces."
I shoot back, we have resorted to eating
 our horses.
Local merchants deny us equipment, assistance,

They only take British money, so sing a song
 of sixpence.

Washington enters. Hamilton stands at attention.

WASHINGTON: The cavalry's not coming.

HAMILTON: Sir!

WASHINGTON: Alex, listen. There's only one
 way for us to win this.
Provoke outrage, outright.

HAMILTON: That's right.

WASHINGTON: Don't engage, strike by night.
Remain relentless 'til their troops take flight.

HAMILTON: Make it impossible to justify the cost of the fight.

WASHINGTON: Outrun.

HAMILTON: Outrun.

WASHINGTON: Outlast.

HAMILTON: Outlast.

WASHINGTON: Hit 'em quick, get out fast.

HAMILTON: Chick-a-plao! [1]

WASHINGTON: Stay alive 'til this horror show is past.
We're gonna fly a lot of flags half-mast.

HAMILTON, LAURENS, LAFAYETTE: Raise a glass!

MULLIGAN: I go back to New York and my apprenticeship.

LAFAYETTE: I ask for French aid, I pray that France has sent a ship.

LAURENS: I stay at work with Hamilton.
We write essays against slavery.
And every day's a test of our camaraderie and bravery.

HAMILTON: We cut supply lines, we steal contraband.
We pick and choose our battles and places to take a stand.
And ev'ry day,
"Sir, entrust me with a command."
And ev'ry day,

[1] Probably a subconscious nod to all the *rigatigatum* and *cracko-jacko* in *West Side Story*, though if I'm being honest, I hear it in Method Man's voice, in that one Wu-Tang skit where they're just talking about how they're going to beat each other up. "And bang them sh*ts with a spiked bat like *blao*."

WASHINGTON: No.

HAMILTON: He dismisses me out of hand.

General Charles Lee enters.

HAMILTON:		ELIZA,
Instead of me[2]		ANGELICA:
He promotes	LEE:	Stay alive.
Charles Lee.	Charles Lee.	
Makes him		
second-in-command:		

LEE: I'm a general. Whee!!!!

HAMILTON: Yeah. He's not the choice I would have gone with.

HAMILTON, LAURENS, LAFAYETTE:
He shits the bed at the Battle of Monmouth.

WASHINGTON: Ev'ryone attack!

LEE: Retreat!

WASHINGTON: Attack!

LEE: Retreat!

WASHINGTON: What are you doing, Lee?
Get back on your feet!

LEE: But there's so many of them!

WASHINGTON: I'm sorry, is this not your speed?!
Hamilton!

HAMILTON: Ready, sir!

WASHINGTON: Have Lafayette take the lead!

[2] I'm playing fast and loose with who gets to be narrator here: I want Hamilton's frustration at being passed over first and foremost, so he gets to tell us this part of the story.

HAMILTON: Yes, sir!

LAURENS: A thousand soldiers die in a hundred degree heat.

LAFAYETTE: As we snatch a stalemate from the jaws of defeat.

HAMILTON: Charles Lee was left behind
Without a pot to piss in.
He started sayin' this to anybody who
    would listen.

LEE: Washington cannot be left alone to
    his devices
Indecisive, from crisis to crisis.
The best thing he can do for the revolution
    is turn 'n
Go back to plantin' tobacco in Mount Vernon.

COMPANY: Ooh!!

WASHINGTON: Don't do a thing. History will prove him wrong.

HAMILTON: But, sir!

WASHINGTON: We have a war to fight, let's move along.

LAURENS: Strong words from Lee, someone oughta hold him to it.

HAMILTON: I can't disobey direct orders.

LAURENS: Then I'll do it.
Alexander, you're the closest friend I've got.

HAMILTON: Laurens, do not throw away
    your shot.

TEN DUEL
COMMANDMENTS[1]

—◆—

MEN: One, two, three, four

FULL COMPANY: Five, six, seven, eight, nine . . .

BURR, HAMILTON, LAURENS, LEE: It's the Ten Duel Commandments.

FULL COMPANY: It's the Ten Duel Commandments.[2]
Number one!

LAURENS: The challenge: demand satisfaction. If they apologize no need for further action.

COMPANY: Number two!

LAURENS: If they don't, grab a friend, that's your second.

HAMILTON: Your lieutenant when there's reckoning to be reckoned.

COMPANY: Number three!

LEE: Have your seconds meet face to face.

BURR: Negotiate a peace . . .

HAMILTON: Or negotiate a time and place.

BURR: This is commonplace, 'specially 'tween recruits.

COMPANY: Most disputes die, and no one shoots. Number four!

LAURENS: If they don't reach a peace,
that's alright.
Time to get some pistols and a doctor on site.

HAMILTON: You pay him in advance, you treat him with civility.

BURR: You have him turn around so he can have deniability.

COMPANY: Five!

LEE: Duel before the sun is in the sky.

COMPANY: Pick a place to die where it's high and dry, number six!

HAMILTON: Leave a note for your next of kin. Tell 'em where you been. Pray that hell or
heaven lets you in.

COMPANY: Seven!

LEE: Confess your sins, ready for the moment
Of adrenaline when you finally face your opponent

COMPANY: Number eight!

LAURENS, LEE, HAMILTON, BURR: Your last chance to negotiate.
Send in your seconds, see if they can set the
record straight . . .

Hamilton & Burr meet center stage. They are the seconds in this duel.

[1] This song owes a huge debt to *Affairs Of Honor,* the book on dueling by Joanne Freeman. She is also one of the world's foremost Hamilton experts, and her insights and friendship have been indispensable.

[2] The entire company narrates this tune—it's the most complex one for our stage manager to call and our sound board op to track because the narrator keeps changing. I did this because I wanted the audience to understand that dueling was simply a way of life, with its own codes and customs. It was almost never a crime of passion—there were steps and ways out.

BURR: Alexander.

HAMILTON: Aaron Burr, sir.

BURR: Can we agree that duels are dumb and immature?

HAMILTON: Sure.
But your man has to answer for his words, Burr. [3]

BURR: With his life? We both know that's absurd, sir.

HAMILTON: Hang on, how many men died because Lee was inexperienced and ruinous?

BURR: Okay, so we're doin' this.

They walk off to their respective corners.

[3] Burr thought dueling was pointless, by the way. He even prevented one between Hamilton and James Monroe. Until, y'know. He didn't.

COMPANY: Number nine!

HAMILTON: Look 'em in the eye,
    aim no higher.
Summon all the courage you require.
    Then count

MEN: One two three four

MEN: Five six seven eight nine

HAMILTON, BURR: Number

COMPANY: Ten paces!

HAMILTON, BURR: Fire!

XII

OF

OSKAR EUSTIS

HIS POLITICS, HIS EVENTFUL CAREER,

HIS THOUGHTS on VERSE DRAMA,

AND HIS STEWARDSHIP OF THE PUBLIC THEATER

with a Word About

THE PHARCYDE

THREE DAYS AFTER LIN AND TOMMY returned from their week in Poughkeepsie, on July 30, 2013, they met producer Jeffrey Seller at Café Luxembourg on Manhattan's Upper West Side to eat lunch and talk strategy. What should *The Hamilton Mixtape*'s next move be? Or, more to the point, *when* and *where*?

Lin and Tommy said that they were ready to plunge ahead. The week at Vassar had been fruitful, the audience effusive. They wanted to go into rehearsal on a full production before the end of 2014.

That seemed aggressive to Jeffrey. Theaters often get booked years in advance. Also, he pointed out, *they still didn't have a second act.*

"Don't worry," Lin said. "I'm going to your house in September." Meaning Jeffrey's home in the Hamptons, where he would churn out the remaining songs.

So much for the question of *when*. But *where* would that production be? Everybody agreed that New York was the best city in which to develop a hip-hop musical

about a Founding Father. But there are dozens of theaters in the city—which one offered the best fit?

A week later, they arranged to visit the three Off-Broadway theaters that seemed like the most promising places to prepare the show for a Broadway run. The "college tour," as they called it, led to a unanimous favorite.

"I want to go to the Public," said Jeffrey. "We're gonna do *A Chorus Line*: It's a new musical, nobody knows anything about it, nobody cares about it—yet."

The Public Theater was indeed the birthplace of *A Chorus Line*, as well as the process that made Michael Bennett's unheralded, unprecedented musical possible: a series of workshops that gave the creative team a chance to refine their show, away from the glare and commercial pressure of Broadway. *A Chorus Line* marks the pinnacle of the Public's half-century tradition of adventurous, socially conscious musicals, including *Hair*; *Bring in 'Da Noise, Bring in 'Da Funk*; *Caroline, or Change*; and *Bloody Bloody Andrew Jackson.*

CHAPTER XII

The inheritor of that tradition is the Public's artistic director, Oskar Eustis. If he were king of the forest—a phrase Oskar uses a lot—life would be what Gonzalo dreams of in *The Tempest*: There would be no riches or poverty, "All things in common nature should produce / Without sweat or endeavor." Like Lin, he had a father involved in Democratic politics; unlike Lin, he had a mother and stepfather in the leadership of the Communist Party of America. To bide his time until the proletariat rises, Oskar develops and produces plays, particularly scripts by new voices. The last theatrical work to do what *Hamilton* has done—leap off the arts pages and become central to the country's cultural conversation—was one that Oskar commissioned and developed 30 years earlier: *Angels in America*. His work with Tony Kushner is a big reason why he is regarded, by people who track such things, as the greatest dramaturg alive.

Oskar already knew Lin, Tommy, and Jeffrey when they arrived for their tour. The Public had hosted a series of developmental concerts for Sting's musical *The Last Ship*, which Jeffrey had produced. And Oskar was two years into an artistic love affair with Lin. At first, his feelings about the young composer weren't exactly cheerful: *In the Heights* had won its four Tony Awards at the expense of *Passing Strange*, which had premiered at the Public. But Oskar liked Lin as soon as they met, and his reaction to the half-dozen demo recordings that Lin sent afterwards was immediate and fierce. Lin seemed a little overwhelmed by this enthusiasm. Oskar is a big man, with a big heart, and at that early stage hardly anybody had heard Lin's *Hamilton* songs, let alone raved about them. "I should do these meetings more often," Lin said after one of those effusions. "They make me feel like a better writer."

Choosing the Public gave Lin and Tommy what they wanted. Oskar and Patrick Willingham, the Public's executive director, scheduled the show for the 2014–'15 season, exactly the time frame they had desired. It gave Lin a year to finish writing the show and Tommy a year to figure out how to stage it. The Public put a couple of workshops on the calendar, intermediate deadlines that Lin and Tommy could work toward. Lin grabbed his dog and his notebooks and headed for the Hamptons, where Jeffrey's upright piano awaited.

Jeffrey got what he wanted, too. Later, when somebody asked him about his marketing campaign for *Hamilton*, he said that going to the Public *was* the marketing campaign: He wanted to brand the show by associating it with what he called "the quintessential New York downtown theater laboratory."

And Oskar got what he wanted, in double measure. From his earliest encounters with the show—listening to Lin's demos, attending the American Songbook concert, making the trek to Vassar—he saw that *Hamilton* could do more than extend the tradition of great Public musicals: Its use of hip-hop would allow it to build on the tradition of Shakespeare in the Park. He calls the show "a perfect example of verse drama."

"Lin does exactly what Shakespeare does," he says. "He takes the language of the people, and heightens it by making it verse. It both ennobles the language and

> **"*Lin does exactly what Shakespeare does* . . . HE TAKES THE LANGUAGE OF THE PEOPLE, AND HEIGHTENS IT BY MAKING IT VERSE."**

the people saying the language. That's precisely what Shakespeare did in all of his work, particularly in his history plays. He tells the foundational myths of his country. By doing that, he makes the country the possession of everybody."

You can see what he means in "Meet Me Inside," Washington's angry confrontation with the hotheaded Hamilton. Music accompanies the dialogue, but the language has a rhythm that strays far from the beat. The exchange shows why, until about 200 years ago, virtually every playwright in the Western tradition wrote in verse. It has lift, concision, drive. It demands, and rewards, your attention.

Here is another *Hamilton* paradox: Half a century after verse storytelling—the technique that worked so well in *Medea*, *Tartuffe*, and *Othello*—was declared dead on the American stage, it has been revived by someone who learned it not in a textbook or in a drama school but from listening endlessly to "Friend or Foe," "Everything Is Fair," and the first album by The Pharcyde.

MEET ME INSIDE[1]

———◆———

[1] This is one of the only hip-hop songs I know in a 7/8 time signature. It's super hard to sustain, but I like that we break into it right after the duel. It feels chaotic, messy.

[2] Jeremy: A remarkably gracious thing for GW to say. Why have him say it?
Lin: *History has its eyes on him, McCarter!*

[3] I always loved the menace at the end of DMX's "Party Up (Up in Here)": "Meet me outside, meet me outside." *What's gonna happen outside, DMX?* I used that menace here.

[4] We're back to 4/4 time here. And this scene is one of my favorites—it's a fully functional scene with two friends at cross-purposes. Hamilton doesn't know, or can't internalize, that Washington wants to keep him safe—all he wants is a command. Washington's logic falls on deaf ears, so he keeps trying to get familiar, which only infuriates Hamilton more. This is where watching every episode of *The West Wing* helps you be a better writer.

HAMILTON: Lee, do you yield!

BURR: You shot him in the side! Yes, he yields!

LAURENS: I'm satisfied.

BURR: Yo we gotta clear the field!

HAMILTON: Go! We won.

COMPANY: Here comes the general!

BURR: This should be fun.

Washington enters.

WASHINGTON: What is the meaning of this?
Mr. Burr? Get a medic for the general.

BURR: Yes, sir.

WASHINGTON: Lee, you will never agree with
    me, but believe me.
These young men don't speak for me.
Thank you for your service.[2]

BURR: Let's ride!

WASHINGTON: Hamilton!

HAMILTON: Sir!

WASHINGTON: Meet me inside.

COMPANY: Meet 'im inside! Meet 'im inside!
Meet 'im inside, meet 'im meet 'im inside![3]

Washington & Hamilton, alone.

WASHINGTON: Son—[4]

HAMILTON: Don't call me son.

WASHINGTON: This war is hard enough
without infighting—

HAMILTON: Lee called you out. We called
his bluff.

WASHINGTON: You solve nothing, you
aggravate our allies to the south.

HAMILTON: You're absolutely right. John
    should have shot him in the mouth.
That would've shut him up.

WASHINGTON: Son—

HAMILTON: I'm notcha son—

WASHINGTON: Watch your tone.
I am not a maiden in need of defending,
    I am grown.

HAMILTON (OVERLAPPING): Charles Lee,
Thomas Conway. These men take your name
and they rake it through the mud.

WASHINGTON: My name's been through a lot,
I can take it.

HAMILTON: Well, I don't have your name.
    I don't have your titles.
I don't have your land.
But, if you—

WASHINGTON: No—

HAMILTON: If you gave me command of a
battalion. A group of men to lead, I could fly
above my station after the war.

WASHINGTON: Or you could die and we need you alive.

HAMILTON: I'm more than willing to die—

WASHINGTON: Your wife needs you alive, son, I need you alive—

Washington reaches out to Hamilton.

HAMILTON: Call me son one more time— 5

Hamilton freezes, aware of the line he has crossed.

WASHINGTON: Go home, Alexander. That's an order from your commander.

HAMILTON: Sir—

WASHINGTON: Go home.

5 Doing this scene with Chris is really different every night. We're best friends, and it takes a lot out of us. Sometimes he screams my head off. Other times he can barely look at me. It's always real though.

XIII

ON

PHILLIPA SOO

AND THE

TROUBLE *with* GOODNESS

THREE TIMES, HOLLYWOOD OPTIONED Ron Chernow's biography of Hamilton. Three times, it came to naught.

"I just don't get it," Ron would tell his agent in the years that followed the book's publication in 2004. "This story has all the ingredients you could possibly want: sex, violence, genius."

When Lin optioned his book, Ron was relieved that the Founding Father who had the most dramatic and least appreciated life story would finally get his due— even though a rap musical was the last way that Ron had anticipated Hamilton getting it. Still, he knew that plenty of traps awaited anybody who wanted to adapt this story. For starters: What do you do about Eliza?

Petite and vivacious, Eliza Schuyler Hamilton won the affection of everyone she met. "She was a most earnest, energetic, and intelligent woman," recalled one of her sons. The letters that Hamilton exchanged with his "Betsey" don't have the lightning-flash quality of his letters to and from the witty Angelica, but they glow all the same. Eliza changed his life, and might have saved it. "I was once determined to let my existence and American liberty end together," he wrote to her during their engagement. "My Betsey has given me a motive to outlive my pride."

Eliza's warmth and vibrancy made her a remarkable woman, but they also make her a challenging character: "It's difficult to make pure goodness compelling," Ron says.

Tommy found a solution before he even realized that they had a problem. In late 2012, he saw Dave Malloy's stage adaptation of *War and Peace,* an electropop musical titled *Natasha, Pierre, & the Great Comet of 1812.* When the lights came up at intermission, he turned to a casting agent sitting nearby and said, "What are you waiting for?"

> *"Eliza's warmth and vibrancy made her a remarkable woman, but they also make her a challenging character: 'IT'S DIFFICULT TO MAKE PURE GOODNESS COMPELLING.'"*

He was talking about Phillipa Soo, the recent Juilliard grad who was making her Off-Broadway debut.

"That girl who played Natasha, she's a star," he told Lin the next day. "There's just something there."

A year later, Pippa was leaving breakfast at a diner in Washington Heights when her phone rang. (The diner had a *Heights* poster on the wall, a tribute to Lin. "He's basically the mayor up here," she says.) Tommy was calling to invite her to read Eliza in a workshop of the still-unfinished Act Two. She said yes, and came to read the role in December 2013, at the first workshop that Jeffrey produced in conjunction with the Public. "Then she was it," says Lin, "and she was it from then on."

Lin liked Pippa for the role because audiences instantly and instinctively warmed to her, just as Eliza's contemporaries had done. "Pippa has this sort of elegance and this lit-from-within quality," he says. "She's so poised, and she's in such control of what she can do, which is kind of amazing for an actor or actress of her age. I certainly wasn't in control of whatever the hell I had at that age."

Though she was young—only a year out of college—she had been performing since her early childhood in Chicago. Her father, who is a doctor, and her mother, who is active in the city's theaters, supported her desire to perform, whether it was acting, singing, or dancing. She even did some modeling: Her half-Chinese heritage gave her a distinctive beauty. Pippa's grandparents—her father's mother and father—had immigrated to this country before they were married. She treasures a photo of her grandfather on the boat that carried him across the Pacific in 1949.

Eliza's devotion was constant, but in the course of her life, and therefore in a single performance of *Hamilton*, virtually everything else about her changes, and fast. The swoony girl who sings "Helpless" reappears a few minutes later as a pregnant young wife, describing what kind of life she wants with her husband in "That Would Be Enough."

As Pippa began to navigate these changes, she asked to meet with Ron Chernow. Their conversation gave her a new understanding of Eliza, as she had hoped it would, but not in the way she expected. "The impression that lasted on me more than the actual facts was how wonderful he thought Eliza was, and how that matched how he felt about his own wife."

Ron told Pippa that during the six years he had spent on the book, Valerie Chernow had developed a powerful identification with Hamilton's wife. "She used to say, 'Eliza is like me: She's good, she's true, she's loyal, she's not ambitious.' There was a purity and a goodness about the character, and that was like Valerie," he says. In 2006, after 27 years of marriage, Valerie passed away. For her gravestone, Ron chose a line from the letter that Hamilton wrote to Eliza on the night before the duel: "Best of wives and best of women."

For all his early worries about the role, Ron knew as soon as he saw Pippa that the show had found its Eliza. Some friends pointed out that Pippa even looks a little like Valerie. Her ballad "That Would Be Enough," in particular, moves him deeply. "Just heartbreakingly beautiful," he says.

CHAPTER XIII

THAT WOULD BE ENOUGH[1]

❖

Hamilton goes home. Eliza enters. She is visibly pregnant.

ELIZA: Look around, look around, at how lucky we are to be alive right now.
Look around, look around . . .

HAMILTON: How long have you known?

ELIZA: A month or so.

HAMILTON: Eliza, you should have told me.

ELIZA: I wrote to the general a month ago.

HAMILTON: No.

ELIZA: I begged him to send you home.

HAMILTON: You should have told me.

ELIZA: I'm not sorry.

I knew you'd fight
until the war was won.   **HAMILTON:**
                           The war's not
                           Done
But you deserve a
chance to meet
Your son.
Look around, look
around, at how lucky
we are to be alive
right now.

HAMILTON: Will you relish being a poor man's wife?
Unable to provide for your life.

ELIZA: I relish being your wife.
Look around, look around . . .

Look at where you are.
Look at where you started.
The fact that you're alive is a miracle.
Just stay alive, that would be enough.

And if this child
Shares a fraction of your smile
Or a fragment of your mind, look out, world!
That would be enough.

I don't pretend to know
The challenges you're facing.
The worlds you keep erasing and creating in your mind.

But I'm not afraid.
I know who I married.
So long as you come home at the end of the day
That would be enough.

We don't need a legacy.
We don't need money.
If I could grant you peace of mind [2]

If you could let me inside your heart
Oh, let me be a part of the narrative
In the story they will write someday.
Let this moment be the first chapter
Where you decide to stay
And I could be enough
And we could be enough
That would be enough.

Hamilton kisses Eliza's hand.

[1] Very few songs come to me as quickly as the first draft of this song did. Words and music together at the piano, from this point to the end of the tune, in about 45 minutes. There is no historical basis for this song. Eliza needed to say it, so she did.

[2] My first draft of this song ended here, but I revisited the tune after writing "Burn" in Act Two. Tommy and I discussed making Eliza even *more* active here—not just expressing this sentiment, but asking to be let into Hamilton's internal life. If she's "erasing herself from the narrative" in Act Two, she needs to be part of it in Act One. I love the way this last section soars—I can't imagine the song without it now.

ON

PAUL TAZEWELL

AND THE

FASHION OF REVOLUTION

"THIS IS A DAY OF FIRSTS," SAID TOMMY. It was May 9, 2014, and he was looking up at the 150 people who packed the top-floor theater at the 52nd Street Project, a program that specializes in plays created for and by kids, and sometimes offers space to shows like *Hamilton*. They had come for what he called "the first time we will have ever done the first act and the second act back to back." Going for a laugh, he said, "You're the first audience *in the history of the world* to have seen that."

The show's title was another first that day. Jeffrey had persuaded Lin to drop "Mixtape" a few months earlier. He joked that it might be the most important contribution he made to the show. "'*Hamilton*' sounds like a blockbuster," he says. "At least it does now."

Tommy warned the audience that Lin had been adding and changing things until the night before. "You'll be hearing things that not even *he* has heard out loud," he said. (Lin couldn't—can't—help himself. "Finishing a tune at 10:30 for actors who are learning it at 11," he had tweeted during a workshop the previous fall. "Horrible horrible when will I stop doing my homework on the bus I'm 33.")

The company had spent five weeks experimenting with different ways to move people (and furniture) around the stage. Five weeks was an unusually long time, but not nearly long enough to figure out how to stage this show. Tommy had been feeling stressed about how to speed up the process when Lac reminded him that nobody was forcing them to do anything. Tommy realized he was right. They decided to stage Act One and fall back to music stands for Act Two.

ABOVE:

Curtain call at the 52nd Street Project—May 9, 2014.

But the biggest first of that workshop, and its real revelation, was what the cast wore. Looking back now, the costume choices of *Hamilton* seem obvious. Nobody thought so in May 2014, not even the man who made them.

In his 20 years on Broadway, Paul Tazewell had designed costumes for shows set in the distant past (*The Color Purple*, *Doctor Zhivago*) and our own time (*Magic/Bird*, *In the Heights*). When he heard Lin's demos, he knew that *Hamilton* would need to combine both sensibilities. But as with Korins's scenic design, the question was: *How?* "The challenge was figuring out where those two eras meet, and what percentage of this world is hip-hop and what percentage is 18th century," he says. He looked at a lot of street fashion from our time and John Trumbull's paintings from Alexander Hamilton's time. He studied the work of fashion icons who had tried to mash up the two eras: Jean-Paul Gaultier, Alexander McQueen, John Galliano. "Everybody has riffed on the 18th century at one time or another," he says.

In spite of his experience, his well-stocked toolkit, and that formidable pile of research, Paul couldn't locate the right point of intersection between past and present. Luckily he and Tommy had collaborated on five productions before this, developing enough mutual trust to remain untroubled by the fact that they weren't sure what to do. "We thought the only way to figure this out is to try it," says Paul.

Since they knew what the cast looked like in contemporary clothes—because that's what the actors wore to rehearsal every day—Paul used the workshop to experiment with an intensely authentic design. "Period

from the neck down, modern from the neck up" became the rule. "I didn't want Chris to be in a powdered wig as Washington," says Paul. "I wanted to see him for who he was."

This choice, by itself, didn't constitute a first. Joe Papp started putting black and Latino actors in period costumes for his free Shakespeare productions more than half a century ago. More recently, visual artists such as Kehinde Wiley—someone whose work Paul consulted during his research—have painted contemporary black men in the trappings of Old Master portraits. Still, the sight of this cast in Paul's costumes made the show seem doubly, triply audacious.

The biggest jolt came toward the end of Act One, when the actors came onstage wearing blue coats with red trim and brass buttons: unmistakably the uniforms of

> *"THERE ARE CERTAIN PLACES WHERE IT RESONATES, WHERE I REMEMBER, 'OH YEAH, I'M A PART OF THIS.' Not this production—I know what I bring to the production—but being an American."*

George Washington's Continental Army. That day, for the first time, 150 audience members had the mind-altering experience of watching black and Latino actors, young men and women from communities that have seen their freedom infringed for hundreds of years, win freedom for us all.

People wept at intermission. They screamed at the finale. In the cramped lobby afterwards, you could hear a potent clatter of emotions: euphoria, disbelief, desperation (this last from people who wanted to invest in the show). There were four presentations between Thursday and Saturday, which meant that 600 people fanned out

ABOVE:
Tommy Kail, Andy Blankenbuehler, and Lin-Manuel Miranda at the 52nd Street Project.

FROM THE
SKETCHBOOK
AND
FABRIC COLLECTION
OF PAUL TAZEWELL

MARIA

HAMILTON

JEFFERSON

ELIZA

ELIZA

"*I didn't want Chris to be in a powdered wig as Washington . . . I WANTED TO SEE HIM FOR WHO HE WAS.*"

that weekend to tell their friends what they had seen. By Monday, *Hamilton* had become the most talked-about not-quite-show in New York.

For Tommy, the experiment of putting actors in period costumes had been a complete success. One choice that had seemed like a concession to the spare nature of workshops, putting all of the actors in parchment-toned clothes, and adding colors only when they distinguished themselves as specific characters, carried all the way to Broadway. Paul was delighted by the outcome too. He had received five Tony Award nominations in his career, but still wanted badly to get this one right.

"This piece is so humbling," he says, tears rising in his eyes. "I really didn't want to fuck it up, and get in the way

of it. There are certain places where it resonates, where I remember, 'Oh yeah, I'm a part of this.' Not this production—I know what I bring to the production—but being an American. I am a part of it, as opposed to being"—he searched for the right word—"an afterthought."

When the Battle of Yorktown sequence ended that day, the largely black and Latino cast (singing a song written by a Puerto Rican composer, wearing costumes selected by an African-American designer) climbed on top of boxes and chairs to celebrate having done the impossible. Andy Blankenbuehler would spend the next 16 months trying to recapture how exhilarating the moment felt. It took him until a week before opening night on Broadway to feel that he had succeeded.

GUNS AND SHIPS

BURR: How does a ragtag volunteer army in need of a shower
Somehow defeat a global superpower?
How do we emerge victorious from the quagmire?
Leave the battlefield waving Betsy Ross' flag higher?
Yo. Turns out we have a secret weapon!
An immigrant you know and love who's unafraid to step in!
He's constantly confusin' confoundin' the British henchmen.
Ev'ryone, give it up for America's favorite fighting Frenchman.

COMPANY: Lafayette!

LAFAYETTE: I'm takin' this horse by the reins makin' redcoats redder with bloodstains.

COMPANY: Lafayette!

LAFAYETTE: And I'm never gonna stop until I make 'em drop, burn 'em up and scatter their remains, I'm—

COMPANY: Lafayette!

LAFAYETTE: Watch me engagin' 'em! Escapin' 'em! Enragin' 'em! I'm—

COMPANY: Lafayette!

LAFAYETTE: I go to France for more funds.

COMPANY: Lafayette!

LAFAYETTE: I come back with more

LAFAYETTE, ENSEMBLE: Guns
And ships

And so the balance shifts.

WASHINGTON: We rendezvous with Rochambeau, consolidate their gifts.

LAFAYETTE: We can end this war in Yorktown, cut them off at sea but
For this to succeed, there's someone else we need.

WASHINGTON: I know.

WASHINGTON, COMPANY: Hamilton!

LAFAYETTE: Sir, he knows what to do in a trench.
Ingenuitive[1] and fluent in French, I mean—

WASHINGTON, COMPANY: Hamilton!

LAFAYETTE: Sir, you're gonna have to use him eventually.
What's he gonna do on the bench, I mean—

WASHINGTON, COMPANY: Hamilton!

LAFAYETTE: No one has more resilience,
Or matches my practical tactical brilliance.[2]

WASHINGTON, COMPANY: Hamilton!

LAFAYETTE:
You wanna
fight for your
land back?   **COMPANY:**
                    Hamilton!
**WASHING-
TON:** I need
my right hand
man back!

---

[1] This is a weird one. *I thought everyone knew this word,* yet I don't know where I've heard it. You should have seen the looks on the faces of my collaborators when I brought the song in. It's apparently a super-archaic word. I really don't know where I met it, but it was there for me when I needed it.

[2] The speed at which Lafayette rhymes here was always meant to be a punchline: Here's Lafayette, the Frenchman, who struggles with the word *anarchy* in "My Shot," and he's a speed demon. It's also meant to demonstrate how Lafayette flourished once he was put in command. He goes from being one of Hamilton's friends to a rap god/military superhero. Doesn't hurt that Daveed is one of the most technically gifted rappers I've ever met, so I knew I could build him tapestries. It was actually his idea to rap this "resilience/brilliance" rap in a triplet rhythm, which is perfect.

	WOMEN:	
LAFAYETTE: Hamilton!		**MEN:**
Ah! Uh, get		Get your right
yah right hand		hand man
man back.		back!
You know you	Hamilton!	Your right
gotta get ya		hand man
right hand		back!
man back.		
I mean ya	Hamilton!	Hamilton!
gotta put some		Ha-
thought into		ha-!
the letter but		
the sooner the	Hamilton	Hamilton
better [3]	Hamilton	Hamilton
to get ya right	Ha- ha-!	Ha- ha-!
hand man back.		

WASHINGTON: Alexander Hamilton,
Troops are waiting in the field for you. [4]
If you join us right now, together we can turn
    the tide.
Oh, Alexander Hamilton,
I have soldiers who will yield for you.
If we manage to get this right
They'll surrender by early light.
The world will never be the same, Alexander . . .

*Hamilton kisses Eliza goodbye. He enters
Washington's office.*

[3] The last line I added to the show. Just *one more fast rap for Lafayette please.*

[4] In real life, Hamilton and his friends *badgered* Washington for a command on his behalf. He felt the war was winding to a close and was desperate to see action before its end. We represent that via Lafayette's crazy fast raps.

HISTORY HAS ITS EYES ON YOU[1]

[1] Once again, I'm in Chernow's debt here. Washington is a hard character to bust out of the marble shell in which history has encased him. When I read Chernow's Washington bio and learned about his disastrous first turn with a command (a slaughter that helped trigger the French and Indian War) it unlocked him for me. This is a man whose first brush with fame was humiliation. History had its eyes on him early, and he never forgot it. You can feel him calcify under the weight of it over the course of his life, ever conscious of it. Restraint: It's a lesson Hamilton never really learns.

[2] Once I wrote this passage, I knew it would be the key to the whole musical. In the words of Tupac, "This be the realest sh*t I ever wrote." We strut and fret our hour upon the stage, and how that reverberates is entirely out of our control and entirely in the hands of those who survive us. It's the fundamental truth all our characters (and all of us) share.

WASHINGTON: I was younger than you are now
When I was given my first command.
I led my men straight into a massacre.

I witnessed their deaths firsthand.
I made every mistake,
And felt the shame rise in me,
And even now I lie awake,

WASHINGTON:	**LAURENS, MULLIGAN:**
Knowing history has its eyes On me.	Whoa, whoa, whoa Whoa . . . Whoa . . . Yeah.

HAMILTON, WASHINGTON:	**COMPANY:**
History has its Eyes on Me.	Whoa, whoa, whoa Whoa . . . . Whoa . . . Yeah.

WASHINGTON: Let me tell you what I wish
   I'd known
When I was young and dreamed of glory.
You have no control.

WASHINGTON, COMPANY: Who lives, who dies, who tells your story.[2]

WASHINGTON: I know that we can win.
I know that greatness lies in you.
But remember from here on in,

WASHINGTON, HAMILTON, MEN:	
History has its	
	ENSEMBLE:
Eyes on you.	Whoa, whoa, whoa Whoa . . . Whoa . . .

COMPANY: History has its eyes on you.

YORKTOWN

(THE WORLD TURNED UPSIDE DOWN)

—◆—

COMPANY: The Battle of Yorktown. Seventeen eighty-one.

Hamilton & Lafayette enter and embrace.

LAFAYETTE: Monsieur Hamilton.

HAMILTON: Monsieur Lafayette.

LAFAYETTE: In command where you belong.

HAMILTON: How you say, no sweat.
We're finally on the field. We've had quite a run.

LAFAYETTE: Immigrants:

HAMILTON, LAFAYETTE: We get the job done.[1]

They high-five.

HAMILTON: So what happens if we win?

LAFAYETTE: I go back to France,
I bring freedom to my people if I'm given
  the chance.

HAMILTON: We'll be with you when you do.

LAFAYETTE: Go lead your men.

HAMILTON: I'll see you on the other side.

LAFAYETTE: 'Til we meet again, let's go!

ENSEMBLE: I am not throwin' away my shot!
I am not throwin' away my shot!
Hey yo, I'm just like my country, I'm young,
  scrappy and hungry

And I'm not throwin' away my shot!
I am not throwin' away my shot!

HAMILTON: 'Til the world turns upside down . . .

ENSEMBLE: 'Til the world turns upside down!

HAMILTON: I imagine death so much it feels
  more like a memory.
This is where it gets me:
On my feet,
The enemy ahead of me.
If this is the end of me, at least I have a friend
  with me.
Weapon in my hand, a command, and my men
  with me.
Then I remember my Eliza's expecting me . . .
Not only that, my Eliza's expecting,[2]
We gotta go, gotta get the job done,
Gotta start a new nation, gotta meet my son!
Take the bullets out your gun![3]

ENSEMBLE: What?

HAMILTON: The bullets out your gun!

ENSEMBLE: What?

HAMILTON: We move under cover and we
  move as one
Through the night, we have one shot to live
  another day.
We cannot let a stray gunshot give us away.
We will fight up close, seize the moment and
  stay in it.
It's either that or meet the business end
  of a bayonet.
The code word is "Rochambeau," dig me?

[1] This just made me laugh: Lafayette and Hamilton, on the verge of the last battle of the war, patting themselves on the back. I never anticipated that the audience response would drown out the next few lines every night. So we added two bars just to absorb the reaction. Cheers still drowned 'em out. So we added four bars. Then it felt like we were *asking* for applause, and they delivered, and it was even worse. We went back to two bars and it is what it is. Why does it get such a delighted response? Because it's true.

[2] This is the kind of thing that happens in hip-hop but not so much in musical theater: breaking the rhyme scheme to highlight a different meaning of the word. Musical theater purists may scoff, but I love that Hamilton's soliloquy here leads him to maturity: He has to put away his martyrdom fantasies because others are counting on him to come home.

[3] This seems so counterintuitive but it's what happened: Leave it to Hamilton to make his men remove their bullets to *ensure* no one would give away their sneak attack. That's some control-freak realness. I can relate.

[4] Part of the inspiration for the structure of "Yorktown" is what I call the "Busta Rhymes soft-loud-soft" technique. On countless songs, Busta will give you the smoothest, quietest delivery and then full-on scream the next verse. It makes for a delightful tension and release, and it's entirely vocal. Same here. "I have everything I wanted but I can't die today/*We're going into battle*/here's what my friends are doing/*Hercules Mulligan*!" Thank you and God bless you, Busta Rhymes.

[5] Laurens actually *was* at the Battle of Yorktown. He didn't head down to South Carolina until later. But I didn't have time to explain that, so I moved him down there early. He spent much of the war trying to get approval for a plan that would allow 3,000 black men to fight alongside the rebels for their emancipation and freedom.

[6] This Mulligan verse includes the greatest lines from a *really long* Mulligan verse I wrote for the first draft of "My Shot." It's much more effective here.

[7] Washington, of course, owned hundreds of slaves, and did not emancipate them until his death at the end of the century.

[8] Per Chernow, this was the name of the tune the British sang as they retreated. I sought out the actual song and it's . . . well, it's a drinking song. It's sprightly and lively and fun to sing with a pint in your hand, but didn't serve me musically. So I wrote my own melody for it. But God, what a great sentiment for the end of the war and the birth of this moment.

ENSEMBLE: Rochambeau!

HAMILTON: You have your orders now, go, man, go!
And so the American experiment begins [4]
With my friends all scattered to the winds.
Laurens is in South Carolina, redefining brav'ry.

HAMILTON, LAURENS: We'll never be free until we end slavery! [5]

HAMILTON: When we finally drive the British away,
Lafayette is there waiting—

HAMILTON, LAFAYETTE: In Chesapeake Bay!

HAMILTON: How did we know that this plan would work?
We had a spy on the inside. That's right,

Mulligan emerges.

HAMILTON, COMPANY: Hercules Mulligan!

MULLIGAN: A tailor spyin' on the British government!
I take their measurements, information and then I smuggle it!

COMPANY: Up.

MULLIGAN: To my brothers' revolutionary covenant
I'm runnin' with the Sons of Liberty and I am lovin' it!
See, that's what happens when you up against the ruffians. [6]
We in the shit now, somebody gotta shovel it!
Hercules Mulligan, I need no introduction,
When you knock me down I get the fuck back up again!

COMPANY: Whoa! Left! Right! Hold!
Go!
What! What! What!

HAMILTON: After a week of fighting, a young man in a red coat stands on a parapet.

LAFAYETTE: We lower our guns as he frantically waves a white handkerchief.

MULLIGAN: And just like that, it's over.
We tend to our wounded. We count our dead.

LAURENS: Black and white soldiers wonder alike if this really means freedom.

WASHINGTON: Not yet. [7]

HAMILTON: We negotiate the terms of surrender.
I see George Washington smile.
We escort their men out of Yorktown.
They stagger home single file.
Tens of thousands of people flood the streets.

There are screams and church bells ringing.

And as our fallen foes retreat,
I hear the drinking song they're singing . . .

ALL MEN: The world turned upside down.

COMPANY: The world turned upside down,[8]
The world turned upside down,
The world turned upside down,
Down,
Down, down, down.

LAFAYETTE: Freedom for America,
freedom for France!

COMPANY: Down, down, down.

HAMILTON: Gotta start a new nation,
Gotta meet my son.

COMPANY: Down, down, down.

MULLIGAN: We won!

LAFAYETTE: We won!

MULLIGAN, LAFAYETTE, LAURENS:
We won!

**MULLIGAN, LAFAYETTE, LAURENS,
HAMILTON, WASHINGTON:** We won!

COMPANY: The world turned upside down!

"**Y**ORKTOWN" COULD HAVE BEEN A rousing finale for Act One, a way to send the audience to the lobby feeling precisely what they wanted to feel about the country's birth. After all, didn't it happen just as the song suggests? The unerring Washington led us to freedom, with military victory and crisp dances, and then everybody lived happily ever after?

That sunny view is radically incomplete, as the founders themselves tried to tell us. John Adams, who lived long enough to see the legend taking root, begged us to remember that the country's birth was painful, contentious, and not remotely finished when the British went home: "It was patched and piebald policy then, as it is now, ever was and ever will be, world without end." The show spends much of Act Two making Adams look like a fat fool, but in refusing to treat the victory at Yorktown as the tidy end of the nation's birth, it takes his side. And the surprise is that good history also makes for good drama.

Instead of letting the audience spend intermission basking in a false view of the founders' infallibility, Lin and Tommy decided to extend Act One with a pair of songs that are explicit about the mistakes that they're going to make, the "patched and piebald" things about to go down. There was only one song that could follow "Yorktown," or at least one character. "After 'Yorktown,' King George is the only person you're willing to have start singing," says Oskar. "Anybody else—" and here he mimed looking at his watch.

Lin could have made "What Comes Next?" a simple comic turn, a lament by a petulant sore loser. Actually, the king *is* a petulant sore loser. But he asks the leaders of the new nation an unexpectedly sobering question: "Do you know how hard it is to lead?" And then he offers a stark bit of wisdom: "It's much harder when it's all your call." Those lines set up the fights that will animate the rest of the show, something "Yorktown" couldn't do. "You have to end an act with a dramatic question," says Tommy. "Ending a war is not a question. What you do *with* that is the question."

Lin paired the king's warning of political dangers with an admission of personal flaws. His research had turned up a coincidence that intrigued him: Alexander Hamilton became a parent at the same time that he was trying to

ABOVE:
Lin-Manuel Miranda and his wife, Vanessa Nadal.

birth a new nation. And—a double coincidence—so did Aaron Burr. Philip Hamilton was born in January 1782, Theodosia Burr in June 1783. Lin wrote "Dear Theodosia," a duet for the new fathers that is joyous but remarkably uncertain: "*If* we lay a strong enough foundation,/We'll pass it on to you," they sing. The only thing that's sure is how much they're going to screw it up. "I'll make a million mistakes," sings Burr.

Chernow was impressed by this refusal to deify the founders—one reason he calls the show "American history for grown-ups." Of course, most people are too busy fumbling for Kleenex during "Dear Theodosia" to admire the song's historiographical rigor. This is particularly true of the people who welcomed new children during the show's development.

Like Jeffrey Seller and Sander Jacobs, Jill Furman is an above-the-title producer of *Hamilton*. She went to Lin's American Songbook concert in 2012, and came away just as exhilarated as she had been on the night she went to the little theater in the basement of the Drama Book Shop and discovered a Nuyorican rapper-actor-composer-playwright who was writing a show about Washington Heights. Jill had a son just before the Public run began, and even now, she turns into what she calls "a total basket base" when she hears the song. Lin can't make eye contact with her until it ends.

So how did he write a song so evocative, one that is both precise and universal, one that made us see our babies' faces? "New fatherhood inspires young composer to write beautiful duet" is a simple, lovely story, but it's just as false as the simple, lovely view of the nation's founding. "I wrote 'Dear Theodosia' the week I adopted our dog," Lin says—although even this isn't the full story, as he explains in his annotations to the song on page 128.

Fatherhood didn't shape the way Lin wrote "Dear Theodosia," but it has changed the way he performs it. On November 10, 2014, Lin's wife, Vanessa, gave birth to their first son, Sebastian. "I play it differently because I have a real kid in my head now. I have access to a new

"*I PLAY IT DIFFERENTLY BECAUSE I HAVE A REAL KID IN MY HEAD NOW. I have access to a new depth of feeling . . .*"

depth of feeling, of 'This is a life I am responsible for, the main purpose of my life is this kid's life, everything else is secondary,'" he says. "It's not an abstract 'my child' now, it's *my child*."

Hamilton's love for Philip was just as deep as Lin's for his son, but, as "Dear Theodosia" anticipates, he sometimes did a lousy job of putting it into effect. A question that recurred in script meetings over the years was: Is the flawed, historically accurate Hamilton too unsympathetic? Were his failures as a husband, leader, and father alienating the audience? That has not been the experience of Javier Muñoz. As Lin's alternate, he needs to embody Hamilton's complexities as fully as the man who dramatized them. But since he only performs the role once a week, he spends most of his working hours getting to observe how an audience responds to them. Nobody associated with *Hamilton* combines a view from

ABOVE:
Lin and Vanessa's son, Sebastian.

those." He knows what he's talking about: Born and raised in Brooklyn, he spent years stringing together gigs in regional theater, finally getting a shot at Broadway as an ensemble member of *In the Heights*. "That's the life I live—I live an openly flawed life," he says. And he thinks these flaws are precisely why Hamilton's story exerts such a potent hold on people. "They allow the audience to say, 'I'm okay the way I am—flawed and human.' It pulls them in closer."

Playing Hamilton presents all sorts of challenges; serving as the *other* Hamilton amplifies those challenges and adds some fresh ones. Since the primary Hamilton was also the show's writer—and a fearless improviser, thanks to Freestyle Love Supreme—Javier had to track Lin's every move throughout rehearsals. There was no telling when he might try something and like it enough to keep it. "If he has done something a certain way two times, that's when I would ask him, 'Is that a change?'" says Javier.

Still "Javilton," as Lin calls him, is palpably grateful for the chance to play the role. "They've given me their baby to take care of and watch," he says. "It feels that precious." When he comes to the theater six times a week to perform the role in the wings—every line, every song— without going on-stage, it's not out of an abstract sense of duty. "This is

"You have to end an act with a dramatic question . . . ENDING A WAR IS NOT A QUESTION. WHAT YOU DO WITH THAT IS THE QUESTION."

live theater," he explains. "It's always changing."

The only way to stay in sync with his castmates as they continually discover new things and deepen their relationships is to change with them. It's not a metaphor to call a play like *Hamilton* a living, changing thing: It has the same surprising life as a baby, or a new nation.

the center and a view from the periphery more completely than he does.

Hamilton's failures don't strike Javier as obstacles: On the contrary, they are how he finds his way into the role. "Most characters in musicals make one or two mistakes, but otherwise they're perfect. I get bored with characters like

ABOVE:
Javier Muñoz.

WHAT COMES NEXT?

We see King George, glum.

KING GEORGE:[1] They say
The price of my war's not a price that they're
    willing to pay.
Insane.
You cheat with the French, now I'm fighting
    with France and with Spain.
I'm so blue.
I thought that we'd made an arrangement when
    you went away,
You were mine to subdue.
Well, even despite our estrangement, I've got a
    small query for you:

What comes next?
You've been freed.
Do you know how hard it is
    to lead?

You're on your own.
Awesome. Wow.
Do you have a clue what happens now?

Oceans rise.
Empires fall.
It's much harder when it's all your call.[2]

All alone, across the sea.
When your people say they hate you,
    don't come crawling back to me.

Da da da dat da dat da da da
Da ya da
Da da dat
Da da ya da . . .

You're on your own . . .

[1] To paraphrase Ashanti and Ja Rule, the king's not always there when you call, but he's always on time. It was a delight to have him pop up at this key moment. He becomes an audience surrogate in a strange way, robbing the revolution of its inevitability and kicking the tires on it: *So you're going to rule yourselves now. Have you figured out how that works yet? Good luck. It's lonely, thankless work.*

[2] This is prep for our second act in a real way: It's not hard to make a revolution exciting onstage. But governing? That takes some doing.

DEAR THEODOSIA[1]

[1] This song arrived in my life in one of those very strange, momentous weeks. To set the scene: 2011. I was on Thanksgiving vacation with my wife's family in the Dominican Republic. My wife's aunt Isolde, across the sea in Austria, was struggling in the final stages of ALS, so the air was heavy: We dreaded/anticipated the news of her passing even as we attempted to make the best of this vacation.

Amidst all this, one day a tiny stray puppy jumped up on my wife's beach chair and nipped at her ankle, with large brown eyes that pleaded, *"Get me off this island."* Vanessa, a lifelong cat person, switched teams in that moment, and Tobillo (Spanish for *ankle)* entered our lives for good. We said to ourselves, "If she comes back tomorrow, she's ours." She came back the next morning, with a little gray sister by her side. That evening, we got the news that Vanessa's aunt passed away (on Isolde's birthday). We cried, we held each other, we made travel plans, and we came home to New York with two small puppies. (Tobillo's sister, the gray dog, lives with a wonderful family in Virginia.)

It was against the backdrop of this week, full of heartbreak and new discoveries and family life, that I wrote "Dear Theodosia." It's the calm in the storm of our show, and it was the calm in the storm of my life in that moment.

Aaron Burr enters.

BURR: Dear Theodosia, what to say to you?
You have my eyes. You have your mother's name.

When you came into the world, you cried and it
    broke my heart.

I'm dedicating every day to you.
Domestic life, was never quite my style.
When you smile, you knock me out, I fall apart.
And I thought I was so smart.
You will come of age with our young nation.
We'll bleed and fight for you, we'll make it right
    for you.

If we lay a strong enough foundation
We'll pass it on to you, we'll give the world to
    you, and you'll blow us all away . . .
    someday, someday.
Yeah, you'll blow us all away,
    someday, someday.

Hamilton enters.

HAMILTON: Oh Philip, when you smile I am
    undone.
My son.
Look at my son. Pride is not the word I'm
    looking for.
There is so much more inside me now.

Oh Philip, you outshine the morning sun.
My son.
When you smile, I fall apart.
And I thought I was so smart.
My father wasn't around.

BURR: My father wasn't around. [2]

HAMILTON:
I swear that
I'll be around for you.

BURR:
I'll be around for you.

HAMILTON: I'll do whatever it takes.

BURR: I'll make a million mistakes.

BURR, HAMILTON: I'll make the world safe
and sound for you . . .
Will come of age with our young nation.

We'll bleed and fight for you, we'll make it right
for you.

If we lay a strong enough foundation [3]
We'll pass it on to you; we'll give the world to
you, and you'll blow us all away . . .
someday, someday.
Yeah, you'll blow us all away,
someday, someday.

[2] Be open to accidents as you write. This bridge came about because while playing back a section in Logic Pro, I accidentally looped a random fragment of a measure in the verse. I liked how it sounded so much that I isolated it and wrote these words over it. I am so moved by "My father wasn't around." Maybe because I don't know a set of parents who don't struggle to learn from their own upbringing, invariably making new mistakes of their own. Maybe because my parents worked such long hours on our behalf, and the blessing/curse of that ethic was lots of time on my own as a kid. The time I spent on my own was when I learned to keep my own company and pursue my own creative endeavors, and I wouldn't trade it for anything, despite any loneliness I might have felt at the time. Mostly, the lyric moves me because they're both new fathers, without role models of their own, vowing to do their best.

[3] This last section used to be sung by the whole company. But between this, "Yorktown," and the upcoming "Non-Stop," we already had a lot of full choral moments, so we simplified it to these two men.

'TOMORROW
THERE'LL BE MORE
OF US'

LAURENS: I may not live to see our glory.

ELIZA: Alexander? There's a letter for you.

HAMILTON: It's from John Laurens. I'll read it later.

LAURENS: But I will gladly join the fight.

ELIZA: No. It's from his father.

HAMILTON: His father?

LAURENS: And when our children tell our story.

HAMILTON: Will you read it?

LAURENS: They'll tell the story of tonight.

ELIZA: "On Tuesday the 27th, my son was killed in a gunfight against British troops retreating from South Carolina. The war was already over. As you know, John dreamed of emancipating and recruiting 3,000 men for the first all-black military regiment. His dream of freedom for these men dies with him." [2]

LAURENS: Tomorrow there'll be more of us . . .

ELIZA: Alexander. Are you alright?

HAMILTON: I have so much work to do. [3]

[1] This is the only scene unrepresented on our cast album, precisely for this reason: It's more of a scene than a song. I wanted to save a surprise for those who see the show. And you, reading this.

[2] John Laurens was the most militant opponent of slavery in this band of brothers. He was also the most reckless in battle (which is saying something, in a crew that includes Lafayette and Hamilton). To me, his death is the greatest What-If? in American history. A voice for emancipation from a surviving Revolutionary War veteran and a favorite of Washington: We'll never know what could have been.

[3] Here's the thing about Hamilton's response: It's more telling when he's quiet than when he has something to say. This was true of the historical Hamilton as well. We have very little written record of his grieving for Laurens. For a man who had an opinion on everything, for him to hold back betrays genuine, life-changing grief. It is possible that Hamilton and Laurens were lovers at some point—Hamilton's letters to Laurens are every bit as flirtatious as his letters to the opposite sex, if not more so. If this is the case, the silence betrays an even more profound loss.

ON "NON-STOP,"

both THE SONG and THE WAY of LIFE,

as Manifest by

ANDY BLANKENBUEHLER

AND THE

PUBLIC THEATER'S PROPS DEPARTMENT

SIX YEARS AFTER LIN READ RON Chernow's book, five years after he rapped at the White House, the *Hamilton* team had only eight working days left to get the show ready for its first audience. They knew it wasn't enough time.

Hamilton was one of the most complex productions ever staged in the Newman Theater, the Public's 290-seat proscenium space. Those eight days in January 2015 were spent doing technical rehearsals—"tech," for short—in which the actors worked through the show onstage, a few seconds at a time, so that every sound level, lighting cue, and movement choice could be tested and tweaked. There was a lot to test and tweak.

"Thirteen-hundred cues," said James Latus, the production stage manager for the downtown run, leafing through his heavily marked-up script, sounding like a man paddling across the Atlantic.

Tech is grueling under the best of circumstances, and these were not the best of circumstances: 12-hour days, heavy woolen costumes, an overhead grid bristling with hot lights. In the dark audience, James and the designers sat at folding tables loaded with laptops, consoles, and assorted abstruse gear. It looked like Mission Control, if NASA's business was launching rockets full of rapping multiracial actors in colonial garb into space.

For the most part, Lin behaved like any other member of the cast, goofing around, singing cartoon theme songs, trying to keep himself and everybody else sane. Lac was out of sight (he and the band were offstage left, in a loft 10 feet off the ground), adjusting the musicians' charts. Tommy kept making circuits around the tables in the audience, checking in with the designers, giving feedback. He didn't stray from what he wears almost every day: an untucked button-down shirt and jeans. He said that he saves his decision-making energy for the choices that count. Those choices came at him all day long.

"Thirteen hundred cues . . ."

EIGHT DAYS BECAME SEVEN AND THEN SIX. Daily, hourly, the show's ambitions were put to the test. All the ideas that had sounded so good in production meetings, or had looked so promising in the rehearsal room, had to survive the proving ground of the actual stage. Everything had to add up to form a complete, coherent reality. For Tommy, the brushwork mattered as much as the broad strokes. "It was really important, in a world where we didn't have roofs and walls, that the

> *"It looked like Mission Control, if NASA's business was* **LAUNCHING ROCKETS FULL OF RAPPING MULTI- RACIAL ACTORS IN COLONIAL GARB INTO SPACE."**

props and clothing were going to root us in time. Especially because of the contemporary language."

Much of the finest brushwork fell to Jay Duckworth, the prop master of the Public, and his colleagues Sara Swanberg and Sydney Schatz. They found or built objects of every size and description that actors carried on David Korins's set. They carried verisimilitude as far it could go, which turns out to be very, very far.

During the "Yorktown" sequence, when Washington consults Comte de Rochambeau's map, Chris Jackson looks at Rochambeau's *actual map,* reproduced on parchment paper treated with Mod Podge, so it resembles sheepskin.

Newspapers figure in several places during the show, and each one includes stories that ran in actual New York newspapers, drawn from the exact month the scene takes place. (Jay and Sara exempted only one kind of paper prop from this fastidious approach: Pamphlets that might end up falling into the audience were filled with nonsense strings of Latin words so as not to distract audience members from watching the show.)

The candles onstage are real wax, because nothing else looks like wax. The seals on the letters by Washington and Hamilton are real wax as well. Each man gets *his own personalized seal.*

Asking Jay why even the tiniest, least visible props deserve this kind of attention is like asking a hawk why he flaps his wings so much. Five seconds pass before he replies, "'Cause it *has* to be." He thinks it's unfair to ask actors to go onstage and expose themselves with anything less than what he calls "ultimate support." Tommy agrees, regarding a personalized wax seal as just as vital to the show's reality as a piece of scenery. "The only people who see it are the actors. But the actors *see* it."

Here again the creators of *Hamilton* are channeling their subject. The inexhaustible Hamilton didn't just organize an army for the new United States, and propose a system of ranks and units for commanding it, he also designed its uniforms, fussing over details as minuscule as the color of George Washington's buttons and his plume (yellow and white, respectively).

———◆———

SIX DAYS BECAME FIVE AND THEN FOUR. Because *Hamilton* was completely sung-through, it was almost completely danced-through. So no matter what else was happening during tech, Andy Blankenbuehler was on his feet, rushing onstage to give a note, rushing back to see how it was playing. Woe to anybody who happened to be in his way: Andy wasn't rude or angry— he smiled a lot, all things considered—but he simply didn't notice any human form between him and the dancers executing his combinations.

The stress on him was enormous. He didn't find it unusual. "I'm kind of always at the same state. A state of general exhaustion. Because my brain never stops. My brain runs at a very fast pace. Pretty much always, I think. I work out constantly, I never sit around, even at home I'm doing my own yard work. I go to the gym every day, I'm warming up all the time, I'm working all the time. I don't sleep enough."

Lin admired this work ethic, and learned from it. On Andy's 45th birthday, in 2015, he tweeted a little tribute to his choreographer: "Happy birthday to Andy Blankenbuehler! You guys know that when I'm playing Hamilton, I'm really just playing him, right? #RELENTLESSGENIUS"

In "Non-Stop," Lin very explicitly asks what makes a genius relentless, what turns a gifted individual into a monster of creativity. The Act One finale covers six furiously productive years in Hamilton's life, from his return to war-ravaged New York City in 1783 to his ascension to Washington's cabinet in 1789. It rips through 12 scenes in six minutes, and staging it demands the same kind of ingenuity that it describes. Luckily, Andy has the same creative metabolism as

Lac. "Twelve ideas for every one we can use," in Lin's estimation.

"What's interesting about 'Non-Stop' is: That's the venom I feel," says Andy.

"The *venom*?"

"That oomph, that vitality. Just keep going until you figure it out."

Andy developed his relentlessness early, and, like Alexander Hamilton, he developed it out of necessity. He moved to New York in 1990 with no job and no contacts, just a determination to dance. (He had grown up in Cincinnati, where his father did community theater, and where nobody could figure out why young Andy worked so hard, or moved so well.) He landed a few Broadway gigs, but got tired of doing *step-touch step-touch* in the back row—he wanted to tell stories that mattered. So he started choreographing his own dances, which taught him, to his surprise, "I didn't know *anything* about what I was doing." He could put together some steps, sure, but what about analyzing a story, or crafting a two-hour arc, or running a meeting, or keeping himself in shape? He flailed.

When *In the Heights* came around, he knew he had to choreograph the salsa-and-hip-hop show, even though—as he admitted to Tommy and Jeffrey—he didn't know anything about salsa or hip-hop. They thought he had a knack for telling stories, so they hired him anyway. To prepare for the show, he moved to Los Angeles, took four hip-hop

"Other choreographers build portraits," explains Stephanie Klemons, dance captain and associate choreographer. "Andy's experience is like a 3-D Imax fresco."

Andy knew the audience wouldn't consciously register a lot of his choices—like the fact that Burr moves in straight lines, because he sees no options, and Hamilton moves in arcs, because he sees all possibilities—but that wasn't the point. "There are very few times when I really want the audience to look at dance," he says. "Dance is just meant to be a framing device that matches emotionally what I want the audience to feel."

In a way, choreographers are like the architects of financial systems: They have to sense how a little change here will shift a balance over there. They need microscopic focus on a macroscopic scale. During tech, Andy would cut across the crowded stage, adjust a performer's elbow, and cross back to the audience, never losing his stride, or breaking his train of thought.

——————◆——————

FOUR BECAME THREE BECAME TWO. Once you've spent a full week in a darkened theater, it begins to seem more real than the real world. You're certainly spending more of your waking hours there than with your loved ones. "It's a great amount of sacrifice for every person here," says Chris Jackson, who called this tech week the most grueling of his career. "You've gotta say *no* a lot. You've gotta say *bye* a lot."

The hours were long, but that doesn't mean they were dull. Learning Andy's choreography had challenged the cast members when they first encountered it in the rehearsal room. When they finally got onstage for those precious eight days of tech, they had to learn it again. Because now the stage was *spinning*.

"There are very few times when I really want the audience to look at dance . . . Dance is just meant to be A FRAMING DEVICE THAT MATCHES EMOTIONALLY WHAT I WANT THE AUDIENCE TO FEEL."

classes a day, soaked up the rhythm of salsa, and devised a hybrid style of his own. It won him a Tony Award.

For *Hamilton*, he needed another new vocabulary. Beyond several varieties of hip-hop dance, you can see little traces of Gene Kelly and Justin Timberlake in the result. When Andy himself dances it, you see a lot of Jerome Robbins. But the movement of *Hamilton*, in its totality, reaches far beyond conventional dance steps, of any tradition. Andy devised a language of what he calls "stylized heightened gesture." It includes everything from the way a chair is moved, to how a shoulder pops, to the bows at the curtain call.

At his first meeting with Tommy, David Korins had proposed using a turntable, a rotating circle at center stage. If the floor spun, it would add energy and motion to the action. It would create more possibilities for the hurricane, the duel, even the evocation of street life in New York. "You can move people magically," he says.

Tommy didn't go for the idea. He'd used a turntable before, in a show that Korins designed, and didn't think *Hamilton* would need one. The May 2014 workshop—

the one at the 52nd Street Project, that left people cheering and crying and pleading to invest—seemed to confirm his instinct. Still, that summer, Korins had raised the possibility one more time. And this time, Tommy thought maybe Korins was onto something. So did Andy. So did Lin, for whom turntables always conjure fond memories of the first musical he ever saw. "They have one turntable," he says of *Les Misérables*. "We have two."

Seeing the two-part turntable installed and spinning at the Public, Andy was delighted with all the subtle effects it could create: Counterclockwise motion, he felt, suggested the passage of time; clockwise suggested resistance to the inevitable. Up on stage, on top of the thing, the actors tried to execute Andy's steps while being carried in two directions. Stephanie watched "the cast's brains melting out of their ears." She spent the week feeling nauseous.

Andy felt the same urgency as everybody else, but the all-consuming demands of tech also gave him a kind of respite. The entire time that he was choreographing *Hamilton*, his five-year-old daughter, Sofia, had been undergoing chemotherapy. She had endured more than two grueling years of treatment by the time he went into tech. Her cancer diagnosis had led Andy and his wife, Elly, to upend their lives. "We stopped living for tomorrow and started living for today," he says. They had sold their apartment, he had given up his office, they had bought

the shell of a brownstone in Harlem, they had moved in with her family in Brooklyn. Almost all of the combinations that proved so taxing to some of the best dancers in New York, the patterns that whirl around the turntable and overflow the stage, Andy had developed alone, on the concrete floor of his mother-in-law's house in Bay Ridge, under a ceiling so low he could reach up and touch it. He would help put Sofia and her brother to bed, open a bottle of wine, head downstairs, and work long into the night, on the part of his life that he could control.

"It was just like the show," he says of that ordeal. "I was living the show. It was a sacrifice that needs to be made. I need to fight for this." Looking back now, he sees that he was "choreographing myself in the show." The way that the 19 actors moved on the Newman stage was, in some ways, a reflection of what one man was suffering, particularly the anguish that awaits Alexander and Eliza in Act Two.

"I'm not making it up," Andy says of the movement that he devised for the cast as the Hamiltons are plunged into despair. He knew what it was like "when someone you love is dying and they're in your arms."

TWO DAYS BECAME ONE BECAME ZERO. On January 20, 2015, the Mission Control tables were packed away, the aisles swept, the stage mopped, and the

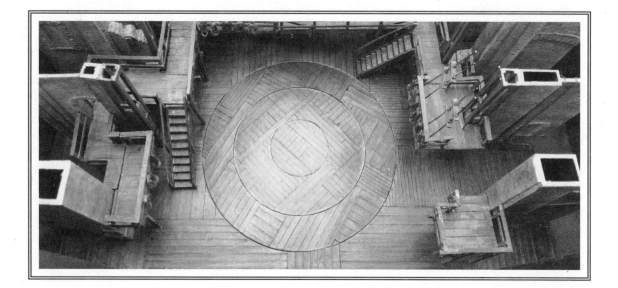

lobby doors propped open. The company did only one complete run of the show before the first audience arrived, but it was a complete run all the same. They had brought *Hamilton* to the stage in time for its world premiere.

The crowd that night came away asking a question that has grown more insistent with time: *How did they do it?* You can ask it of those eight days in January. You can ask it of the seven-year development of the show. If you feel like being deep, you can ask it just as profitably of what happened in the years depicted in "Non-Stop," when the victorious rebels had to learn how to govern themselves. These things unfolded on very different scales, obviously. Still they each tell a story of something unprecedented and implausible becoming real. And they all suggest the same answer.

Alexander Hamilton was indispensable to the infant republic, as Lin dramatizes. But you could say the same about Washington, Madison, and half a dozen other founders. It's possible that some of them could have won the war without the others, but would they have ratified the Constitution? And vice-versa. The Founding Fathers did the impossible twice in 10 years because they did it together: supporting, inspiring, challenging, and correcting each other.

Hamilton is Lin's show to an extent that almost no Broadway musical in living memory is one person's show: idea, story, music, lyrics, lead performance. But it's impossible to imagine it working without his core group of collaborators. In those frenetic days in January—and across those long years leading up to the Broadway opening night—he depended on what he calls his Cabinet: Tommy, Andy, and Lac. "Our shorthand is very short," says Tommy. It needed to be.

"Non-stop" ends with a whirl of virtuosity. Lin and Lac pile up two melodies, then three, then four, and Andy puts the whole company and even part of Korins's set in motion. The reason why Lin can call this sequence a "colonial clusterfuck" without suggesting that it's a problem that needs to be solved is Tommy. No matter how hyperactive things got onstage, or how stressful the time crunch became, Tommy kept everybody clicking along. In fact, for all the stress of tech, the Newman came to feel (in its quiet moments, anyway) like a model society in miniature: a bunch of very talented people who knew their jobs and did them, giving their best in the service of a worthy common goal. It takes all kinds to make a revolution.

At that first preview, it was disorienting to watch more than 200 strangers stream into the theater, hailing from God-knows-where. They didn't know they were obstructing what had very recently been Andy's path to the stage, or occupying the spot where Tommy liked to preside, arms crossed, a couple of fingers to his lips. But as Alexander Hamilton kept trying to tell us, even the best-ordered societies need infusions of new blood to thrive. Keep it in mind the next time you go to the theater: Some gifted men and women have built a community in that room, and the immigrant is you.

NON-STOP

BURR: After the war I went back to New York.

HAMILTON: A-after the war I went back to New York.

BURR: I finished up my studies and I practiced law.

HAMILTON: I practiced law, Burr worked next door.[1]

BURR: Even though we started at the very same time,
Alexander Hamilton began to climb.

BURR:
How to account for
his rise to the top?
Maaaaan, the man is   **ENSEMBLE:**
non-stop.   Non-stop!

HAMILTON: Gentlemen of the jury, I'm curious, bear with me.
Are you aware that we're making hist'ry?
This is the first murder trial of our brand-new nation.

HAMILTON:
The liberty behind   **BURR, ENSEMBLE:**
deliberation—   Non-stop!

HAMILTON: I intend to prove beyond a shadow of a doubt
With my assistant council—

BURR: Co-council.
Hamilton, sit down.
Our client Levi Weeks is innocent. Call your first witness.[2]
That was all you had to say!

HAMILTON: Okay!
One more thing—

BURR: Why do you assume you're the smartest in the room?
Why do you assume you're the smartest in the room?
Why do you assume you're the smartest in the room?[3]
Soon that attitude
May be your doom!

ENSEMBLE: Awwww!

BURR: Why do you   **ENSEMBLE:** Why do
write like you're   you write like you're
running out of time?[4] running out of time?
Write day and night
like you're running
out of time?
Ev'ry day you fight,   Ev'ry day you fight,
like you're running   like you're running out
out of time.   of time.
Keep on fighting. In
the meantime—

                                       Non-stop!

HAMILTON: Corruption's such an old song that we can sing along in harmony[5]
And nowhere is it stronger than in Albany.
This colony's economy's increasingly stalling and

HAMILTON: **BURR, ENSEMBLE:**
Honestly that's why   He's just
public service seems to   Non-stop!
be calling me

HAMILTON: I practiced the law, I practic'lly perfected it.
I've seen injustice in the world and I've corrected it.

[1] They really did set up their law practices in the same 'hood around the same time.

[2] This trial didn't occur until way later, but it's such a perfect way to introduce their postwar lives—two lawyers, fundamentally different, meeting up in court—that I moved it up. Love them as a legal dream team too.

[3] Once again, dancehall rhythms for Burr, just as in "Wait For It." I wrote much of this song in Nevis, where I did research on Hamilton's life, so my pulse was already on island rhythm time.

[4] This sentence sums up how I think most of us feel in the face of Hamilton's remarkable output. Same as Shakespeare or the Beatles: *How on Earth did you do that with the same 24 hours a day that everyone else gets?*

[5] 'Twas always true. Pick up the paper today and you can read about more corruption hijinks. There's actually an Albany Museum of Political Corruption. A museum!

Now for a strong central democracy,
If not then I'll be Socrates

HAMILTON:
Throwing verbal
rocks at these
mediocrities.   **ENSEMBLE:**
                           Awww!

BURR: Hamilton, at the Constitutional
Convention

HAMILTON: I was chosen for the
Constitutional Convention.

BURR: There as a New York junior delegate:

HAMILTON:
Now what I'm going
to say may sound   **COMPANY:**
indelicate . . .   Awwww!

BURR:
Goes and proposes
his own form of
government!   What?
His own plan
for a new form of
government!   What?

BURR: Talks for six hours! The convention
is listless! [6]

ENSEMBLE MAN: Bright young man . . .

ANOTHER ENSEMBLE MAN: Yo, who the eff
is this?

BURR:
Why do you always
Say what you believe?   **COMPANY:**
Why do you always   Why do you always
Say what you believe?   Say what you believe?

Ev'ry proclamation
guarantees
Free ammunition for
your enemies!   Awww!

BURR, MEN: Why do
you write like it's   **WOMEN:**
Going out of style?   Going out of style, hey!

Write day and night
like it's
Going out of style?   Going out of style, hey!

BURR, COMPANY: Ev'ry day you fight like it's
     going out of style.
Do what you do.

Hamilton at Burr's doorstep.

BURR: Alexander?

HAMILTON: Aaron Burr, sir.

BURR: It's the middle of the night. [7]

HAMILTON: Can we confer, sir?

BURR: Is this a legal matter?

HAMILTON: Yes, and it's important to me.

BURR: What do you need?

HAMILTON: Burr, you're a better lawyer than me.

BURR: Okay.

HAMILTON: I know I talk too much,
     I'm abrasive.
You're incredible in court. You're succinct,
     persuasive.
My client needs a strong defense.
     You're the solution.

[6] I wish you could hear my non-miked conversations with Chris Jackson as Washington after this moment. Usually, in character, I say to him, "Well, I meant to talk for an hour, but it just got away from me . . ." as he looks at me with pity.

[7] Another great *What if*? Historically, we know that Hamilton asked other people to contribute to *The Federalist Papers*: Madison and John Jay agreed, but Gouverneur Morris declined. I extended that into this fictional scene, wherein Hamilton invites Burr to write. This is the equivalent of asking someone to invest in Pixar just before *Toy Story* drops. It's plausible, as Burr traveled in the same circles and held similar views to Hamilton, but it gets at the root of their fundamental difference: Burr is not willing to expose himself or his legacy to something this risky.

THE FEDERALIST:

ADDRESSED TO THE

PEOPLE OF THE STATE OF NEW-YORK.

NUMBER I.

Introduction.

AFTER an unequivocal experience of the inefficacy of the subsisting federal government, you are called upon to deliberate on a new constitution for the United States of America. The subject speaks its own importance; comprehending in its consequences, nothing less than the existence of the UNION, the safety and welfare of the parts of which it is composed, the fate of an empire, in many respects, the most interesting in the world. It has been frequently remarked, that it seems to have been reserved to the people of this country, by their conduct and example, to decide the important question, whether societies of men are really capable or not, of establishing good government from reflection and choice, or whether they are forever destined to depend, for their political constitutions, on accident and force. If there be any truth in the remark, the crisis, at which we are arrived, may with propriety be regarded as the æra in which

A   that

THE FEDERALIST
NO. I
*written by Alexander
Hamilton under the
pen name "Publius."*

BURR: Who's your client?

HAMILTON: The new U.S. Constitution?

BURR: No.

HAMILTON: Hear me out.

BURR: No way!

HAMILTON: A series of essays, anonymously
     published
Defending the document to the public.

BURR: No one will read it.

HAMILTON: I disagree.

BURR: And if it fails?

HAMILTON: Burr, that's why we need it.

BURR: The Constitution's a mess.

HAMILTON: So it needs amendments.

BURR: It's full of contradictions.

HAMILTON: So is independence.
We have to start somewhere.

BURR: No. No way.

HAMILTON: You're making a mistake.

BURR: Good night.

HAMILTON:[8] Hey.
What are you waiting for?
What do you stall for?

BURR: What?

HAMILTON: We won the war.
What was it all for?
Do you support this Constitution?

BURR: Of course.

HAMILTON: Then defend it.

BURR: And what if you're backing the
wrong horse?

HAMILTON: Burr, we studied and we fought
     and we killed
For the notion of a nation we now get to build.
For once in your life, take a stand with pride.
I don't understand how you stand to the side.

BURR: I'll
keep all my
plans close to
my chest.

ENSEMBLE:
Wait for it, wait for it,
wait . . .

I'll wait here and see
which way the wind
will blow
I'm taking my time,
watching the after-
birth of a nation
Watching the tension
grow.

Which way the wind
will blow.
I'm taking my time,
watching the afterbirth
of a nation
Watching the tension
grow.

Angelica enters, arm in arm with Hamilton.

ANGELICA: I am sailing off to London.[9]
     I'm accompanied by someone
Who always pays
I have found a wealthy husband who will keep
     me in comfort for all my days.
He is not a lot of fun, but there's no one who
     can match you for turn of phrase.
My Alexander.

[8] This section was added later. Originally it ended with the two of them stalking off to their separate quarters, but now Hamilton really challenges Burr at his core: *What are you waiting for?* It's the more malignant version of "I will never understand you" from after the wedding. This difference will only escalate over the course of their lives.

[9] We're moving chess pieces here: Angelica across the sea.

HAMILTON: Angelica.

ANGELICA: Don't forget to write.

ELIZA: Look at where you are.
Look at where you started.
The fact that you're alive is a miracle.
Just stay alive, that would be enough.

And if your wife could share a fraction of
    your time
If I could grant you peace of mind
Would that be enough?

BURR: Alexander joins forces with James
Madison and John Jay to write a series of essays
defending the new United States Constitution,
entitled *The Federalist Papers*.[10]

The plan was to write a total of 25 essays, the
work divided evenly among the three men. In
the end, they wrote 85 essays, in the span of six
months. John Jay got sick after writing 5. James
Madison wrote 29. Hamilton wrote the other 51.

BURR:
How do you write
Like you're   **WOMEN:**
Running out of time? Running out of time?

Write day and night
Like you're
Running out of time? Running out of time?

BURR, MEN: Ev'ry
day you fight,
Like you're
Running out of time   Running out of time?
Like you're
Running out of time, Running out of time?
Are you
Running out of time? Awwww!

COMPANY: How do you write like tomorrow
    won't arrive?[11]
How do you write like you need it to survive?
How do you write ev'ry second you're alive?
Ev'ry second you're alive ev'ry second
    you're alive.

WASHINGTON: They are asking me to lead.
I am doing the best I can
To get the people that I need,
I'm asking you to be my right hand man.

HAMILTON: Treasury or State?

WASHINGTON: I know it's a lot to ask,

HAMILTON: Treasury or State?

WASHINGTON: To leave behind the world
you know . . .

HAMILTON: Sir, do you want me to run the
Treasury or State department?

WASHINGTON: Treasury.

HAMILTON: Let's go.

ELIZA: Alexander . . .

HAMILTON: I have to leave.

ELIZA: Alexander—

HAMILTON: Look around, look around at
how lucky we are to be alive right now.

ELIZA: Helpless . . .

HAMILTON: They are asking me to lead.[12]

ELIZA: Look around, isn't this enough?[13]

[10] We drop into plain speech here because the facts are so extraordinary that no amount of spin on the ball can make them land any harder.

[11] I wish writing were really like the way Andy staged it here: Me in a mania at a desk while a group of people stand around cheering in awe. More realistically, it's me pooping around on Twitter until I get an idea.

[12] In the space of two lines, Hamilton takes other people's themes and flips them to make his own argument. He throws Eliza's refrain back at her, and volleys with Washington's words and melody. He will do *anything* to get what he's after, and we underscore that melodically here.

[13] This all-skate came from tons of trial and error between me, Andy, Tommy, and Lacamoire. Take pieces from five different puzzles and make something new, that sets us sailing into intermission: That's what's at play here. As the guy who gets to play Hamilton, let me also say, it's a helluva view from the center of it.

ANGELICA:
He will never be
satisfied,
He will
Never be satisfied,

Satisfied,
Satisfied . . .

ELIZA:
What would be
enough
To be
Satisfied,
Satisfied,
Satisfied . . .

Look around,

Look around,

WASHINGTON:
History has its
Eyes . . .

On . . .

You!

BURR:
Why do you assume
you're the smartest
in the room?

Why do
you assume you're
the smartest in the
room?
Why do
you assume you're the
smartest in the
room?

ENSEMBLE:
Non-
Stop!

Non-

He will
Never be satisfied,

Satisfied,

Satisfied . . .

Isn't this

enough?
What would be
enough?

WASHINGTON,
MULLIGAN,
LAURENS,
LAFAYETTE:
History has its
Eyes . . .
On . . .
You . . .

Soon that
attitude's
gonna
Be your doom!
Why do you fight
Like you're
Running out of time?

stop!

Non-

ANGELICA:	ELIZA:	WASHINGTON, MULLIGAN, LAURENS, LAFAYETTE:	BURR:	ENSEMBLE:
Why do you fight like	Why do you fight like		Why do you fight	stop!
History has its eyes on you . . .	History has its eyes on you . . .	History has its eyes on you . . .	History has its eyes on you . . .	History has its eyes on you . . .

HAMILTON:
I am not throwin'
away my
Shot!

MEN:
Just you wait!

I am not throwin'
away my
Shot!
I am
Alexander
Hamilton!

FULL COMPANY:
Just you wait!

Alexander
Hamilton
Hamilton, just you wait!

I am not throwin'
away
My shot!

ACT II

❦

*"Am I then more of an American than those who
drew their first breath on American ground?"*

—Alexander Hamilton, 1795

XVII

YOU CAN BE A NEW MAN

OR,

THE STORY OF

OAK & DAVEED

THOMAS JEFFERSON (OUR THIRD president) and James Madison (our fourth president) had a partnership so close that it reminded John Quincy Adams (our sixth president) of "the invisible and mysterious movements of the magnet." They had the same background—they were both rich slaveholding aristocrats from Virginia—and they shared a political goal: destroying Alexander Hamilton.

Lin and Tommy liked the idea of having Hamilton's enemies in the second half of the show be played by his friends in the first half. But to make the idea work, they would need a couple of supremely dynamic actors, who would be totally convincing in two roles, not one.

At the Public, the audience spent Act One watching Daveed Diggs play the swashbuckling, speed-rapping Marquis de Lafayette, a freedom fighter who launches himself off the top of a desk on his way to war. When he swanned back onstage at the start of Act Two, he had let his hair down—literally—to transform into the super-smooth Jefferson, aloof and debonair.

Tommy knew that Daveed's laid-back charisma would suit both roles: They had worked together in Freestyle Love Supreme, a trial by fire. Anyway, the 34-year-old Daveed had plenty of experience with split identities. He grew up in a tough part of Oakland but went to Brown, he was raised by a black father and a white Jewish mother, he has had one career as an actor (including a performance at the Public's Under the Radar Festival) and another as a rapper. These contradictions have been a rich

subject for his songs, both as a solo artist and as the lead MC for Clipping, the avant-garde hip-hop group. "I'm American-working-class split persona," he raps on one of them, "Party like a rock star, introverted loner." Which sounds like Jefferson, except for the working-class part.

Okieriete Onaodowan, known to all as Oak, made an even more drastic transformation halfway through the show. In Act One, he played the muscle; in Act Two, the brains. The Hulk before intermission, Bruce Banner after it. As Hamilton's friend Hercules Mulligan, Oak rapped in a booming growl and pretended that he had trouble controlling his powerful limbs; as James Madison, he shrank his 5'11", 235-pound frame and adopted a nasal voice, diminishing himself to play Jefferson's shy, sickly partner. Both of his performances seemed effortless, even though they were totally different types, and neither was much like Oak in real life. If *Hamilton* had five acts, Oak would play five roles.

Daveed and Oak, Oak and Daveed. A good way to chart the growth of *Hamilton* mania during those first weeks at the Public was to watch what happened when the two of them appeared in the lobby after each show— the crowds that grew around them, the multiplying requests for selfies, a new sensation for them both. Daveed had long since given up his boyhood Broadway dreams, since the place didn't seem to have a place for him. "I used to have dreams about flying one day all the time, too," he says. He didn't even have an agent when performances began.

"Daveed thinks that SEEING A BLACK MAN PLAY JEFFERSON or MADISON or WASHINGTON when he was a kid in Oakland MIGHT HAVE CHANGED HIS LIFE."

The acclaim was just as unexpected for Oak. Growing up in West Orange, New Jersey, school plays and community theater were mainly ways to stay out of trouble when it wasn't football season. This didn't always work: He stole, he mouthed off to teachers, he got suspended a lot. His parents, both of whom had immigrated from Nigeria, didn't have much money, but he managed to afford some training after he graduated. It was during that shaky early stretch of his career that a director advised him to try another line of work. Even after some regional credits and a couple of small Broadway roles, that memory stung.

Beyond the newfound acclaim, and the chance to have New York apartments for the first time, Daveed and Oak both saw a special opportunity in playing a Founding Father. Oak says he is "hyperconscious" about the roles he takes. He is allergic to doing "another show about a messed-up black kid." Madison has been a godsend: "I'm a black man playing a wise, smart, distinguished future president." Daveed thinks that seeing a black man play Jefferson or Madison or Washington when he was a kid in Oakland might have changed his life. "A whole lot of things I just never thought were for me would have seemed possible," he says. Even now, the show is changing him, making him feel more American. "I always felt at odds with this country," he says. "You can only get pulled over by the police for no reason so many times before you say, 'Fuck this.'"

Don't be too quick to count a kid out. There are plenty of debatable lessons to be drawn from Alexander Hamilton's life, but that one is clear. The poor bastard orphan from the islands ought to have died a dozen times but somehow lived to help to found the nation. As a leader of the new republic, he fought to make it easier for people like him to travel as far as their talent would take them.

"There are strong minds in every walk of life that will rise superior to the disadvantages of situation and will command the tribute due to their merit," Hamilton wrote in *The Federalist No. 36*. Look no further than his own life for proof of that statement. Or Oak's. Or Daveed's.

ABOVE:
Okieriete Onaodowan, Daveed Diggs, and Christopher Jackson.

WHAT'D I MISS?

———◆———

COMPANY: Seventeen. Se se seventeen
Se se seventeen

BURR: Seventeen eighty-nine.
How does the bastard orphan,
Immigrant decorated war vet
Unite the colonies through more debt?
Fight the other Founding Fathers 'til he has
    to forfeit?
Have it all, lose it all,
You ready for more yet? [1]
Treasury secretary. Washington's the president.
Ev'ry American experiment sets a precedent.
Not so fast. Someone came along to resist him.
Pissed him off until we had a two-party system.
You haven't met him yet, you haven't had
    the chance.
'Cause he's been kickin' ass as the ambassador
    to France
But someone's gotta keep the American promise.
You simply must meet Thomas. Thomas! [2]

COMPANY (EXCEPT HAM, PEG, PHIL):
Thomas Jefferson's coming home!
Thomas Jefferson's coming home!
Thomas Jefferson's coming home!
Thomas Jefferson's coming home!
Thomas Jefferson's coming home [3]
Lord he's been off in Paris for so long!
Aaa-ooo!
Aaa-ooo!

Thomas Jefferson enters.

JEFFERSON: France is following us to revolution
There is no more status quo
But the sun comes up and the world still spins.

ENSEMBLE: Aaa-ooo!

JEFFERSON: I helped Lafayette draft a
    declaration,
Then I said, I gotta go.
I gotta be in Monticello, now the work at
    home begins . . .

ENSEMBLE: Aaa-ooo!

JEFFERSON: So what'd I miss? [4]
What'd I miss?
Virginia, my home sweet home, I wanna
    give you a kiss.
I've been in Paris meeting lots of different
    ladies . . .
I guess I basic'lly missed the late eighties.
I traveled the wide, wide world and came
    back to this . . .

ENSEMBLE: Aaa-ooo!

JEFFERSON: There's a letter on my desk
    from the president.
Haven't even put my bag down yet.
Sally be a lamb, darlin', won'tcha open it? [5]
It says the president's assembling a cabinet
And that I am to be the secretary of state, great.
And that I'm already Senate-approved . . .
I just got home and now I'm headed up to
    New York.

ENSEMBLE: Headin' to New York!
Headin' to New York!

JEFFERSON:
Lookin' at the rolling
fields
I can't
Believe that we are free.   ENSEMBLE:
Ready to face   Believe that we are free
whatever's awaiting
Me in N.Y.C.   Me in N.Y.C.

---

[1] I mean, you can't say Burr didn't warn you ish was gonna get real.

[2] I *sometimes* say this to Thomas Kail.

[3] I can't tell you how thrilled I was when I first saw Kail and Blankenbuehler's staging for this moment: Jefferson descending a staircase, with our ensemble scrubbing the floors and getting his bags. It's the paradox of Jefferson made flesh: The writer who articulated liberty so clearly was an active participant in the brutal system of slavery.

[4] Figuring out the "sound" of Thomas Jefferson was a fun challenge. My reasoning: He's a full generation older than Hamilton, and he was absent for much of the fighting of the Revolutionary War, though certainly an architect of some of the founding documents. So I wrote him in sort of a Lambert/Hendricks/Ross/Gil Scott-Heron mode—jazzy, proto-hip-hop, but not the boom bap of Hamilton. He has just as much fun with words, but they swing and they sing.

[5] Our Sally Hemings shout-out.

CHAPTER XVII

JEFFERSON: But who's waitin' for me when I step in the place?
My friend James Madison, red in the face.

JEFFERSON:
He grabs my arm and
I respond,   ENSEMBLE:
"What's goin' on?"   Aaa-ooo!

MADISON: Thomas, we are engaged in a battle for our nation's very soul.
Can you get us out of the mess we're in? [6]

ENSEMBLE: Aaa-ooo!

MADISON: Hamilton's new financial plan is nothing less than government control.
I've been fighting for the South alone.
Where have you been?

JEFFERSON: ENSEMBLE:
Uh . . . France. [7] Aaa-ooo!

MADISON: We have to win.

JEFFERSON: ENSEMBLE:
What'd I miss?   Wha? Wha? What'd I miss?
What'd I miss?   I've come home to this?
Headfirst into a
political abyss!

                             Head first, into the abyss!

I have my
first cabinet
meeting today,   Chick-a-pow!

I guess I better think
of something to say

I'm already on my way,   On my way.
Let's get to the
bottom of this . . .

                             What did I miss?
                             Ahhh ah!

WASHINGTON: Mr. Jefferson, welcome home.

HAMILTON: Mr. Jefferson? Alexander Hamilton.

WASHINGTON, ENSEMBLE: Mr. Jefferson, welcome home.

COMPANY: Mr. Jefferson, welcome home.
Sir, you've been off in Paris for so long!

JEFFERSON: So what did I miss?

[6] It's to my regret that Madison's friendship and fallout with Hamilton land firmly in our act break. They wrote *The Federalist Papers*, but Hamilton's financial plans left war vets who sold their bonds with nothing, and Madison's disgust with this arrangement began their falling out. Madison and Jefferson were in absolute lock-step for much of their relationship, and it worked very well. Jefferson was the charisma, Madison was the wonk. We do our best to convey that quickly here.

[7] This was a Daveed improv that made it into the song.

AN ACCOUNT OF

RAPPING *for the* CHILDREN

WHO WILL ONE DAY

RAP FOR THEMSELVES

*H*AMILTON OPENED AT THE PUBLIC Theater on February 17, 2015, earning the kind of critical acclaim that theater artists dream of receiving. The popular reaction was even more jubilant than the reviews: The demand for tickets was so oppressive that at least one member of the cast changed her name on Facebook to duck the requests.

A few weeks after opening night, Lin nevertheless tweeted that he was terrified about what the next day would bring. Teenagers from New York public high schools would be in the audience the following after-

> "*Perform a musical for one of those conventional audiences and you know what to expect: Put it on for A COUPLE HUNDRED KIDS who have never set foot in a theater before . . . and THERE IS NO GUESSING.*"

noon—they would, in fact, be the *entire* audience. "Kids, like Shakira's hips, don't lie," he tweeted.

The students would be attending *Hamilton* as part of the Public Theater's partnership with the Theater Development Fund. Since 1995, the TDF Stage Doors program has brought more than 62,000 students to see plays and musicals at theaters around New York City. Because TDF tries to create opportunities for schools that lack resources, the students tend to be a vivid mix of races, religions, and national origins. They are much closer to the face of the new 21st-century America than, say, your

typical Off-Broadway subscriber audience. Perform a musical for one of those conventional audiences and you know what to expect: Put it on for a couple hundred kids who have never set foot in a theater before—which is true of many TDF participants—and there is no guessing.

The teachers and TDF teaching artists had started preparing their classes to see *Hamilton* weeks before that matinee. Bill Coulter, who teaches a sophomore English class at (wait for it) Fort Hamilton High School in southwestern Brooklyn, had his class read the Declaration of Independence, the Universal Declaration of Human Rights, even the Haitian Declaration of Independence. They delved so deeply into these documents that the students started to wonder if he was teaching a social studies class.

At John Adams High School in Queens, the TDF teaching artist Joe White had read his class the first lines of *Hamilton*—about "a bastard orphan son of a whore and a Scotsman / Dropped in the middle of a forgotten / Spot in the Caribbean"—then asked the students to describe what kind of person that might be. They said he sounded Dominican ("There are a lot of Dominicans in the class," White says), or West Indian. They guessed that he had come to New York because he had a bad life.

"Then I read the line about 'the ten-dollar Founding Father without a father, who got a lot farther by being a self-starter,'" White recalls. "They said, 'He worked his way up. He started as an immigrant, somebody who wanted to make something of himself.' But they said, 'What is a ten-dollar Founding Father?' So I showed them a $10 bill and said, 'This is the guy—this is who we're talking about. He was kind of a gangsta.' They couldn't believe it."

On the day of the show, the students arrived enthusiastic and stayed that way. "*Excited* isn't the right word," says Ginger Bartkoski Meagher of TDF. "They were engaged, moved, amazed." She tries to avoid the word *transformative* because it sounds so corny, but concludes that it's the best description. "It's theater telling them a story about themselves, a story that they didn't know. That's huge—that's amazing."

"They went absolutely crazy," says White. "It was like the feel at Shea Stadium. The play is in language they understand. Most of these kids have earbuds and listen to music pretty much 24 hours a day, so they totally got it."

Onstage, the actors rode the wave of adolescent energy as best they could. The mood was particularly electric during the Cabinet rap battles. Chris Jackson says that when he stepped to the front of the stage to announce the first one, he could feel a sense of delight and surprise radiating from the crowd.

"Battles are definitely part of youth culture now," says Daveed. "There are YouTube channels for rap battles." That means that the kids felt empowered to let the competing rappers know what they thought. As Hamilton and Jefferson traded arguments (and insults), the actors heard a lot of *OHHHHH*s and cheers. Daveed loves to perform for audiences that don't know the rules, but says that it was painful to play Jefferson in the Cabinet battle that day: "They're so vocal, it hurts so much more when I lose."

After the show, the kids waited in the lobby for the actors to appear. Lin signed autographs and posed for pictures. He accepted a Fort Hamilton High T-shirt from Bill Coulter's students. "The student matinees are, it turns out, the highlights of my life," he tweeted later. "I can't begin to describe how it feels."

> "IT'S THEATER TELLING THEM A STORY ABOUT THEM-SELVES, *a story that they didn't know. That's huge—that's amazing.*"

For the kids, the show wasn't over. Back in their classrooms, in the Bronx, Brooklyn, and Queens, the students followed the TDF approach, which asks them to devise performances based on the plays they've seen. The *Hamilton* script had made Joe White mull some ideas for his students: "What political issues are important to the students? What are we dealing with now that would be open to debate? I thought it would be cool to have them do rap battles with each other." He paired up his students, and asked them to come up with pro and con positions on some tough issues, like gun control and same-sex marriage. Then they turned those arguments into raps, and squared off in front of the class. He even asked them to incorporate a line from the show.

A RAP WRITTEN FOR A DEBATE ON

MARRIAGE EQUALITY

It's 2015, can't you see?
Everyone can be loved, including me.
We live for the new, we live for the now
And while you are hating on gays
I say go ahead and finish your vows.
You say everyone is scared, even the children
I say there's a lesson to be learned,
So let's teach them — . . . L-O-V-E
That's what everyone wants, you and me
We have to be together and bring the peace
And join together in equality.
They put a ban on gay marriage and here I stand
Ready to go with you, hand in hand
Because I want to be in the room where it happens.

WRITTEN BY

ESTEISY SEIJAS

of

JOHN ADAMS HIGH SCHOOL

At Fort Hamilton High, Susan Willerman asked students to choose an issue they were passionate about, then improvise words and movement that allowed them to present different views on the issue to their classmates. "Having seen the show, they had a much greater sense of what this could be. I was pretty much blown away by the creativity." A hearing-impaired student who usually shied away from getting in front of the class was excited to take part. "Seeing how much energy and enthusiasm those performers had must be very inspiring for anybody who has stage fright," says Willerman of the *Hamilton* cast. "The kids must have thought, *They're really putting themselves out there—maybe I can do that, too.*"

Bill Coulter's class in Brooklyn spent their last session talking about the connection between *Hamilton* and the work they had done. "Some of them were just absolutely blown away," he says. "They were saying, 'George Washington wasn't black, Mr. Coulter!' I said, 'Obviously he wasn't, guys.'" He asked the kids how the casting affected them. "They said, 'It just made me really proud, and feel good about being American. Like I belong here.'"

DAVEED HAS MORE STINGING DEFEATS in Cabinet battles ahead of him. A few months after those student matinees at the Public, Jeffrey Seller announced a radical expansion of *Hamilton*'s outreach to students. Thanks to a $1.5 million grant from the Rockefeller Foundation, 20,000 students from New York public schools—specifically, schools in which a high percentage of kids qualify for free lunches—will get to see the show on Broadway in 2016. That is *35 times* as many who saw it via TDF at the Public. They will pay a Hamilton—that is, $10—to attend a matinee, and to participate in educational programming designed by the Gilder Lehrman Institute of American History. Daveed doesn't mind. On the contrary. When the news was announced, he called it "the most important and exciting moment in the journey thus far."

The sheer size of those numbers means that reckoning with *Hamilton*'s impact now, in the first year of its public performances, is a bit like judging your harvest in the middle of May. Jeffrey plans to expand a version of the program to other cities when the show begins to tour. What will happen when hundreds of thousands of kids, all around the country, have the experience that Bill Coulter's students did?

Lin doesn't know, but he is very familiar with the power of plays to shape young minds. "I know how deep in the DNA musicals get because they're deep in *my* DNA," he says. At the press conference for the announcement of the student program, he evoked *Les Misérables*, the first Broadway musical he ever saw: "I know that show like I know my family tree."

Sometime early in the next decade, give or take a few years, *Hamilton's* influence on students will take another big leap—bigger by order of magnitude. The show will be licensed for student and amateur productions. So in addition to watching from the dark in vast numbers, college and high-school kids will get to learn it and perform it for themselves. Executives at two organizations that lead the field of theatrical licensing, Theodore S. Chapin of the Rodgers and Hammerstein organization and Drew Cohen of Music Theatre International, say that *Hamilton* will almost certainly be one of the most licensed musicals in the country when it becomes available. Its subject matter will appeal to history teachers, its array of juicy roles will appeal to young actors, and its mélange of musical styles will appeal to almost everybody. In a given school year, they imagine, that might mean 600 or 700 student productions around the United States.

What will it mean when thousands of students step into these roles at age 15 or 18 or 20—roles that have changed the lives of the original cast members, who encountered them at a significantly later age? Leslie says that playing a Founding Father has made him feel newly invested in the country's origins, something that always seemed remote from his life as a black man in America. "The empathy that requires, the connections you make, the lines you draw between the things you want and the things they wanted, that you love and they loved, I never found all that connective tissue before this show."

Lin hopes those student productions will strive for the diversity of the original production, the ethnic mix that makes *Hamilton* look like a message beamed back from Future America. It means that whatever impact the show might have on Broadway, and however long it might run, the biggest impact won't be in New York: It'll be in high-school and college rehearsal rooms across America, where boys learn to carry themselves with the nobility of George Washington, girls learn to think and rap fast enough to rip through "Satisfied," and kids of either gender (Lin isn't doctrinaire) summon the conviction of John Laurens, the freedom-fighting abolitionist, who sings, "Tomorrow there'll be more of us."

ABOVE:
Lin-Manuel Miranda at the press conference where Hamilton's
partnership with the Rockefeller Foundation was announced.

CABINET BATTLE #1

—◆—

Microphones emerge.

WASHINGTON: Ladies and Gentlemen, you coulda been anywhere in the world tonight, but you're here with us in New York City. Are you ready for a cabinet meeting???[1]

The Company cheers.

WASHINGTON: The issue on the table: Secretary Hamilton's plan to assume state debt and establish a national bank. Secretary Jefferson, you have the floor, sir.

JEFFERSON: "Life, liberty and the pursuit of happiness."
We fought for these ideals; we shouldn't settle for less.
These are wise words, enterprising men quote 'em.
Don't act surprised, you guys, cuz I wrote 'em.

JEFFERSON, MADISON: Owwwwwwwwww.

JEFFERSON: But Hamilton forgets
His plan would have the government assume states' debts.
Now place your bets as to who that benefits
The very seat of government where Hamilton sits.

HAMILTON: Not true!

JEFFERSON: Ooh, if the shoe fits, wear it.
If New York's in debt—
Why should Virginia bear it?
Uh! Our debts are paid, I'm afraid.
Don't tax the South cuz we got it made in the shade.
In Virginia, we plant seeds in the ground.
We create. You just wanna move our money around.[2]
This financial plan is an outrageous demand.
And it's too many damn pages for any man to understand.
Stand with me. In the land of the free.
And pray to God we never see Hamilton's candidacy.
Look, when Britain taxed our tea, we got frisky.
Imagine what gon' happen when you try to tax our whiskey.

WASHINGTON: Thank you, Secretary Jefferson. Secretary Hamilton, your response.

HAMILTON: Thomas. That was a real nice declaration.
Welcome to the present. We're running a real nation.
Would you like to join us, or stay mellow,
Doin' whatever the hell it is you do in Monticello?
If we assume the debts, the Union gets a new line of credit, a financial diuretic.[3]
How do you not get it? If we're aggressive and competitive
The Union gets a boost. You'd rather give it a sedative?
A civics lesson from a slaver. Hey neighbor.
Your debts are paid cuz you don't pay for labor.
"We plant seeds in the South. We create." Yeah, keep ranting.
We know who's really doing the planting.[4]
And another thing, Mr. Age of Enlightenment,
Don't lecture me about the war, you didn't fight in it.
You think I'm frightened of you, man? We almost died in a trench
While you were off, getting high with the French.
Thomas Jefferson, always hesitant with the President

[1] I was always excited to write these Cabinet battles: In fact, I wrote these before many of the other songs in the show. Battle rapping incorporates a lot of elements: moving the crowd, flipping your opponents' insults, verbal prowess—but the stakes are rarely as high as the direction your country takes. I wanted to write battle raps with exactly those stakes in mind. Also love Washington serving as Mekhi Phifer in *8 Mile* here.

[2] The fun in writing these debates is of course articulating the perspectives of these men in a way that feels contemporary. Jefferson echoes the feelings of many Wall Street critics today when he says, "We create. You just wanna move our money around." If I were watching that in a rap battle, I'd nod my head. Jefferson had a way of making himself the man of the people, and I tried to honor that in his battle raps.

[3] The first thing I did here was to look up the etymology of *diuretic* and make sure it existed in this era. *Whew.*

[4] I cannot tell you how cathartic it is to get to express this to Jefferson every night. The audience's reaction is similarly cathartic.

[5] I find that people react one of two ways when they're angry: They run hot or they run cold. Most of us run hot: We lose our temper, and our wits often leave us as well. I don't get angry easily (I'm really 5,000 times as mellow as Hamilton) but when I *do*, I run *cold*: Time slows down, and the exact right words click into place to destroy what's in front of me. Not proud of it, but it's how I'm wired. I gave this trait to Hamilton, and I think it suits him well: He rhymes the craziest when he is backed into a corner.

[6] This line alone makes the student matinees worth it. *They lose their minds.*

Reticent—there isn't a plan he doesn't jettison.[5]
Madison, you're mad as a hatter, son, take your
    medicine.
Damn, you're in worse shape than the national
    debt is in,
Sittin' there useless as two shits.
Hey, turn around, bend over, I'll show you
    where my shoe fits.[6]

WASHINGTON: Excuse me? Jefferson, Madison, take a walk! Hamilton, take a walk! We'll reconvene after a brief recess. Hamilton!

HAMILTON: Sir!

WASHINGTON: A word.

MADISON: You don't have the votes.

JEFFERSON, MADISON: You don't have the votes.

JEFFERSON: Aha-ha ha ha!

JEFFERSON, MADISON: You're gonna need congressional approval and you don't have the votes.

JEFFERSON: Such a blunder sometimes it makes me wonder why I even bring the thunder.[7]

MADISON: Why he even brings the thunder . . .

Washington & Hamilton, alone.

WASHINGTON: You wanna pull yourself together?

HAMILTON: I'm sorry, these Virginians are birds of a feather.

WASHINGTON: Young man, I'm from Virginia. So watch your mouth.

162

HAMILTON: So we let Congress get held hostage by the South?

WASHINGTON: You need the votes.

HAMILTON: No, we need bold strokes. We need this plan.

WASHINGTON: No, you need to convince more folks.

HAMILTON: Well, James Madison won't talk to me, that's a nonstarter.

WASHINGTON: Winning was easy, young man. Governing's harder.[8]

HAMILTON: They're being intransigent.

WASHINGTON: You have to find a compromise.

HAMILTON: But they don't have a plan, they just hate mine![9]

WASHINGTON: Convince them otherwise.

HAMILTON: What happens if I don't get congressional approval?

WASHINGTON: I imagine they'll call for your removal.

HAMILTON: Sir—

WASHINGTON: Figure it out, Alexander. That's an order from your commander.

[7] Our audiences are of all ages and walks of life, but *everyone* gets the Grandmaster Flash reference, even if they don't know how they know it. This feels incredible from onstage.

[8] Nice bit of symmetry with "Dying is easy, governing's harder" from Act One. Or as Mario Cuomo put it, "You campaign in poetry. You govern in prose."

[9] This is familiar in contemporary politics.

DID THEY
or
DIDN'T THEY?

OR,

SOME DISCOURSE ON AFFAIRS

RON CHERNOW SAW *HAMILTON* MORE than 20 times at the Public. It sounds a little crazy, he realizes, but he had his reasons. During previews, he kept seeing it so he could give notes as the show took shape. After opening night he went back to witness history (a break from his day job, writing history), and to find new treats amid the dense complexity of Lac's orchestrations and Andy's dances. Also friends kept hitting him up to take them along.

After one performance, he and a guest greeted Lin, who told them how much fun he was having onstage.

"I get to be pure id for two and a half hours," he said. "I get to have an affair."

"*Two* affairs," said Ron's friend.

Lin looked perplexed.

There's one affair in the show for sure: Hamilton's tryst with Maria Reynolds in the middle of Act Two. The second affair, if it happened, was with his sister-in-law, Angelica. It was hot gossip at the time, furnishing John Adams with the last item in one of his lists of Hamilton's misdeeds—his "fornications, adulteries, and his incests." But conclusive proof never came to light—at least not after one of Hamilton's sons tore passages out of their letters. The surviving facts establish only that Alexander and Angelica enjoyed what Ron calls "a subtle, delicate, ambiguous flirtation."

One of the little pleasures that kept Ron coming back was Lin's willingness to honor this ambiguity. Ron's friend thought there was an affair, but plenty of other theatergoers didn't. "I'm convinced that anyone else dramatizing the story would have Hamilton sleeping with his sister-in-law," says Ron. "That would have spiced things up."

Yet here is one place where Lin the Writer left a puzzle for Lin the Actor to solve. Writing an ambiguous relationship is one thing, but how do you perform it? Seven times a week, Lin and Renée had to do *something* up there. That meant they had to decide what really happened between Alexander and Angelica. Or did they?

Ask Renée if the brilliant, alluring Angelica was having an affair with the brilliant, charming Hamilton, and she volleys back, Angelica-style: "So, what *is* an affair?"

ABOVE:
John Trumbull's portrait of Angelica Schuyler Church, her son, Philip, and a servant (top).

Inclose My dear friend is a letter from
your sister; which she has written to supply
my deficiency. Tomorrow I open the budget &
you may imagine that to day I am very
busy and not a little anxious. I could not
however let the Packet sail without giving
you a proof, that no degree of occupation
can make me forget you.

We hope to hear shortly that
you are safe arrived & that every thing.
is to your wish. That Mr Church is
well, young and spreightly. And that
your Sons promise all to be great
men, and your Daughters to be like
yourself. Adieu love to Mr Church

& believe me always   Yr Affectionate friend
                                        & brother

                                        A Hamilton

New York January 7. 1789

Mr A Church

"Even if it hasn't been consummated, I'm 100 percent playing it as an *emotional* affair," she says. "As a married person, that almost seems worse to me."

"It's an emotional affair," Lin agrees. "It's an intellectual affair."

They were sitting on the couch in Lac's dressing room one afternoon: It looked like couples counseling.

"It's emotional and intellectual," continues Renée, "and I think that the next step would definitely be sexual. But I don't *know* that, and I don't know that she knows that. I don't think you tell yourself when you're doing something so wrong."

"It feels wrong?"

"It feels wrong—and *right*," she says, laughing. "It feels wrong, but it's also necessary and crucial for her existence. He gives her something that she gets nowhere else, and she has to have it. I don't know that there's a choice."

"This is someone who has incredible intellectual curiosity, who's desperate for news of America, and she's stuck with a banker in London," says Lin. "Her letters are not only, 'How are you doing?' and 'How is the family doing?' but '*What's the dirt?*'"

Lin dramatized those letters in "Take a Break," another express bus of a song, zipping its characters through seven or eight plot points in four and a half minutes. As preparation, he read all of Alexander and Angelica's correspondence. He wanted to show that the flirtation didn't end when she moved to London, that he kept trying to impress her, that the tension was real. He also wanted to underscore that she is the smartest character in the show, making her a political counselor to Hamilton as he fights to enact his debt plan, a woman who lavished her wit on flirty letters because the strictures of her era denied her other outlets.

Lin took his share of liberties: There was no trip upstate like the one Angelica and Eliza propose, and Angelica's chronology has been shuffled around. (In real life, she eloped with her rich British businessman before meeting Hamilton—something Renée says she puts out of her mind.) But Lin thinks that his version, which gives the two of them a moment of acute mutual attraction before Hamilton meets Eliza, makes the rest of their relationship feel truer to life.

"You have a moment with a girl, then your best friend marries the girl. You might love your best friend, and hug your best friend, but you and the girl *both know* that you said some shit that you can't unsay," says Lin. "Everyone has a version of that in their life."

"At least one," says Renée.

And these sorta-kinda affairs, these wrong-yet-right, not-quite-relationships are much easier today than in the 1790s, Lin and Renée agree, thanks to technology. It's easier to be present physically without being present emotionally when a beloved non-lover is a quick text message away.

"This can happen really easily with wit, with flirting back and forth," says Renée. "Why do you think I turned my instant messenger off in the '90s, or whenever it was?"

If pushed, they both say they don't know if Alexander and Angelica were sleeping together. Nor can they guess what would have happened if the characters had made that trip upstate. Renée doubts it would have been con-

---

"For all of Angelica's BEAUTY and BRILLIANCE, Lin is sure that Hamilton MARRIED THE RIGHT SCHUYLER SISTER."

---

summated. "I think that sometimes people do this kind of thing because you can't go there, because it feels in some ways safe, because there's something that would stop you." The thing, in this case, is the love they share for Eliza.

For all of Angelica's beauty and brilliance, Lin is sure that Hamilton married the right Schuyler sister. "Eliza ended up being this nonstop source of warmth and forgiveness and kindness. Also they had eight kids together, which is a pretty good testament that they liked being around each other."

Renée, surprisingly, agrees that Hamilton was better off with Eliza. "To me, the best and most exciting surprise in the show is that Angelica's the only one that always knew Eliza was the better woman. Every great thing that Angelica does in her life is because she knows what her sister would do." In "Satisfied," after all, Angelica decides to give up on Alexander—"this man she desperately loves, and needs"—because that's what her sister would do.

"The love affair for Angelica really is Eliza," says Renée, "and loving Alexander through her."

TAKE A BREAK[1]

[1] A musical theater composer I love and admire came to a workshop of *Hamilton* and gave me notes. One of them: "Take a Break." It's as well-written as your other songs, but you don't need it. I sat with this for a week (I admire this composer very much) but then took the note as a challenge to *earn* the song's place in the show. It's our only personal check-in with Hamilton's family in a politically heavy second act. I felt like I needed it. So it does exactly what I need it to do, without an ounce of fat: introduce us to Philip, let us know that Angelica and Hamilton are still letter-flirting, and see that Hamilton's work is driving him to distraction. Aaaand out.

[2] This is the same melody as the lead-in to "Ten Duel Commandments." When you start learning piano (I started at age six), these are the kinds of pieces you learn, simple stuff to make you practice scales. Foreshadowing, but also what a nine-year-old would be learning.

[3] This used to be a *really obscure* Macbeth quote: "They have tied me to a stake; I cannot fly, but, bear-like, I must fight the course." (It's from a *really* short scene in Act Five where Macbeth kills Young Seward.) Then Oskar Eustis said, "Lin, I run the Shakespeare Festival and *even* I don't get this reference." He was correct. I was being willfully esoteric. So I went with one of the greatest hits. *But I still like my Act Five reference better.*

Eliza joins young Philip Hamilton at the piano.

ELIZA:
Un deux trois quatre
Cinq six sept huit neuf.

PHILIP HAMILTON:
Un deux trois quatre

Cinq six sept huit neuf.

Good!
Un deux trois quatre
Cinq six sept huit neuf.

Un deux trois quatre

Cinq six sept huit neuf.

He sings the last three notes differently. Eliza corrects him, but he sings it his way.

ELIZA:
Sept huit neuf—

PHILIP:
Sept huit neuf—[2]

Sept huit neuf—

PHILIP:
Sept huit neuf—

ELIZA, PHILIP: One two three four five six seven eight nine!

In an adjacent room, Hamilton composes a letter.

HAMILTON: My dearest Angelica,
"Tomorrow and tomorrow and tomorrow
Creeps in this petty pace from day to day."[3]
I trust you'll understand the reference to another
     Scottish tragedy
Without my having to name the play.
They think me Macbeth, ambition is my folly.
I'm a polymath, a pain in the ass, a massive pain.
Madison is Banquo, Jefferson's Macduff
And Birnam Wood is Congress on its way to
     Dunsinane.

HAMILTON, ANGELICA: And there you are,
     an ocean away.

Do you have to live an ocean away?
Thoughts of you subside
Then I get another letter
I cannot put the notion away . . .

Eliza enters.

ELIZA: Take a break.

HAMILTON: I am on my way.

ELIZA: There's a little surprise before supper
And it cannot wait.

HAMILTON: I'll be there in just a minute, save
my plate.

ELIZA: Alexander—

HAMILTON: Okay, okay—

ELIZA: Your son is nine years old today.
He has something he'd like to say
He's been practicing all day
Philip take it away—[4]

*Eliza ushers Hamilton to the piano, where
Philip leaps off the piano bench.*

PHILIP:
Daddy, Daddy, look—
My name is Philip.
I am a poet.
I wrote this poem just to show it.
And I just turned nine.
You can write rhymes but you can't write mine.

	HAMILTON:
PHILIP:	What!
I practice French	
and play	
Piano with my	
mother.	
	Uh-huh!
I have a sister but I	
want a little brother. [5]	
	Okay!
My daddy's trying to	
start America's bank.	
Un deux trois quatre	
cinq!	
	Bravo!

ELIZA: Take a break.

HAMILTON: Hey, our kid is pretty great.

ELIZA: Run away with us for the summer.
Let's go upstate.

HAMILTON: Eliza, I've got so much on my plate.

ELIZA: We can all go stay with my father.
There's a lake I know . . .

HAMILTON: I know.

ELIZA: In a nearby park.

HAMILTON: I'd love to go.

ELIZA: You and I can go when the night
gets dark . . .

HAMILTON: I will try to get away.

*Fade up on Angelica. She is writing a response
to Hamilton's letter.*

ANGELICA: My dearest Alexander,
You must get through to Jefferson.
Sit down with him and compromise.
Don't stop 'til you agree.
Your fav'rite older sister,
Angelica, reminds you
There's someone in your corner all the way
      across the sea.
In a letter I received from you two weeks ago
I noticed a comma in the middle of a phrase.
It changed the meaning. Did you intend this? [6]
One stroke and you've consumed my waking days.
It says:

Fade up on Hamilton, reading the letter.

HAMILTON, ANGELICA: "My dearest, Angelica."

ANGELICA: With a comma after "dearest."
You've written

HAMILTON, ANGELICA: "My dearest, Angelica."

ANGELICA: Anyway, all this to say
I'm coming home this summer
At my sister's invitation,
I'll be there with your fam'ly
If you make your way upstate.
I know you're very busy
I know your work's important
But I'm crossing the ocean and I just can't wait.

[4] When people ask me about the most autobiographical scene in the show, I point to this one. There's no history book in which you'll read about Philip doing a recital for Alexander. This came out of me, and looking at it, I see myself, almost painfully, in every character onstage. As Alexander, I relate as a father with an enormous workload. As Eliza, I relate because of the pains I take to slow down and carve out time for my family. But most of all, I'm Philip: I've written something and I'm proud of it and I want to show it to the people I love. You didn't expect these notes to turn into my therapy session, did you?

[5] And, boy, did he get little brothers! Five of them, actually, and two sisters. But if you want to see a musical with eight kids, go watch *The Sound of Music.*

[6] This took weeks to figure out, but it's based on actual correspondence between Alexander and Angelica. They'd slip commas between words and change the meaning. The passage that inspired this verse was actually in French. Comma sexting. It's a thing. Get into it.

HAMILTON, ANGELICA: You won't be an ocean away.
You'll only be a moment away.

Eliza calls from the other room.

ELIZA: Alexander, come downstairs. Angelica's arriving today!

Angelica enters.

ELIZA: Angelica!

ANGELICA: Eliza!

They embrace. Hamilton enters.

HAMILTON: The Schuyler sisters!

ANGELICA: Alexander.

HAMILTON: Hi.

ANGELICA: It's good to see your face.

ELIZA: Angelica, tell this man John Adams spends the summer with his family.

HAMILTON: Angelica, tell my wife John Adams doesn't have a real job anyway.

ANGELICA: . . . You're not joining us? Wait.

HAMILTON: I'm afraid I cannot join you upstate.

ANGELICA: Alexander, I came all this way.

ELIZA: She came all this way—

ANGELICA: All this way—

ELIZA, ANGELICA: Take a break.

HAMILTON: You know I have to get my plan through Congress.

ELIZA, ANGELICA: Run away with us for the summer.
Let's go upstate.

HAMILTON: I lose my job if we don't get this plan through Congress.

ELIZA, ANGELICA: We can all go stay with our father.

ELIZA:	ANGELICA:
There's a lake I know	I know we'll miss your face—
In a nearby park.	Screw your courage To the sticking place—7
You and I can go	
	Eliza's right—
Take a break And get away—	Take a break.
	Run away with us For the summer—
Let's go upstate Where we can stay.	Let's go upstate.
	We can all go stay with our father, If you take your time—
Look around, look around, At how lucky we are to be alive right now—	You will make your mark.
	Close your eyes and dream—
We can go—	
When the night gets dark. Take a break.	When the night gets dark. Take a break.

HAMILTON: I have to get my plan through Congress.
I can't stop 'til I get this plan through Congress.

7 And this is why cast albums (all of 'em, not just mine) are so useful. Maybe one in a thousand people will catch that Angelica's responding with a Lady Macbeth quote, thus referencing Hamilton's *Macbeth* quote at the top of the song. Also, I *first* heard "Screw your courage to the sticking place" in *Beauty and the Beast*, not knowing as a child that the great Howard Ashman was quoting Shakespeare. So it's my nod to both.

IN WHICH ADVANTAGES ARE DERIVED

from Listening to the

BROADWAY OLD MASTERS

and

JASMINE CEPHAS JONES

HAMILTON **MADE A LEAP IN AMBITION** and sophistication over its predecessor, *In the Heights*. Partly this is the natural course of a career, the result of Lin having matured as a man and an artist. But it also reflected a changed relationship to the Broadway traditions that inspired him.

Beneath all the flashy rapping of *In the Heights*, Lin's ballads showed a serious apprenticeship to his illustrious forebears. His lyrics were precise, evocative, moving. When he wrote *Hamilton*, he wasn't just listening to their cast albums anymore: He was listening to *his actual forebears*. The final form of *Hamilton* reflects the counsel he received from some living legends of musical theater, a kitchen cabinet of his heroes.

In 2007, John Kander saw *In the Heights*, then did something he almost never does: He stuck around to meet the guy who wrote it. He and Lin became friends. "I was terrifically impressed with him, with his energy and his talent," says the composer of *Cabaret* and *Chicago*—an all-around giant of the profession since before Lin was born.

As *The Hamilton Mixtape* began to emerge, Lin invited him to the American Songbook concert and other early workshops, which afforded Kander a rare pleasure: "I came away feeling like writing. Not writing like Lin, or doing a project like that—it was just that really, really good work makes me want to go to work." In the audience after one presentation, Kander shared his enthusiasm with his friend Mike Nichols—the last conversation they had before the great director's death. (It meant a lot to Tommy to spend time with Nichols, one of the directors on his personal Mt. Rushmore. The other is Hal Prince, who directed *Cabaret*, *Sweeney Todd*, and *The Phantom of the Opera* on his way to racking up a record 21 Tony Awards. "It's those two guys on the mountain, twice," Tommy says.)

Spending time with Kander reinforced Lin's natural tendency toward extreme diligence. "This guy is 80-plus years old and he's still chasing moments, and chasing the way to articulate those moments perfectly," marvels Lin. And he found in Kander a model of how to do this without being eaten alive. "The myth of 'You have to be a tortured artist' is a *myth*," says Lin. "You can have a happy, healthy life and still go to all these crazy dark places in your writing, and then go play with your child and hug your wife."

ABOVE:

Stephen Sondheim and Lin-Manuel Miranda.

John Weidman first came to know Lin as a talented and apparently inexhaustible schoolmate of his daughter at Hunter College High School. The librettist (that is, the person who wrote the scenes and dialogue that accompany the songs) of three shows with Stephen Sondheim found it "slightly disorienting, in a pleasing way," to watch that young man grow up to take a spot next to him in the front ranks of Broadway storytellers. He was glad to help Lin get there.

In 2009, when Lin was at what he called a crossroads in the show's creation, he reached out to Weidman for advice. He admired the way that Weidman and Sondheim had distilled sprawling history into the concise drama of *Pacific Overtures* (about the first contact between America and Japan) and *Assassins* (about men and women who have tried to kill a president). How did they do it?

Weidman answered Lin's many questions at length. He took him to lunch for what Lin called "hummus and knowledge." He shared technical insights derived from 40 years of facing precisely the challenges that Lin faced. He reassured Lin that it would be provocative—

KNOWLEDGE & INSPIRATION:

EXCERPTS FROM AN EMAIL EXCHANGE

Lin-Manuel Miranda to John Weidman, 11/9/09

I wanted to pick your brain about how you winnowed down the shape of *Assassins* and *Pacific Overtures*, given the wealth of historical material and historical perspectives available. I'm trying to turn Hamilton's life into a hip-hop album. Inevitably, the more research I do, the more daunting the project seems.

I have three songs written, and I'm at a crossroads.... Do you recommend writing about the sections of Hamilton's life that are most attractive personally, and writing the connective tissue later, if I find that there are large, Buick-sized holes in the storytelling?

John Weidman to Lin-Manuel Miranda, 11/23/09

Absolutely. Particularly since you are talking about a concept album first and then maybe a theater piece afterwards. Let your imagination go to the places where it naturally wants to go and turn it loose. Each song then gets added to the other ones, each created from a pure idea and a place of pure enthusiasm and at some point as the songs accumulate——and this is key——the songs themselves start to become the "research." Inevitably, they'll start to suggest patterns, what's missing. But it won't be what's missing from some documentary-like take on Hamilton's life. It'll be what's missing from why *you* were so taken with his life and why *you* needed to write about it. Does that make sense?

Lin-Manuel Miranda to John Weidman, 11/26/09

Thanks so much for this wealth of knowledge and inspiration. Thanks for the tacit permission to write my way into the most interesting sections of his life and find the patterns there. It's thrilling to go forward with that as the game plan.

---

and significant—to reveal what a Founding Father had in common with somebody like Kanye West.

"By writing about Hamilton you're really writing about America today," he wrote after listening to a new *Hamilton* song in 2011. "In the end I guess I'm saying stay with this even when it seems opaque and impossible and drives you crazy."

The result of Lin's persistence gave Weidman hope. "If you've done this work for most of your life, and you care about it, to see something like this, which represents where a next-generation artist can take it, is both thrilling and reassuring," he says. When the show reached Broadway, *New York* magazine asked Lin to list the top influences on its creation. Weidman was number eight. "People in my life—not excluding my wife—consider this the pinnacle of my career," Weidman says.

"... Lin made something that COMBINED TRADITION AND INNOVATION SO SEAMLESSLY ... he listened to his young castmates with the same absorbing interest he lavished on the old masters, and let himself be guided by both."

Another special influence on the show came from the writer who looms largest in Lin's Hall of Fame—bigger even than Big Pun. In fall 2008, he got to meet Stephen Sondheim, the composer/lyricist whose name is synonymous with what's best and most boundary-pushing in musical theater, thanks to *Gypsy*, *Sweeney Todd*, *Sunday in the Park with George*, and other masterworks dating back to the 1950s. Sondheim remembers that first conversation with Lin, and how much he liked the *Hamilton* idea, even though "I didn't know what a mixtape was."

During the next few years, when Lin was laying the groundwork for the show, he was also spending a lot of time in Sondheim's brain. They had that meeting in 2008 because Lin had been hired to do Spanish translations of the lyrics that Sondheim had written for the Puerto Rican characters in *West Side Story*. "It's an unusual assignment, like when I did crossword puzzles," Sondheim says, referring to the contributions he made to *New York* magazine in its first year of publication. (Eminem has drawn a similar comparison between lyric-writing and puzzle-solving, a coincidence that doesn't surprise Sondheim, or even seem remarkable: "Every

creative act is a puzzle. It's trying to make form out of chaos.")

Lin was proud of his work on *West Side Story*, but felt that its real value lay in forging a relationship with "The God MC Sondheezy," as he called him in a tweet. (Lin had heard Sondheim laugh at the "bursar" line in "Aaron Burr, Sir," and tweeted: "I wish I could bottle that laugh.") Lin gave him a hip-hop name because more than anybody else on Broadway, Sondheim writes lyrics that achieve the density and ingenuity of the best rap verses. In fact, when the early audiences for *Hamilton* marveled at how hip-hop allowed Lin to deliver a lot of exposition very quickly, they were only catching up to something Sondheim had grasped 30 years earlier, when he decided to have the Witch rap her backstory in the opening number of *Into the Woods*: "It's an attempt to delight the ear while filling it full of information, which ordinarily would be extremely boring," he explains.

Sondheim knew the rat-a-tat power of hip-hop, but he warned Lin of its limitations. After listening to some *Hamilton* demos, he imparted a lesson that Lin took to heart: "The only caution I can raise is monotony of rhythmic and verbal attack over the evening—and, occasionally, over the song," he wrote. In other words: Musicals depend on variety. Like republics, they need a multiplicity of voices to thrive.

When Lin achieved the kind of variety that Sondheim liked, the enthusiastic response meant the world to him. The reaction that struck him the most in the early going was Sondheim's enthusiasm for "Say No to This." Here is all the variety that you could desire: Hamilton raps about his affair with Maria Reynolds, who sings her side of the story in R&B. Now and then Maria's husband pops up to extort money from Hamilton in another rap, and the rest of the company chimes in by singing "No!" in disbelief. The variety in the music helps to express the rich and shadowy complexity of the subject. No wonder the guy who wrote *Company* liked it.

Jasmine Cephas Jones liked it too. *"This is my jam,"* she said the first time she heard it, when she was preparing to audition for Maria. On the page, her affair with Hamilton could be a mere scheme of extortion, a trap she sets

because it'll help her survive in her abusive marriage. "What makes 'Say No to This' interesting is the possibility that she's also falling in love with him," she says. "That's what makes the stakes so high."

Jasmine admired the song's variety too, but the word meant something different to her than it did to Sondheim. She had grown up in New York theater, tagging along to rehearsals with her father, the actor Ron Cephas Jones, doing her homework backstage, studying acting at the Neighborhood Playhouse. When she went to Berklee College of Music to train as a singer, she gravitated toward jazz and contemporary music—styles closer to the Miles Davis, Prince, and Stevie Wonder records she had grown up with, and the songs she had heard her mother sing. (Kim Lesley, a jazz singer, played gigs while pregnant with Jasmine, which brings her near to being the embodiment of the old showbiz accolade that a performer was born onstage.)

Maria Reynolds stood apart from many of the roles that Jasmine auditioned to play: Here was a great musical-

theater character that wasn't tailored for a conventional musical-theater voice. "I just went into the audition like Jasmine, and how I would normally sing," she says. It made her feel good to land a role not in spite of her distinctive R&B voice but because of it. "No one is trying to be something else," she says of her castmates, many of whom had similar experiences.

Like Daveed and Oak, Jasmine plays two roles in the show: She's Peggy, the youngest Schuyler sister, before she reemerges as Maria. One night during the run at the Public, Lin heard Jasmine and her onstage sisters, Renée and Pippa, singing R&B songs in their dressing room. He loved their harmonies so much that he rearranged "The Schuyler Sisters" to showcase them better.

If you want to know how Lin made something that combined tradition and innovation so seamlessly, a big reason is that he listened to his young castmates with the same absorbing interest he lavished on the old masters, and let himself be guided by both. "We are influencing the piece by just being who we are," says Jasmine.

SAY NO TO THIS

[1] This originally started with an LL Cool J quote from his seminal '80s' classic "I Need Love." It got a great laugh, but I realized we don't need a laugh here, we really need to focus.

[2] Hamilton's the only one who can narrate the song at this point in the story: It happened to him, in secret, and we don't know Maria or James Reynolds yet. So he does it. It's an all-hands-on-deck approach to the storytelling: The person closest to the action addresses the audience.

[3] In real life, Hamilton described the moment this way: "Some conversation ensued from which it was quickly apparent that other than pecuniary consolation would be acceptable." Wink, wink.

Maria Reynolds enters. Burr enters.

BURR: There's nothing like summer in the city.
Someone under stress meets someone
    looking pretty.
There's trouble in the air, you can smell it.
And Alexander's by himself. I'll let him tell it.

Hamilton at his desk.

HAMILTON: I hadn't slept in a week.
I was weak, I was awake. [1]
You've never seen a bastard orphan
More in need of a break.
Longing for Angelica.
Missing my wife.
That's when Miss Maria Reynolds walked into
    my life, she said:

MARIA REYNOLDS: I know you are a man of
    honor,
I'm so sorry to bother you at home
But I don't know where to go, and I came here
    all alone.

HAMILTON: She said:

MARIA: My husband's doin' me wrong
Beatin' me, cheatin' me, mistreatin' me.
Suddenly he's up and gone
I don't have the means to go on.

HAMILTON: So I offered her a loan, I offered
to walk her home, she said: [2]

MARIA: You're too kind, sir

HAMILTON: I gave her thirty bucks that I had
socked away, she lived a block away, she said:

MARIA: This one's mine, sir:

HAMILTON: Then I said, "Well, I should head
back home," she turned red, she led me to her
bed, let her legs spread and said: [3]

MARIA: Stay?

HAMILTON: Hey

MARIA: Hey

HAMILTON: That's when I began to pray:
Lord, show me how to
Say no to this
I don't know how to
Say no to this.

HAMILTON: But my God, she looks so helpless
And her body's saying, "Hell, yes."

MARIA: Whoa . . .

HAMILTON: Nooo, show me how to

HAMILTON, ENSEMBLE: Say no to this.

HAMILTON: I don't know how to

HAMILTON, ENSEMBLE: Say no to this.

HAMILTON: In my mind, I'm tryin' to go

ENSEMBLE: Go! Go! Go!

HAMILTON: Then her mouth is on mine, and
I don't say

ENSEMBLE: No! No!
Say no to this!

No! No!
Say no to this!

No! No!
Say no to this!

No! No!
Say no to this!

Hamilton & Reynolds kiss and embrace.

HAMILTON: I wish I could say that was the
  last time.
I said that last time. It became a pastime.
A month into this endeavor I received a letter
From a Mr. James Reynolds, even better, it said:

Lights up on James Reynolds.

JAMES REYNOLDS: Dear sir, I hope this letter
  finds you in good health,
And in a prosperous enough position to
  put wealth
In the pockets of people like me: down on
  their luck.
You see, that was my wife who you decided to

HAMILTON: Fuuuu—

JAMES REYNOLDS: Uh-oh! You made the
  wrong sucker a cuckold.
So time to pay the piper for the pants
  you unbuckled
And hey, you can keep seein' my whore wife
If the price is right: if not I'm telling your wife.

HAMILTON: I hid the letter and I raced to her place, screamed "How could you?!" In her face, she said

MARIA: No sir.

HAMILTON: Half dressed, apologetic. A mess, she looked pathetic, she cried:

MARIA: Please don't go, sir.

HAMILTON: So was your whole story a setup?

MARIA: I don't know about any letter.

HAMILTON: Stop crying goddamn it get up.

MARIA: I didn't know any better.

HAMILTON: I am ruined.

MARIA:	HAMILTON:
Please don't leave me with him helpless.	I am helpless—how could I do this? [4]
Just give him what he wants and you can have me.	
	I don't want you.
Whatever you want	I don't want you.
If you pay,	I don't . . . .
You can stay.	

	HAMILTON:	
	Lord, show me how to	ENSEMBLE:
	Say no to this.	Say no to this!
Tonight		
	I don't now how to Say no to this.	Say no to this!

4 This used to be "How could you do this?" Tommy Kail suggested the change, and it's a good one—Hamilton's realization of his own culpability in this situation is far more compelling than blaming Maria.

	Cuz the situation's Helpless.	
Helpless.		
	And her body's Screaming hell yes.	
Whoa!		
	No, show me how to say no to this.	Say no to this!
How can you say no to this?	How can I Say no to this?	Say no to this!
	There is nowhere I can go. When her body's on mine	Go! Go! Go!
	I do not say . . .	
		No!
		No!

They kiss. It escalates.

HAMILTON:		ENSEMBLE:
Yes.	MARIA: Yes!	Say no to this!
		No!
Yes.		No!
	Yes!	
		Say no to this!
Yes.	Yes!	No!
		No!
		Say no to this!
Yes.	Yes!	No!
		No!

ENSEMBLE: Say no to this!

Hamilton staggers.

HAMILTON:
Say no to
this. I—
Don't say no to this,

There is nowhere I
can go.

MARIA REYNOLDS:
Don't say no to this.

ENSEMBLE:
Go go go . . .

James Reynolds swaggers in.

JAMES REYNOLDS: So?

Hamilton pays James Reynolds.

HAMILTON: Nobody needs to know.[5]

Hamilton walks away from them both.
Burr enters.

[5] So imagine you're me, and you get to the end of this song. And you know that there's a really timeless song about the guilt of infidelity in the musical theater canon: "Nobody Needs to Know," by Jason Robert Brown, from his brilliant show *The Last Five Years*. And you realize that "know" is a *great* twist/ending to a song about not saying "no." What do you do? You do what I did: frantically call JRB and ask his permission to quote his work.

XXI

ON BEING IN

"THE ROOM WHERE IT HAPPENS"

WITH THE CAST OF A CHORUS LINE

Plus a Brief Account of

NEVIN STEINBERG

BRINGING BOOM-BAP TO BROADWAY

WITH SPEAKERS THE SIZE OF REFRIGERATORS

AFTER THE BOWS AND THE CLAPPING and the cheering on April 16, the members of the *Hamilton* cast formed a line that stretched the full width of the Newman Theater stage. They raised their headshots (the glossy photos that performers give to casting directors at auditions) and held them in front of their faces. They were standing on the same spots where the original cast members of *A Chorus Line* had struck that iconic pose for the first time exactly 40 years earlier.

The connection between *Hamilton* and its legendary predecessor meant the world to people involved with the show. Early in his career, Jeffrey saw *A Chorus Line* again and again, trying to understand how Michael Bennett had given the struggles of Broadway dancers such a powerful, universal appeal. Andy says that even amid the commotion of tech rehearsals at the Public, he would get chills when he thought about working on the same stage where Bennett had worked: *A Chorus Line* is the show that inspired him to forgo acting, and to commit his professional life to choreography.

There was even a physical connection between the two. In 2012, on the night that Marvin Hamlisch died, Jay Duckworth honored the composer of *A Chorus Line* by lighting a candle on the Newman stage, and playing the original cast album in its entirety. That candleholder sat on Hamilton's desk throughout the run at the Public.

On the night of the 40th anniversary, arrayed across the stage, the members of the *Hamilton* ensemble led a rendition of "What I Did for Love," Hamlisch and Ed Kleban's song about the sacrifices that artists make for their art. Tommy thought this would be a powerful way to honor the dancers whose lives had formed the basis of Bennett's show, 19 of whom returned to the Public that night. It was also a way to showcase the men and women of the *Hamilton* ensemble itself.

That ensemble—the actors and dancers who weren't playing the lead roles—had been working nightly wonders of dancing, singing, and endurance, performing the exhausting combinations that sprang from Andy's inexhaustible brain. Their skills had allowed them to be stars and featured performers in other shows: "an ensemble of soloists," Andy calls them. Here, they merged their talents to create a powerful cumulative effect, a living embodiment of Alexander Hamilton's energy and the dynamic young country he helped to found. There were five men and four women in the *Hamilton* ensemble at the Public, badasses all.

At some points in the show you would see them front and center, as when Carleigh Bettiol sashayed through the room, champagne in hand, elegantly setting the stage for "A Winter's Ball," or when Ariana DeBose seemed to pinch a bullet in her fingers, tracing its slow and deadly trajectory toward Hamilton's body.

At other times, their exuberance enlivened a scene, as when Jon Rua would slingshot himself under a wooden plank, spin on one heel, and flex a bicep to catch Angelica's eye in "The Schuyler Sisters," or Thayne Jasperson flung himself up the side of the set to spread revolutionary fervor in "My Shot."

Their moves could be small and evocative, as when Sydney James Harcourt slowly raised a hand to quiet the chattering Hamilton, who had come to seek his blessing to marry Eliza, or when Sasha Hutchings held herself ramrod straight in a lift, high over her castmates' heads, as the memory of Hamilton's mother flashed through his mind. They could also be flashy, brilliantly so, as when Seth Stewart loaded, twirled, and fired a musket with precise grace, or Ephraim Sykes spun through a bending, whirling, sliding combination in "My Shot," all precise limbs and pyrotechnics.

You could also watch, throughout the show, the three female dancers with distinctive short blond hair. Actually there was only one such dancer, she just had a remarkable capacity for seeming to be everywhere all the time. That would be Betsy Struxness. In an onstage ceremony just before the first performance on Broadway, she was awarded the Gypsy Robe, which recognizes a chorus member with the most Broadway credits—the one whose career resembles the stories that make up *A Chorus Line*.

When "What I Did for Love" ended that night, the *Chorus Line* veterans walked onstage to join the full *Hamilton* cast. The audience stood for a long, loud ovation. It was a tribute and a torch-passing, a union of past and present. It was a chance to thank the dancers who weren't in the spotlight, but still made a triumphant musical possible—and their predecessors who had done it 40 years before.

———— • ————

THE *CHORUS LINE* CELEBRATION WAS glorious, and it almost didn't happen.

Back in February, Jeffrey and Oskar had called a press conference in the Public's lobby to announce plans for *Hamilton*'s future. Press conferences in downtown theater lobbies are about as rare as rapturously received hip-hop musicals about the Founding Fathers, so most people assumed that the show would cancel the extension it had announced, and make a dash for Broadway. It was the safe bet, and maybe the smart one. If *Hamilton* could reopen before the Tony Award deadline in late April, it stood a good chance to win Best Musical, which might make the difference between a long run and a quick exit. Who knew how much momentum the show could sustain, or what next season might bring?

When Oskar climbed on top of the bar that day in February, he surprised the crowd by saying that *Hamilton* was going to finish its run as planned, then restart performances on Broadway at the Richard Rodgers Theatre in July. By staying downtown a little longer, Lin and Tommy were making the same calculation that had brought Michael Bennett to the Public 40 years earlier: Before going to Broadway, let's take the time to get it right. For if *Hamilton* had made the quick move to Midtown, there would have been no time to make changes. Tommy and Andy would have needed to scramble to replicate what they had done at the Public. Jeffrey calls the decision "a powerful expression of Tommy's self-assurance."

With that gamble, the last busy phase of *Hamilton*'s development began. Lin and his collaborators had bought themselves five months. They would use it to rewrite, restage, and refine the show. They would add two new members to the ensemble, Emmy Raver-Lampman and Austin Smith. The critics liked what they had seen the first time, but Lin and his Cabinet planned to keep working until the critics saw it again—the moment in late July when the calendar was going to tell them "Pencils down," in Tommy's words. In short, they were going to apply one of the ringing lessons of *A Chorus Line*—and of Alexander Hamilton's life, for that matter: Your time is short, use it all.

ABOVE:

Oskar Eustis announcing the Broadway transfer of Hamilton *in the Public Theater lobby—February 24, 2015.*

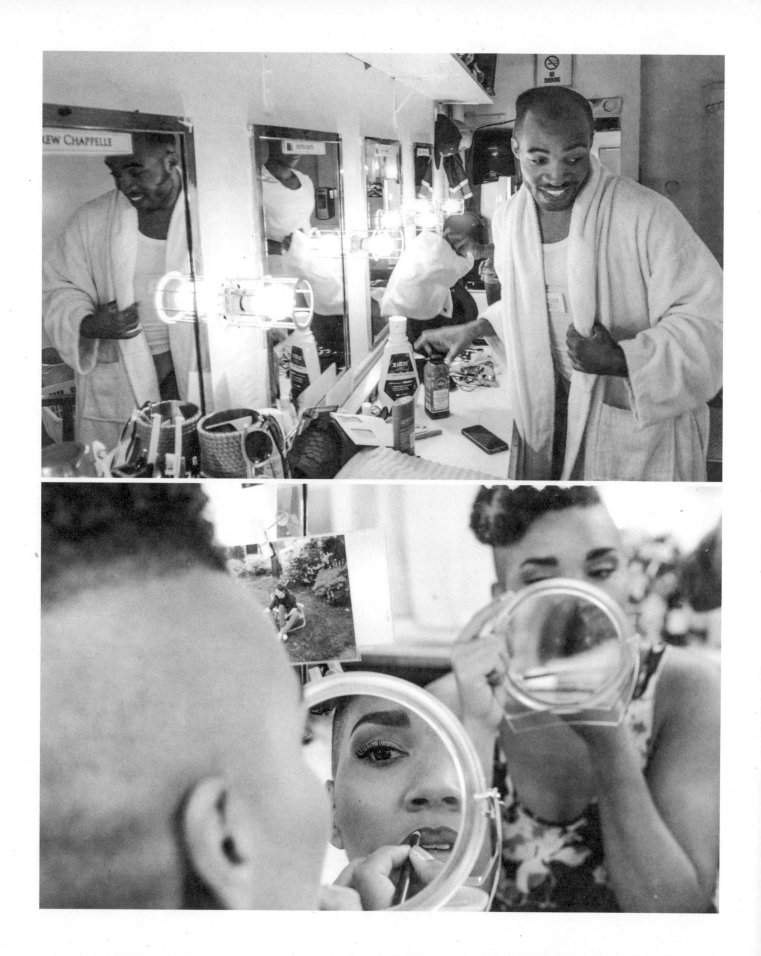

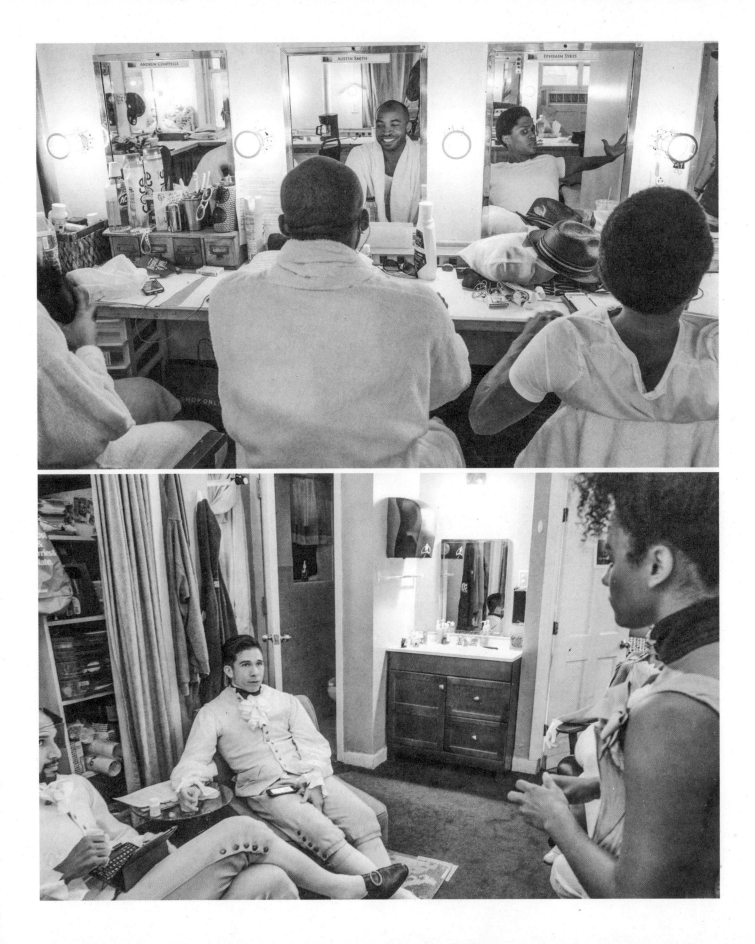

All that spring and summer, Tommy and his collaborators fine-tuned *Hamilton*, both figuratively and, in one case, literally. Just as Andy worked wonders large and small in weaving together his dancers, the sound designer Nevin Steinberg needed to find intricate ways to coordinate amps, mics, and wires to produce the clarity that Lin's score demanded. In his two decades on Broadway, he had designed dozens of shows, including *In the Heights*, but *Hamilton* made him feel the same pressure that Paul Tazewell felt when designing the costumes.

"It's a constant challenge to live up to what Lin wrote," Nevin says. "To make sure people hear it and understand it and feel it in way that you know is possible. It haunts me." Like Paul, he tears up as he talks about it.

You can hear a compact demonstration of why *Hamilton* proved so tricky, and how Nevin's labors paid off, in "The Room Where It Happens." Lin wrote the song to dramatize a dinner that Hamilton, Madison, and Jefferson shared on June 20, 1790, that decided the location of the United States capital. (The conversations that cemented the plan to move uptown resembled that momentous dinner: In a series of meetings in the days leading up to the press conference, a handful of people—Lin, Tommy, Jeffrey, and Oskar—had made big decisions in a little room.)

One morning after the Public run ended, Nevin sat in the audience of the empty Richard Rodgers Theatre, with Lac by his side. All around them, the familiar Mission Control tables had reappeared for *Hamilton*'s final round of tech rehearsals. The 10 members of the band were getting situated in the orchestra pit beneath the stage, and Nevin and Lac were trying to find the right levels and balances to bring out every color and texture in their playing.

Since the Lincoln Center concert three years earlier, the lineup had remained consistent: a rock band with a string section. For "The Room Where It Happens," though, Lac wanted something extra. Lin's demo recording had reminded him of Kander and Ebb, which had made him think of their show *Chicago*, which had given him a crazy idea. "If I want to be remembered for anything in the show," he says, "I want people to say, 'Hey, that's the guy that put a banjo in *Hamilton*.'"

Nevin was trying to balance that twangy banjo sound against the fact that "The Room Where It Happens" is one of the most banging, boom-bap, straight-ahead hip-hop songs in this show—or in any that preceded it. That morning, he was experimenting with how best to use the new and fearsome toys he had acquired for the move uptown: a pair of refrigerator-sized Meyer 1100-LFC subwoofers. He had positioned them on either side of the proscenium arch, trying to make these chest-high speaker cabinets as inconspicuous as possible. (This model is designed for stadiums, not Broadway theaters, since why would a Broadway show need this much sonic energy in ranges so low that you can feel them? "It's a monster," promises the brochure.) As the band began to play, Nevin flicked the iPad on his lap, then flicked it again. The subwoofers started booming; a water bottle on the table began to shake.

That's when Lin walked in.

He was carrying his lunch and wearing a red "Where's Waldo?" T-shirt. (Waldo peeked over the text "You can't see me.") He didn't know that after six years of hearing his *Hamilton* songs in his head, or on headphones, or in a medium-sized downtown theater, he was about to hear them on an exactingly calibrated, extraordinarily powerful Broadway sound system for the very first time.

Jason Bassett, who stage managed *Hamilton* on Broadway (and *In the Heights* before that) has noticed that Lin has a distinctive way of reacting to such moments: "What I've always loved about him is that he's as much an observer of his remarkable life as everybody else. His excitement is genuine, so you can genuinely share it with him."

The band paused just as Lin arrived, so the theater was quiet as he took a seat at one of the tables in the audience. He said his hellos and unwrapped his burger. Then Lac cued the band, and "The Room Where It Happens" came roaring out of Nevin's system again: the rinky-dink banjo, the booming bass, the thumping drums.

Lin froze, burger halfway to his face. He gaped at the stage. He shouted to no one in particular, "Oh fuck *everybody*!"

—◆—

[1] My father is a political consultant: These kinds of conversations are very common. "Can you believe they named/honored/venerated this guy?".

[2] Sometimes a rhyme leads you to a wonderful, unexpected place. I'm playing with rhymes for "Burr, Sir" in the whole show. So I get to "Mercer" and think, who even is Mercer? Google Mercer. General who died during the Revolutionary War. But doesn't he have a street named after him downtown, in the Village? What was it called before he died? Google. Clermont Street. Wait, wait, this is perfect! In a song about legacy, we can begin with Hamilton and Burr bitching about how the guy who doesn't even survive the war gets a street named after him, while they're still alive and hustling. And Burr has legacy on his mind at the top of this song about being on the outside of power and legacy, looking in. Thanks, Mercer!

[3] Again, we're tipping Burr toward where he needs to get by the end of this song. Hamilton is saying, "If I act like you, I can get this deal done." Which leaves Burr asking the unspoken question, "Why am I, *who act like me all the time*, not invited to this dinner?"

BURR: Ah, Mr. Secretary.

HAMILTON: Mr. Burr, sir.

BURR: Didja hear the news about good old General Mercer? [1]

HAMILTON: No.

BURR: You know Clermont Street?

HAMILTON: Yeah.

BURR: They renamed it after him. The Mercer legacy is secure. [2]

HAMILTON: Sure.

BURR: And all he had to do was die.

HAMILTON: That's a lot less work.

BURR: We oughta give it a try.

HAMILTON: Ha.

BURR: Now, how're you gonna get your debt plan through?

HAMILTON: I'm guess I'm gonna fin'lly have to listen to you. [3]

BURR: Really?

HAMILTON: Talk less. Smile more.

BURR: Ha-ha.

HAMILTON: Do whatever it takes to get my plan on the Congress floor.

BURR: Now, Madison and Jefferson are merciless.

HAMILTON: Well, hate the sin, love the sinner.

Madison & Jefferson enter.

MADISON: Hamilton!

HAMILTON: I'm sorry, Burr, I've gotta go.

BURR: But—

HAMILTON: Decisions are happening over dinner.

BURR: Two Virginians and an immigrant walk into a room.

BURR, ENSEMBLE: Diametric'lly opposed, foes.

BURR: They emerge with a compromise, having opened doors that were

BURR, ENSEMBLE: Previously closed, bros.

BURR: The immigrant emerges with unprecedented financial power
A system he can shape however he wants.
The Virginians emerge with the nation's capital.
And here's the pièce de résistance:

BURR:
No one else was in
The room where it
happened.

The room where it
happened.
The room where it
happened.
No one else was in

ENSEMBLE:

The room where it   The room where it
happened.   happened.
The room where it
happened.
The room where it   The room where it
happened.   happens.
No one really knows
how
The game is played.   The game is played.
The art of the trade,
How the sausage gets   How the sausage gets
made.   made.
We just
Assume that it   Assume that it happens.
happens.
But no one else is in
The room where it   The room where it
happens.   happens.

BURR, COMPANY: Thomas claims—

JEFFERSON: Alexander was on Washington's
    doorstep one day
In distress 'n disarray. [4]

BURR, COMPANY: Thomas claims—

JEFFERSON: Alexander said—

HAMILTON: I've nowhere else to turn!

JEFFERSON: And basic'lly begged me to join
the fray.

BURR, COMPANY: Thomas claims—

JEFFERSON: I approached Madison and said—
"I know you hate 'im, but let's hear what he has
    to say."

BURR, COMPANY: Thomas claims—

JEFFERSON: Well, I arranged the meeting.
I arranged the menu, the venue, the seating,

BURR: But!
No one else was in

BURR, COMPANY: The room where it
    happened.
The room where it happened.
The room where it happened.

BURR: No one else was in

BURR, COMPANY: The room where it
    happened.
The room where it happened.
The room where it happened.

BURR:
No one really knows
how the   COMPANY:
Parties get to yesssss.   Parties get to yesssss.
The pieces that are
sacrificed in
Ev'ry game of   Ev'ry game of chesssss.
chesssss.
We just
Assume that it   Assume that it happens.
happens.

But no one else is in
The room where it   The room where it
happens.   happens.

BURR, COMPANY: Meanwhile—

BURR: Madison is grappling with the fact that
not ev'ry issue can be settled by committee.

COMPANY: Meanwhile—

BURR: Congress is fighting over where to put
    the capital—

[4] The only account we
have of this dinner is
Jefferson's, so we start
the *Rashomon* sequence
with him.

The company screams in chaos.[5]

BURR: It isn't pretty.
Then Jefferson approaches with a dinner and invite.
And Madison responds with Virginian insight.

MADISON: Maybe we can solve one problem with another.
And win a victory for the southerners, in other words—

JEFFERSON: Oh-ho!

MADISON: A quid pro quo.

JEFFERSON: I suppose.

MADISON: Wouldn't you like to work a little closer to home?

JEFFERSON: Actually, I would.

MADISON: Well, I propose the Potomac.

JEFFERSON: And you'll provide him his votes?

MADISON: Well, we'll see how it goes.

JEFFERSON: Let's go.

BURR: No!

COMPANY: –One else was in
The room where it happened.

BURR, COMPANY: The room where it happened.
The room where it happened.
No one else was in
The room where it happened.
The room where it happened.
The room where it happened.

BURR: My God!

BURR, COMPANY: In God we trust.
But we'll never really know what got discussed.
Click-boom then it happened.

BURR: No one else was in the room where it happened.

COMPANY: Alexander Hamilton!

BURR: What did they say to you to get you to sell New York City down the river?

COMPANY: Alexander Hamilton!

BURR: Did Washington know about the dinner? Was there presidential pressure to deliver?

COMPANY: Alexander Hamilton!

BURR: Or did you know, even then, it doesn't matter where you put the U.S. capital.

HAMILTON: Cuz we'll have the banks,
We're in the same spot.

BURR: You got more than you gave.

HAMILTON: And I wanted what I got.[6]

Hamilton faces Burr.

HAMILTON: When you got skin in the game, you stay in the game.
But you don't get a win unless you play in the game.
You get love for it. You get hate for it.
You get nothing if you . . .

HAMILTON, COMPANY:
Wait for it, wait for it, wait!

HAMILTON: God help and forgive me,
I wanna build something that's gonna
Outlive me.

[5] I asked the cast to shout any city within the original 13 colonies, but they kinda shout whatever they want.

[6] Originally, this section ended with:
HAMILTON: Cuz we'll have the banks. The city's undiminished
BURR: You got more than you gave.
HAMILTON: Checkmate: Game finished.
And that was the end of the section. On my second go-round of revisions, I seized the opportunity to play out the Hamilton-Burr dynamic inside Burr's mind. It also allowed me to play with the trumpet sample I'd created for the song (that refrain that plays between each section is deliberately treated and processed to sound like an old jazz sample, but it's original). Anyway, this is my favorite part of the show to act as Hamilton.

HAMILTON, JEFFERSON, MADISON, WASHINGTON:	COMPANY:
What do you want, Burr?	What do you want, Burr?
What do you want, Burr?	What do you want, Burr?
If you stand for nothing, Burr, what do you fall for?	What do you want, Burr? What do you want?

BURR: I
Wanna be in
The room where it happens. [7]
The room where it happens.
I
Wanna be in
The room where
it happens.
The room where
it happens.

I	I wanna be in the room Where it happens.
Wanna be	The room where it happens. The room where it happens.
In the room where it happens.	I wanna be in The room where it happens.
I	The room where it happens. The room where it happens.
I wanna be in the room . . . Oh [8]	I wanna be in
	the room where it happens.
Oh	The room where it happens.
	The room where it happens.

[7] Burr unbound! This is Oskar Eustis's favorite section, because Burr answers the company's question in the most Burr-like way possible. *What do you want? What do you believe in?* Burr: I want to be in the room. For the sake of it.

[8] Both Lacamoire and Blankenbuehler petitioned me for more time in this section, and thank God they did. Boy does it bring the number home.

I wanna be
I wanna be

     I wanna be in the
     room
     Where it happens.

I've got to be

     The room where it
     happens.

I've got to be

     The room where it
     happens.

in that room
In that big ol' room

COMPANY: The art of the compromise—9

BURR: Hold your nose and close
your eyes.

COMPANY: We want our leaders to
save the day—

BURR: But we don't get a say in what
they trade away.

COMPANY: We dream of a brand new start—

BURR: But we
dream in the
dark, for the
most part.

BURR, COMPANY: Dark as a tomb where
it happens.

BURR:	**COMPANY:**
I've got to be	The room where
in the room . . .	it happens.
I've got to be . . .	
	The room where
	it happens.
I've got to be . . .	
	The room where
	it happens.

Oh, I've got to be
in the room where
it happens . . .

I've got to be, I've
gotta be, I've gotta
be . . .
in the room!

Click-boom!

     The room where
     it happens.
     The room where it
     happens.

     I wanna be in
     The room where it
     happens.

     Click-boom!

9 **I'm perhaps proudest of these three couplets in the whole show: They encapsulate everything the number is about, are fully in character, and also speak to something fundamentally true about contemporary politics that I'd never been able to verbalize until these lines showed up.**

SCHUYLER
DEFEATED

—◆—

Eliza enters. Philip Schuyler enters with a newspaper.

PHILIP: Look! Grampa's in the paper! "War hero Philip Schuyler loses Senate seat to young upstart Aaron Burr!"

Grampa just lost his seat in the Senate.

ELIZA: Sometimes that's how it goes.

PHILIP: Daddy's gonna find out any minute.

ELIZA: I'm sure he already knows.

PHILIP: Further down,

PHILIP, ELIZA: Further down

PHILIP: "Let's meet the newest senator from New York . . ."

ELIZA: New York—

ELIZA, PHILIP: Our senator! . . .

Hamilton storms up to Burr. The cabinet forms around them.

HAMILTON: Burr!

HAMILTON: Since when are you a Democratic-Republican?

BURR: Since being one put me on the up and up again.

HAMILTON: No one knows who you are or what you do.

BURR: They don't need to know me. They don't like you.

HAMILTON: Excuse me?

BURR: Oh, Wall Street thinks you're great. You'll always be adored by the things you create But upstate,

HAMILTON: Wait.

BURR: People think you're crooked! And Schuyler's seat was up for grabs, so I took it.

HAMILTON: I've always considered you a friend.

BURR: I don't see why that has to end!

HAMILTON: You changed parties to run against my father-in-law.

BURR: I changed parties to seize the opportunity I saw. I swear, your pride will be the death of us all! Beware it goeth before the fall . . .

CABINET BATTLE #2

— ◆ —

Washington, Hamilton & Jefferson, back in the cabinet.

WASHINGTON: The issue on the table. France is on the verge of war with England. Do we provide aid and troops to our French allies or do we stay out of it?[1] Remember, my decision on this matter is not subject to congressional approval. The only person you have to convince is me. Secretary Jefferson, you have the floor, sir.

JEFFERSON: When we were on death's door.
When we were needy.
We made a promise. We signed a treaty.
We needed money and guns and half a chance.
Uh, who provided those funds?

MADISON: France.

JEFFERSON: In return, they didn't ask for land.
Only a promise that we'd lend a hand.
And stand with them if they fought
     against oppressors,
And revolution is messy but now is the time
     to stand.
Stand with our brothers as they fight
     against tyranny.
I know that Alexander Hamilton is here and he
Would rather not have this debate.
I'll remind you that he is not secretary of state.
He knows nothing of loyalty.
Smells like new money, dresses like fake royalty.
Desperate to rise above his station,
Everything he does betrays the ideals of
     our nation.

ENSEMBLE: Ooh!!

JEFFERSON: And if ya don't know, now ya know, Mr. President.[2]

WASHINGTON: Thank you, Secretary Jefferson. Secretary Hamilton, your response.

HAMILTON: You must be out of your goddamn
     mind if you think
The president is gonna bring the nation to the
     brink
Of meddling in the middle of a military mess,
A game of chess where France is queen and
     kingless.
We signed a treaty with a king whose head is
     now in a basket.
Would you like to take it out and ask it?
"Should we honor our treaty, King Louis' head?"
"Uh . . . do whatever you want, I'm super dead."[3]

WASHINGTON: Enough. Enough. Hamilton is right.

JEFFERSON: Mr. President—

WASHINGTON: We're too fragile to start another fight.

JEFFERSON: But sir, do we not fight for freedom?

WASHINGTON: Sure, when the French figure out who's gonna lead 'em.

JEFFERSON: The people are leading—

WASHINGTON: The people are rioting.
There's a difference. Frankly, it's a little
     disquieting that you would let your ideals
     blind you to reality.
Hamilton.

HAMILTON: Sir.

WASHINGTON: Draft a statement of neutrality.

---

[1] This was a natural fit for the second rap battle, because it was the subject in which Hamilton and Jefferson clashed most directly. Much of the poison that came from their respective pens stemmed from this issue, and as Jefferson says, State Department matters are really not in Hamilton's job description.

[2] This is a famous line from Biggie's classic song "Juicy." Daveed, the first time he got the lyric: "It's *so* hard not to say n***a at the end of this sentence. I'm fighting muscle memory!"

[3] Originally, Hamilton's argument was as long as Jefferson's, but I realized I wasn't gonna top this punchline. Also, Washington cutting him off and agreeing with him leads us nicely into the next song: Hamilton is winning without trying, because he and Washington are in lockstep on this issue.

Washington exits.

JEFFERSON: Did you forget Lafayette?

HAMILTON: What?

JEFFERSON: Have you an ounce of regret?
You accumulate debt, you accumulate power,
Yet in their hour of need, you forget.

HAMILTON: Lafayette's a smart man,
     he'll be fine.
And before he was your friend, he was mine.
If we try to fight in every revolution in the
     world, we never stop. [4]
Where do we draw the line?

JEFFERSON: So quick-witted. [5]

HAMILTON: Alas, I admit it.

JEFFERSON: I bet you were quite a lawyer.

HAMILTON: My defendants got acquitted.

JEFFERSON: Yah. Well, someone
oughta remind you.

HAMILTON: What?

JEFFERSON: You're nothing without
Washington behind you.

Washington re-enters.

WASHINGTON: Hamilton!

JEFFERSON: Daddy's calling.

Hamilton exits after Washington, eyes on Jefferson.

[4] This line gets a really wild-card reaction every night, depending on the audience. Sometimes nothing. Sometimes applause. Once a profound "Oh, sh*t." We still recognize ourselves in this one.

[5] Originally, this was an exchange about Jefferson and Hamilton's mutual friend Angelica (Jefferson met her in Paris). It didn't serve our transition into the next song, but it was definitely soapy and fun:
     HAMILTON: She's never mentioned you.
     JEFFERSON: She's not the type who shares.
     But since you're so interested in foreign affairs . . .
Ooooohhhhh . . .

A PICTURE OF

THE RECORDING STUDIO

Featuring Learned Comments by

QUESTLOVE

AND A THROWN SHOE

I F QUESTLOVE ISN'T THE POPE OF hip-hop, he's at least a high-ranking cardinal: He's the drummer of The Roots, the author of the argumentative memoir *Mo'Meta Blues*, the leader of Jimmy Fallon's house band, an all-around musical savant.

A man of his stature ends up sitting through a lot of pitches from people who want to bring hip-hop to Broadway. These long ago took on a wearying familiarity: "You know, aerosol spray cans, 'up in da Bronx,' breakdancing in the first act— that sort of thing," he says. When people told him about *Hamilton*, he assumed it had to be another entry in this

grim parade. Seeing it at the Public left him shocked. No corny Broadway overacting, no hip-hop clichés, no spray cans. "It sucker-punches everybody that's ever seen it," he says—himself included. And it left him asking a question that lingered long after the show moved uptown: "Is this the most revolutionary thing to happen to Broadway, or the most revolutionary thing to happen to hip-hop?"

"It's been a while since hip-hop has been able to show its brilliance," he says. "Now it's sort of coasting. In the

mid- to late-'80s, when hip-hop was a teenager, it was discovering itself, and we were discovering it too. But hip-hop is now 40 years old. I feel like *Hamilton* is hip-hop saying, 'See, *we still got it*! We still got some tricks up our sleeve!' I would *neeeever* have thought that this is how you would shock people. Only a brilliant nerd like Lin would even think to take a Hamilton book on vacation."

Lin felt, when he wrote *Hamilton*, that it could legitimize hip-hop in musical theater. He didn't want do a rap version of *Hair*, the show that introduced rock to Broadway. He aimed at having an impact like *Rent*, which, in his words, "ended the conversation of whether rock music belonged on Broadway. If you look at half the scores on Broadway today, they use rock—it's just in the DNA now. And this was my injection of hip-hop into the DNA." (Don't forget how recently this would have sounded like a provocation or a joke. As late as the summer of 2014—in the wake of the early closing of *Holler If Ya Hear Me*, a new musical featuring 2Pac songs—two *New York Times* critics mused in a podcast about whether hip-hop would ever work on Broadway.) Questlove agrees that *Hamilton* can

ABOVE:

Questlove, Pac-Man, Alex Lacamoire, and Clyde the Ghost at Atlantic Records.

demonstrate hip-hop's value, but he puts the show in the context of all of American culture, not merely Broadway. "Just from the way the story is told, I feel like hip-hop is now a legitimate filter—though it's always been legitimate to me. It's as vital and important as dancing or poetry or singing," he says.

Of all the improbable things about *Hamilton*, the fact that so many hip-hop luminaries share Questlove's affection for the show brings it closest to the realm of science fiction. The greatest and most famous MCs (Busta Rhymes, Q-Tip, Common, Queen Latifah, Talib Kweli, Missy Elliott, Hammer, Chance the Rapper, Jay Z) and producers (RZA, DJ Premier, Salaam Remi, Pharrell Williams) came to see it, and stayed afterwards to tell the cast how much they loved it. "After seeing *Hamilton* it may be reasonable to put @Lin_Manuel in your top 5 MCs list," tweeted Peter Rosenberg, the influential radio DJ for Hot 97 in New York. The BET Hip-Hop Awards invited Lin, Renée, and Daveed to participate in a cypher, trading freestyle rhymes alongside Questlove and Black Thought, the lead MC and co-founder of The Roots.

Daveed may be in the best position to appreciate how strange this embrace has been, since he's not just a fan of these giants but a fellow hip-hop artist. "They're all people I've wanted to meet and interact with," he says. "If you told me I would get to meet them from doing a musical, I would've said that's ludicrous."

Questlove came to see the show again and again at the Public, bringing different friends each time. No matter what their background was, they kept loving it. "If I read this quote it would look like hyperbole, but I lived during the *Thriller* era, and it was almost the same thing," he says. "Rarely did I see something that could unite demo-

graphics that had nothing to do with each other. My English teacher loved *Thriller*. The rambunctious kids who before November 30th, 1982"—the release date of Michael Jackson's album—"were calling me racial slurs in the playground suddenly were saying, 'Teach me how

---

"Is this THE MOST REVOLUTIONARY THING TO HAPPEN TO BROADWAY, or the most revolutionary thing to happen to hip-hop?"

to do the moonwalk.'" He didn't just sing the show's praises, he got involved. With Black Thought, he agreed to executive produce the cast album for Atlantic Records.

On a long Sunday, Questlove came to Avatar Studios in Midtown to hear Lin, Leslie, Oak, Daveed, and Chris record their vocals. It was a day of discovery for those guys. Hearing the music every night through onstage monitors didn't prepare them for the full complexity of Lin's score and Lac's orchestrations, which the band had recorded the week before.

"Yo this band is cold," said Daveed when he heard "Non-Stop" for the first time.

"This sounds so cold I need a jacket," said Oak when he heard "Cabinet Battle #1."

After performing together eight times a week, they knew each other's rhythms so well that when they went into the booth to record "My Shot," the Sons of Liberty sounded like an actual rap group. "There's chemistry

ABOVE:
Alex Lacamoire recording ensemble vocals at Avatar Studios.

there," Questlove said, admiring the effect. He also admired the way that Lac ran the studio, marveling at how certain he was of the sound he was after, how eloquently he could describe it, and how persistent he was in pushing until he got it. "Wow, he makes me feel like a lazy schlub," he said.

When it was Leslie's turn to record "Wait for It," his castmates stood in the control booth, listening with Lac, Tommy, Questlove, and Bill Sherman, one of the album's producers. They were so impressed that somebody took off a shoe and threw it at the window, a sign of admiring faux-outrage. Lac told them it was time to record their harmony vocals. "I don't want to sing shit right now," said Oak.

If the hip-hop world has a favorite track in the show, it's probably "Washington On Your Side." Lin was delighted when Busta Rhymes told him that he loved the old-school way that Burr, Jefferson, and Madison finished each other's sentences as they concocted a plan to destroy Hamilton. Talib Kweli told *New York* magazine that when he heard the song, he immediately thought, *I want to know who wrote these lyrics.* Questlove called it a "tug of war" song, which he has missed hearing in hip-hop lately. (Lac even put a Questlove homage in the song: The kick drum and bass swing way, way back behind the beat, a feel that Lac loved hearing on D'Angelo's album *Voodoo*, which Questlove helped to mastermind.)

Lin knew the song had the potential to be a blazing hip-hop track. When he heard Daveed tearing through Lafayette's verses, he realized that Lin the Writer didn't need to abide by Lin the Rapper's speed limit. It inspired him to write the blistering resignation speech that Jefferson delivers near the end of this song. What's particularly impressive about the version on the cast album is that Daveed recorded it early on a Sunday, a time when the only actors awake in the whole city might have been in that studio. He was sipping tea and spitting fire from take one.

From the beginning, Lin wanted a cast album that would hold up as a pop album in its own right. He, Lac, and the other producers pursued this goal with the same relentlessness as every other aspect of the show. Most cast albums are recorded in three or four days: Lac insisted on two weeks, to get every vocal and instrumental part exactly right. Most ensembles are recorded in groups, by "miking the room." Lac and his engineer Derik Lee recorded each performer separately.

He brought in Tim Latham to mix the album (that is, to balance, sharpen, and fine-tune the recorded tracks): Not many mixers have mixed Broadway records but also gotten shout-outs from A Tribe Called Quest, as Tim has. "The #BoomBap master," Questlove called him on Instagram.

The most noticeable departure from the Broadway norm may be that unlike many cast albums, where the sound balance might be 70 percent vocals and 30 percent music, Tim estimates this album is 55 vocal and 45 instrumental. It owes a lot to Questlove's input. As Lac and his team rushed to get the final mixes ready, he and Black Thought came to Atlantic Records to listen and give notes. Some of Questlove's ideas were subtle, technical—an array of suggestions that encouraged Lac, Bill, and Tim to take more chances. One of them was simple, and was delivered with all the authority that a man of Questlove's eminence possesses: "Turn the drums up."

◆

THERE'S AN OLD COMPLAINT AROUND Broadway that pop stars don't adopt songs from musicals anymore, the way that Frank Sinatra and Ella Fitzgerald did. The reception of the *Hamilton* album made this complaint seem quaint. When it dropped, it charted higher in its first week of release than any Broadway album since Lerner and Loewe's *Camelot* more than half a century earlier. *Rolling Stone* gave it four-and-a-half stars, declaring that it "proves that a cast soundtrack LP can work as a powerful, cohesive, exhilarating pop experience in the 21st century." *Billboard* gave the album a five-star review, the first the editors had awarded since instituting the star system a few years earlier.

More intriguing, *Billboard* declared it the best rap album of the year. (And 2015 was a strong year for rap albums: It included, among others, Kendrick Lamar's *To Pimp a Butterfly*, another dazzling extension of what hip-hop can do.) Framing the *Hamilton* record as a rap album among other rap albums increases the odds that this musical could have the most ridiculous-sounding impact of all: Beyond legitimizing hip-hop on Broadway, and changing the way the public thinks about hip-hop, it might change hip-hop itself.

"This play's just a baby right now," says Questlove. "Who knows what it'll do?"

WASHINGTON ON YOUR SIDE[1]

BURR: It must be nice, it must be nice to have Washington on your side.
It must be nice, it must be nice to have Washington on your side.

JEFFERSON: Ev'ry action has its equal, opposite reaction.
Thanks to Hamilton, our cabinet's fractured into factions.
Try not to crack under the stress, we're breaking down like fractions.
We smack each other in the press, and we don't print retractions.
I get no satisfaction witnessing his fits of passion.
The way he primps and preens and dresses like the pits of fashion.[2]
Our poorest citizens, our farmers, live ration to ration
As Wall Street robs 'em blind in search of chips to cash in.[3]
This prick is askin' for someone to bring him to task.
Somebody gimme some dirt on this vacuous mass so we can at last unmask him.
I'll pull the trigger on him, someone load the gun and cock it.
While we were all watching he got Washington in his pocket.

JEFFERSON, BURR: It must be nice, it must be nice to have Washington on your side.
It must be nice, it must be nice to have Washington on your side.

Look back at the Bill of Rights.

Madison enters.

MADISON: Which I wrote.

JEFFERSON, MADISON, BURR: The ink hasn't dried.
It must be nice, it must be nice to have Washington on your side.

MADISON: So he's doubled the size of the government.
Wasn't the trouble with much our previous government size?[4]

BURR: Look in his eyes!

JEFFERSON: See how he lies.

MADISON: Follow the scent of his enterprise

JEFFERSON: Centralizing national credit.[5]
And making American credit competitive.

MADISON: If we don't stop it we aid and abet it.

JEFFERSON: I have to resign.

MADISON: Somebody has to stand up for the South!

BURR: Somebody has to stand up to his mouth!

JEFFERSON: If there's a fire you're trying to douse,

MADISON, JEFFERSON: You can't put it out from inside the house.

1 I'm crazy about the music in this thing. It's this weird swing beat, not really common in hip-hop, and I probably spent more time building it from scratch in Logic than any other song in the show, with the exception of "Satisfied." Originally, the song was much longer and had a section where Jefferson, Madison, and Burr spread rumors about Hamilton. But we realized it was more powerful to keep the action to the three of them plotting and scheming, so the gossip section was cut and replaced with the ratatat back and forth of the second verse.

2 One of my go-to conversational gambits is switching the letters of someone's name. "Jeremy McCarter? More like Meremy Ja*k*arta." It's not funny, but it makes me laugh, and I find my brain is doing it all the time. Anyway, I stumbled on Pits of Fashion/Fits of Passion, realized that they'd both work, and worked backwards to earn them.

3 Jefferson may be Hamilton's antagonist, but he's not wrong: Hamilton's plan left veterans who sold their war bonds out in the cold and at the mercy of those who bought them knowing the government would buy them back at cost.

4 Madison used to have his own verse, wherein he said: "I used to write with him/Imbibe with him and ride with him/I find myself on this side of a sizable divide with him./We used to fight for the right to be left alone./But left alone to his own devices, he's a crisis all his own." Ended up cutting everything but these lines, as a lead-in to the group verse.

5 This section is so
exciting and personal to
me because the interplay
between these guys
captures how we made
the show: good ideas
cascading off each other
and leading to action.

6 Like I've said before,
having Daveed gave me
the confidence to write
this intricately, knowing
I had a ringer to pull it
off. This section is very
Kendrick-Lamar
inspired—he's the
master of these
polysyllabic gems that
seem to go off the rails
but are so perfect that
the music has no choice
but to stop and meet
him on the other side.

JEFFERSON: I'm in the cabinet I am
    complicit in
Watching him grabbin' at power and kiss it.
If Washington isn't gon' listen
To disciplined dissidents, this is the difference.
This kid is out! 6

MADISON, BURR, JEFFERSON:
Oh!
This immigrant isn't somebody we chose.
Oh!
This immigrant's keeping us all on our toes.
Oh!
Let's show these Federalists who
    they're up against!
Oh!

JEFFERSON, MADISON: Southern mother-
fuckin'—

JEFFERSON, MADISON, BURR:
Democratic-Republicans!

ENSEMBLE: Oh!

JEFFERSON, MADISON, BURR: Let's follow
the money and see where it goes.

ENSEMBLE: Oh!

JEFFERSON, MADISON, BURR: Because every second the Treasury grows.

ENSEMBLE: Oh!

JEFFERSON, MADISON, BURR: If we follow the money and see where it leads. Get in the weeds, look for the seeds of Hamilton's misdeeds.

JEFFERSON, MADISON, BURR: It must be nice. It must be nice.

MADISON: Follow the money and see where it goes.

JEFFERSON, MADISON, BURR: It must be nice. It must be nice.

JEFFERSON: The emperor has no clothes. [7]

JEFFERSON, MADISON, BURR: We won't be invisible. We won't be denied. Still. It must be nice, it must be nice to have Washington on your side.

[7] The line at the Public was "It's nice to have something to really oppose." But I like this better. It's more of a riddle.

THE PEN & THE PAD II

From Lin's Notebooks

———◆———

TOP LEFT:
Well, I always knew what the punchline would be.

TOP RIGHT:
King George's logic in this early draft of "Guns and Ships" is the same logic our country has applied to any number of ill-advised foreign policy misadventures. (History Spoiler: People almost never greet invading soldiers as liberators.) We eventually changed this section because King George's re-emergence after the war is such a delightful surprise, we didn't want to have him pop up any earlier.

BOTTOM LEFT:
I'm fiddling with the imagery for the end of "The Room Where it Happens." This is all good stuff, and it occurs to me that the last four lines (which didn't make the show) are a riff on "Just To Get A Rep" by Gang Starr.

BOTTOM RIGHT:
I wanted this song to start as simply as a joke: "Three guys walk into a bar . . ." It will ease us into the complexity that follows.

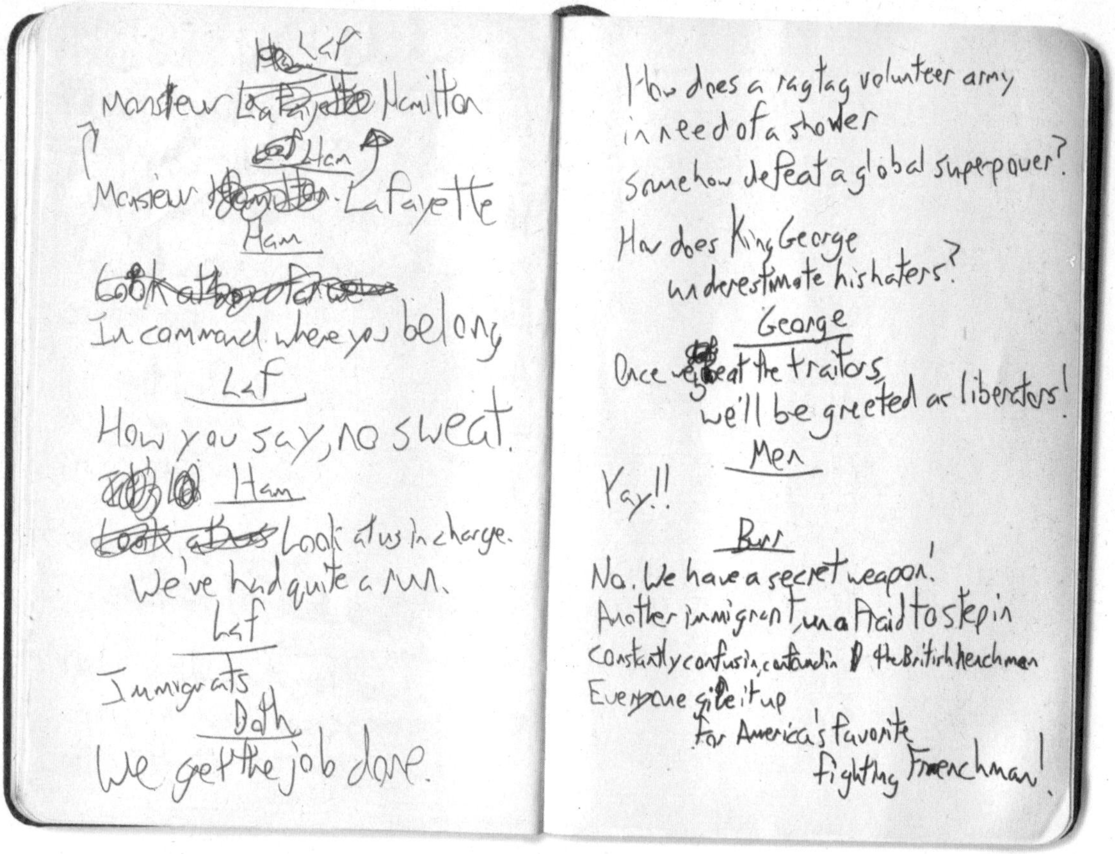

[Handwritten notebook pages:]

[Top left page:]
Monsieur ~~Lafayette the~~ Hamilton
Monsieur ~~Hamilton~~ Lafayette
Ham
~~Look at your love~~
In command where you belong,
Laf
How you say, no sweat.
Ham
~~Look at this~~ Look at us in charge.
We've had quite a run.
Laf
Immigrants
Both
We get the job done.

[Top right page:]
How does a ragtag volunteer army
in need of a shower
somehow defeat a global superpower?
How does King George
underestimate his haters?
George
Once we ~~greet~~ beat the traitors,
we'll be greeted as liberators!
Men
Yay!!
Burr
No. We have a secret weapon!
Another immigrant, unafraid to step in
constantly confusing, confounding the British henchmen
Everyone give it up
for America's favorite
fighting Frenchman!

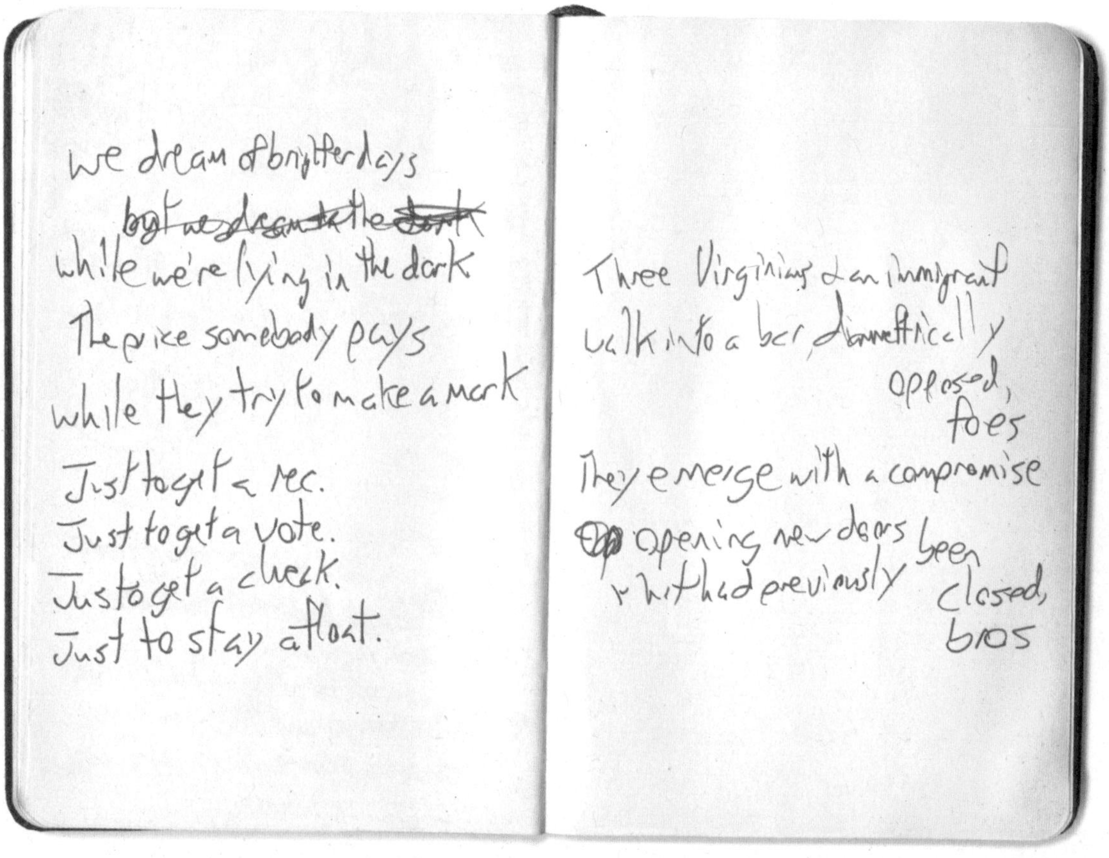

[Bottom left page:]
We dream of brighter days
~~but we dream in the dark~~
while we're lying in the dark
The price somebody pays
while they try to make a mark
Just to get a rec.
Just to get a vote.
Just to get a check.
Just to stay afloat.

[Bottom right page:]
Three Virginians & an immigrant
walk into a bar, diametrically
opposed,
foes
They emerge with a compromise
opening new doors
& with had previously been
closed,
bros

My dearest, Angelica,

In a letter I recieved from you
two weeks ago, I
noticed a comma in the middle
of a phrase
a comma, out of place
It changed the meaning.
Did you intend this?
Nevertheless it has consumed my   restless
One stroke and you're   past few days.

My Dearest, Angelica
with a comma after
'dearest,

"My dearest, comma, Angelica"
Is the letter I hold nearest to
my heart

Burr   that the words don't
There are moments when the world reach

There is suffering that has no name
too terrible to

Hold your child as tight as you can

And push away the unimaginable
There are moments when you're in so deep
It seems easier to just swim down

The Hamiltons have moved uptown
And try to live with the unimaginable

TOP RIGHT:
I'm working out the
clearest way to convey
the importance of
comma placement and
its usage in surrepti-
tious flirting in
"Take a Break."
The notion of comma
placement as flirting
knocked me out when I
first read about it.
I had to get it in there.

BOTTOM:
I got exactly this far
with Burr singing
"It's Quiet Uptown"
when it occurred to me
that not only is Angel-
ica the only choice to
narrate this moment,
it completes her arc in
the most unexpected,
satisfying way possi-
ble. For her to bear
witness to the lives of
Alexander and Eliza
is the role she chose
in "Satisfied". . . she
fulfills it here, at their
lowest moment.

XXIII

ON THE
ORIGIN & PERSISTENCE
of Our
NATIONAL
SHAME

AFTER CLOSING NIGHT AT THE Public, the *Hamilton* company took a few weeks off, then got back to work. Through the sixth-floor windows of New 42ⁿᵈ Street Studios, where they reconvened for rehearsals, they had a view that was captivating and bizarre, even by Times Square standards: They could look directly across 42ⁿᵈ Street to Madame Tussaud's. Over there, crowds lined up to see lifelike wax replicas with no actual life; over here, actors who looked nothing like their historical counterparts were bursting with it.

Almost everyone in the company that summer was in their 20s or 30s, and the handful who were a little older could pass for 30-something. *Do the grown-ups know what's happening here?* The rapturous reviews at the Public contributed to the loose, upbeat vibe: The cast and creative team had work to do, but they also knew the show was very unlikely to fail—a rare and enviable position for theater artists, or anybody else.

In the larger of the two rehearsal rooms at New 42—the one with circles on the floor, which marked the location of the turntable, and made the place look like a high school gym—Andy drilled the ensemble. He added two swings (Neil Haskell and Morgan Marcell) to the three from downtown (Andrew Chappelle, Stephanie Klemons, and Voltaire Wade-Greene). They needed to be ready to jump in when a member of the ensemble missed a show because of illness or injury, which always

happens in shows as demanding as this one. Alysha Deslorieux likewise stayed ready to jump in as one of the Schuyler sisters or Maria. Andy cleaned and sharpened everybody's work, spending part of one day trying to achieve a tighter elbow drop in "Non-Stop." He also chased a phantom.

"My whole career I've been wanting to make a 'Sit Down You're Rocking the Boat,'" he says. The showstopping number from *Guys and Dolls* knocked him out when he saw it on the 1992 Tony Award telecast. He thought he might finally have it within reach, thanks to the final chorus of "The Room Where It Happens." It might sweep the audience away, it might create that kind of roof-shaking release.

"It killed me when I heard it, I loved it so much," he says of Lin's song. In workshops and at the Public, Andy never felt that his choreography did it justice. He wanted to find sharper ways to physicalize the envy that gnaws at Burr, who seethes at being left out of that famous dinner. He attacked it again at New 42, and kept after it when they got onstage at the Rodgers.

"You have to become a laser beam, not a spotlight," he told the ensemble one day. "Think of ripping somebody's flesh off their body."

When someone asked him to demonstrate the arm extension he wanted, Andy seemed less like a dancer playing to the back row and more like a monster flexing

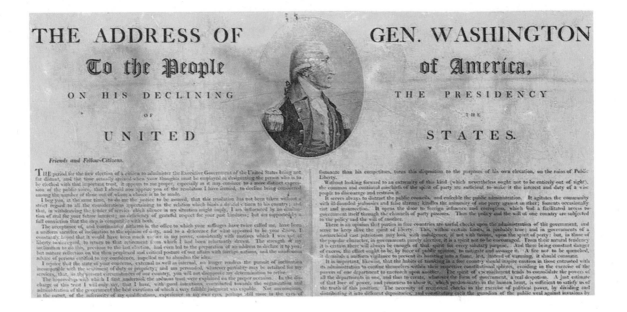

its limbs: tight, chiseled, scary. Day by day, tweak by tweak, he kept coaxing the dancers into making Burr's song a demonstration of how disfiguring ambition can be, and how sexy.

While Andy worked with the ensemble, Tommy rehearsed with the principals in a room next door. Actors would perform a scene or part of a song, then he would amble up to them, crack some jokes, toss off an observation or an idea, and walk back to his seat, having shaped the scene without appearing to have done so. The best part of directing, Tommy says, is "code-switching," relating to dozens of different artists in dozens of different ways, finding the specific approach that will unlock each person's most creative self. He's a fan of Phil Jackson's books.

"Open the bag up," Tommy said to Renée one afternoon. He meant: Keep playing with different ways to perform one of Angelica's scenes with Alexander.

That was his gospel throughout the development process. For if the most essential trait of the *Hamilton* team was relentless creativity, a close second was ruthless pragmatism. Lin, Tommy, and their collaborators shared an eagerness to try things—to try *everything*—to find what worked best. "New discoveries, new mistakes" was the daily goal that Tommy had announced for the company at their first rehearsal the previous November. It's a way of affirming the very American view that Benjamin Franklin offered in 1786, when someone asked him how the new

Union was getting along: "We are, I think, in the right road of improvement, for we are making experiments."

Watching the show at the Public had revealed to Lin and the Cabinet many more things to try. Some changes came quickly, as when Tommy worked with Oak to retool his depiction of James Madison, giving the author of the Bill of Rights more stature, more strength. ("A testament to Oak's nimbleness," Tommy says of how easily the shift happened.) Other changes took weeks to click into place. Lin and Tommy thought that 25 things in the script needed fixing. Most were so small that the average audience member probably wouldn't notice the change, but a few were substantial, none more so than "One Last Ride."

At the Public, the song skipped from Washington asking Hamilton to draft his Farewell Address, to the two of them marching out to fight in the Whiskey Rebellion, to Washington singing the lofty words of Hamilton's speech. The song had its delicious moments—Lin, standing at Chris Jackson's elbow, always got a laugh when he screamed at the rebels, "Pay your fucking taxes!"—but it never did everything that Lin and Tommy wanted it to do. "You run out of time," Tommy explains. "Chris made it work, and we did our best."

The rewrite to "One Last Ride" illustrates what all those creative impulses, all those pragmatic experiments, were trying to achieve: to ensure that every single element in the show, at every moment, was serving The Story. The

ABOVE:
George Washington's Farewell Address.

CHAPTER XXIII

Story was not a list of events on a historical timeline, in Tommy's view, it was the emotional journey that Hamilton and the other key characters needed to make. Partly at Oskar's urging, Lin and Tommy decided to rework the event-heavy song for something simpler, more expressive. It needed to reveal how Hamilton was affected when his friend, mentor, and father figure retired from public life. That was an easy thing to say, a hard thing to do.

One day, Tommy ducked out of dance rehearsal to check on Lin, who had sequestered himself in a little side room at New 42, trying new approaches to the song, rejecting them, trying again. They kicked around some ways to musicalize Washington's desire to go home, but didn't get anywhere. As he was leaving, Tommy mentioned "the vine and fig stuff."

Lin sat up in his chair. "I don't know what you're talking about."

This was unusual. They almost always caught each other's references, finished each other's thoughts. Tommy explained that Washington's favorite verse from Scripture dealt with finding peace in seclusion, under each person's own vine and fig tree.

"Where is this?" said Lin. "*What is this?*" He started googling.

Tommy went back to rehearsal. A few minutes later, Lin appeared.

"I got it," he said.

The new song would be called "One Last Time." Out went the Whiskey Rebellion, in came Micah 4:4, the Scripture passage so dear to Washington. Just as the revised lyrics came from Lin's collaboration with Tommy, the new music was shaped by his friendship with Chris. "I know his voice really well—I know the sweet spot," says Lin. When he turned the Bible passage into a lyric, he built the phrase "their own vine and fig tree" on the intervals that Chris sings best—which, if you think about it, is pretty much what Hamilton did for Washington when he drafted the Farewell Address.

Lin and Tommy liked the personal nature of the Biblical verse: Washington wanted badly to return to

---

"'NEW DISCOVERIES, NEW MISTAKES,' is the daily goal that Tommy had announced for the company at their FIRST REHEARSAL the previous November."

"*Chris knows that* PLENTY OF PEOPLE IN AMERICA ARE UNCOMFORTABLE WITH A BLACK PRESIDENT. *He also knows the symbolic power of* Hamilton *having three of them.*"

that the struggle continues. The idea is perfect, the execution is not. It's never been perfect."

From the beginning of the show's development, Chris had been wrestling with the founders' failure to eradicate slavery when they formed the Union. "They lied about it. They lied to themselves about it. It's the great shame of our glorious country," he says. "It's still affecting me, my parents, our lives."

He tried to rationalize Washington's slaveholding for the sake of stepping into the man's shoes, but after a lot of inward struggle, he had to give it up. "I won't reconcile that," he concluded. "But it doesn't keep me from getting to the heart of who he was, and trying to portray the truth in that." In the last moments of the show, when Eliza sings that Hamilton would have done more to fight slavery if he'd had more time, Chris, as Washington, bows his head in shame. It's his way of having Washington accept responsibility for what he did and didn't do.

Chris knows that plenty of people in America are uncomfortable with a black president. He also knows the symbolic power of *Hamilton* having three of them. As the show rehearsed that summer, the aftermath of the Charleston shootings demonstrated how real symbolic power can be. Activists renewed their efforts to remove Confederate flags from statehouses, stores, and everywhere else.

From the day Alexander Hamilton arrived in what would become the United States, he fought against everything that flag would come to stand for. "If they break this Union, they will break my heart," he said on his deathbed. His fight isn't over, Chris thinks: "It's living and breathing." When he looks around today, he sees a battle of ideas going on, one in which even a Broadway musical has a role to play, in every word, note, and gesture. "This is our own form of protest."

Mt. Vernon, to depart what he called "the great theater of action." But those lines from Scripture had a public meaning for him, too. In 1790, he cited the verse in a letter to a Jewish community that had immigrated to Rhode Island to seek relief from persecution. He was stating the principle that all men and women should find a safe haven in America, no matter who they are or where they come from.

This second meaning of the song took on unexpected weight in the summer of 2015. The night before the full company of *Hamilton* reassembled, a white supremacist violated the safest haven of all: He gunned down nine worshipers at Emanuel A.M.E. Church in Charleston, South Carolina, one of the oldest black churches in the South.

"It stopped me cold," says Chris. It was a brutal reminder of the gap that yawns between the hope he sings about in "One Last Time" and contemporary American reality. "To me, it encapsulated the thought

ONE LAST TIME[1]

— ◆ —

Washington's office. Hamilton enters.

HAMILTON: Mr. President, you asked to
see me?

WASHINGTON: I know you're busy.

HAMILTON: What do you need, sir? Sir?

WASHINGTON: I wanna give you a word
of warning.

HAMILTON: Sir, I don't know what you heard,
but whatever it is, Jefferson started it.

WASHINGTON: Thomas Jefferson resigned
this morning.

HAMILTON: You're kidding.

WASHINGTON: I need a favor.

HAMILTON: Whatever you say, sir, Jefferson
will pay for his behavior.

WASHINGTON: Shh. Talk less.

HAMILTON: I'll use the press,
I'll write under a pseudonym, you'll see what
    I can do to him—

WASHINGTON: I need you to draft an address.

HAMILTON: Yes! He resigned. You can finally
speak your mind—

WASHINGTON: No. He's stepping down so he
can run for president.

HAMILTON: Ha. Good luck defeating you, sir.

WASHINGTON: I'm stepping down. I'm not
running for president.

HAMILTON: I'm sorry, what?

WASHINGTON: One last time.
Relax, have a drink with me
One last time.
Let's take a break tonight
And then we'll teach them how to say goodbye,
    to say goodbye.
You and I.

HAMILTON: No, sir, why?

WASHINGTON: I wanna talk about neutrality.

HAMILTON: Sir, with Britain and France on
the verge of war, is this the best time—

WASHINGTON: I want to warn against partisan
fighting.

HAMILTON: But—

WASHINGTON: Pick up a pen, start writing.
I wanna talk about what I have learned.
The hard won wisdom I have earned.

HAMILTON: As far as the people are concerned
You have to serve, you could continue to serve—

WASHINGTON: No! One last time
The people will hear from me
One last time
And if we get this right
We're gonna teach 'em how to say goodbye,
You and I—

HAMILTON: Mr. President, they will say
you're weak.

[1] Keeping what I loved about "One Last Ride" while rewriting it as "One Last Time" (see page 207) was a little like merging a vanishing bar of soap to a new bar of soap. Takes a lot of strength and I'd like to end the metaphor here now, please.

WASHINGTON: No, they will see we're strong.

HAMILTON: Your position is so unique.

WASHINGTON: So I'll use it to move them along.

HAMILTON: Why do you have to say goodbye?

WASHINGTON: If I say goodbye, the nation
    learns to move on.
It outlives me when I'm gone.
Like the Scripture says:
"Everyone shall sit under their own vine and
    fig tree
And no one shall make them afraid."
They'll be safe in the nation we've made.
I want to sit under my own vine and fig tree.
A moment alone in the shade.
At home in this nation we've made.
One last time.

HAMILTON: One last time.

Washington hands Hamilton the pen.

*He starts writing Washington's Farewell
Address.*

HAMILTON: Though, in reviewing the
incidents of my administration, I am uncon-
scious of intentional error, I am nevertheless too
sensible of my defects not to think it probable
that I may have committed many errors. I shall
also carry with me

HAMILTON:	**WASHINGTON:**
The hope that my	The hope [2]
country will	
view them with	View them with
indulgence	indulgence
And that	
after forty-five years	After forty-five years
of my life dedicated	of my life dedicated
to its service with an	to its service with an
upright zeal,	upright zeal

[2] Reading Washington's Farewell Address, this section jumped out at me. In it, Washington seeks to do exactly what we aim to do with this musical: paint himself as human, and capable of mistakes. Which makes his ode to "The Benign Influence Of Good Laws Under A Free Government" all the more moving. And moving in stereo, because they're Hamilton's sentiments as well. The music underpinning it is "The Story of Tonight," which we have not heard since Laurens's death, so it evokes a nostalgia for a more idealistic time in the lives of all these men.

the faults of	
incompetent abilities	
will be	
consigned to	Consigned to
oblivion, as I myself	oblivion, as I myself
must soon be to the	must soon be to the
mansions of	mansions of
rest.	rest.
I anticipate with	I anticipate with
pleasing	pleasing
expectation that	expectation that
retreat in which	retreat in which
I promise myself to	I promise myself to
realize, the	realize, the
sweet enjoyment of	sweet enjoyment of
partaking, in	partaking, in
the midst of my	the midst of my
fellow-citizens,	fellow-citizens,
the benign	the benign
influence of good	influence of good
laws	laws
Under a free	Under a free
government, the	government, the
ever-favorite object	ever-favorite object
of my heart,	of my heart,
and the happy	and the happy
reward, as I trust,	reward, as I trust,
of our mutual cares,	of our mutual cares,
labors, and	labors, and
dangers.	dangers.

WASHINGTON: One last time.

WOMEN: George Washington's going home!

HAMILTON: Teach 'em how to say goodbye.

WASHINGTON:	**COMPANY:**
You and I	George Washington's
	Going home

Going home

History has its eyes
on you.

We're gonna teach
'Em how to say
Goodbye!

George Washington's
Going home

George Washington's
Going home

George Washington's
Going home

Teach 'em
How to say
Goodbye!

Teach them
How to say
Goodbye

To say goodbye!

Say goodbye!

One last time!

Teach 'em how!

Say goodbye!

Say goodbye!

One last time!

THE SLAVERY DEBATE:

Cut Lyrics of "Cabinet Battle #3"

JEFFERSON/MADISON/BURR

The people don't know what we know.

The scene changes. We are back in WASHINGTON'S CABINET.

Song: "BATTLE NUMBER THREE."

WASHINGTON

The issue on the table: a petition from a Quaker delegation
in Philadelphia calling on Congress to end the African slave
trade and abolish slavery, in all its forms. If this comes to
a vote in Congress, what is the White House's position? Secre
tary Jefferson, you first. Tread lightly.

JEFFERSON

The constitution clearly states
That the states have to wait
Until eighteen oh eight to debate

HAMILTON

Sir—

JEFFERSON

Wait!
That's the price we paid
For the southern states to participate
In our little independence escapade
We made concessions to the south to make them less afraid
You take away our property? Secession talk will escalate
But for a second let us say that we can legislate
Unanimous empancipation. Freedom reigns and, yes it's great.
We cannot cure prejudice or righteous, desperate hate
So back to Africa or do they get a separate state?
It's a sin. It's growing like a cancer
But we can't address the question, if we do not have an answer.

HAMILTON

Is it my turn? Good.
Plantation states are packed with promise makers
Do you realize the precious time these legislators wasted?
Institutionalizing slavery only multiplies our troubles
Wait till the 1800's, and their population doubles
You all know

This is the stain on our soul and democracy
A land of the free? No it's not. It's hipocrisy
To subjugate, dehumanize a race, call 'em property
And say that we are powerless to stop it. Can you not forsee?
Sir, even you, you have hundreds of slaves
Whose descendants will curse our names when we're safe in our
Graves
How will the south find labor for its businesses?
How will Thomas Jefferson find his next mistresses?

JEFFERSON

How dare you.

HAMILTON

Yet still, people follow like lemmings
All your hemming and hawing, while you're hee-hawing with
Sally Hemings

WASHINGTON

That's enough.

MADISON

Hamilton, if we support emancipation
Every single slave owner will demand compensation
And as for slandering Jefferson with talk of mistresses.
Do you really wanna—

MADISON/JEFFERSON

Do you really wanna have that conversation?

HAMILTON

No.

WASHINGTON

I've heard enough, gentlemen. You can go.
Slavery's too volatile an issue. We won't get through it.

MADISON

Sir, we'll keep it off your desk.

WASHINGTON

Good. Do it.

     Room where it happened reprise possibly.

40

XXIV

O F

JONATHAN GROFF

HIS ROYAL CHARACTER,

HIS NOTABLE CAREER,

HIS DRESSING ROOM DÉCOR &c.

"THE FOUR GRANDPARENTS OF THE show are *Sweeney Todd, Jesus Christ Superstar, Evita,* and *Gypsy,*" says Tommy.

It was dinner break at the Richard Rodgers, where tech rehearsals were underway. The cast had seized the chance to get out of the building, since their workday was scheduled to last until midnight. The place was as deserted as a Broadway theater can be when there are only four days left before the first audience arrives. Power tools whirred; laptops clicked.

"*Gypsy* and *Sweeney* are the story of monsters," he continues. "They're both about somebody who has already been judged by history, but the shows still create mystery about why the monsters do what they do. *Evita* and *Jesus Christ Superstar* showed that music could lead the way"—meaning that they had started as concept albums, and were virtually sung-through, like *Hamilton.* "They both took mythical figures and humanized them."

"What about *Les Mis?*"

"That might be the grandparent that raised us. There's a lot of Javert and Valjean in there," he says. "*Les Misérables* is fundamentally about somebody who says, 'You have to live by these rules,' and somebody else who says, 'Sometimes you have to break those rules.' Burr's inability to understand how Hamilton lives is one of his great obstacles of Act One. At the end of Act Two, he

absorbs Hamilton's energy, and kills him. And Hamilton acts in a way that is much more Burr-like."

Something onstage caught Tommy's eye. An actor who had just returned from dinner was performing a grandiose bow toward the mezzanine. He touched his heart; he looked rapt; he bowed again. It was a parody of communing with the space, or some mystical actorly crap like that.

"Groff, you are *back on Broadway!*" Tommy shouts to him.

"Literally," Groff replies.

"There are *dozens* of people excited about that," says Tommy.

The joke is that 31-year-old Jonathan Groff is, by far, the show's biggest star. In 2007, he collected a Tony nomination and the hearts of pretty much everybody who saw him for his breakout role in the rock musical *Spring Awakening.* He led the cast of *Hair* at Shakespeare in the Park a year later, and notched a few other Off-Broadway credits, but for the most part he spent his late 20s getting famous on film and TV: He played a recurring role on *Glee,* he supplied the voice of Kristoff in *Frozen,* he landed a lead role in the HBO drama *Looking.* The announcement that Groff would be returning to Broadway as *Hamilton*'s King George III, the charming sociopath who threatens and taunts the

Americans, constituted big news. Many more than dozens were excited about it.

But once again, luck and good timing had to intervene. Groff was the last principal to join the company of *Hamilton*, and he almost didn't join at all.

On opening night at the Public, the king had been played by Brian d'Arcy James. He stole the show, but he was already committed to another role that began in a few weeks. Lin and Tommy thought of Groff as a potential replacement. They liked his comic sensibility, his boyish impudence—what Tommy called his "King Groffrey" quality, a reference to the sadistic teen-aged tyrant of *Game of Thrones*. But King George III is a strange role to offer to a rising young star. He sings only three variations on one song. They keep him onstage for just nine minutes.

Groff considered the offer mainly because he had gotten to know Lin when they were both breaking out in their Broadway debuts. "I thought, *Yeah, I'll go do something at the Public*, mostly because I loved him. He's a nerd, he's a theater fan, he's a genuinely good person." He listened to a demo recording of "You'll Be Back," the king's first song, and signed up for the show.

"And then I saw it," he says. "And it was like—," and here words fail him. "I was weeping, and I did not expect to be weeping. It was a transformative experience. I felt like I'd really won the lottery."

On the day before Groff's first performance at the Public, the cast held a coronation ceremony onstage. It was Brian's idea—a generous gesture from one well-liked actor to another, both silly and heartfelt. (A garter was involved.) That likability, Tommy says, is the key to both actors' ability to bring the role to life. "How much more interesting is it to have a king who's going to do the most horrible things, and is The Other, and yet we love him?" When Groff was in *Spring Awakening*, he

GEORGE III

Being Eldest Son of Frederick *late* Prince of Wales, *he was* Born *June,* 4th 1738. Created Prince of Wales, 1751 — Succeeded *his* Grandfather, George II. *Oct.* 25 1760 *was* Proclaimed *the next day* — Married Charlotte Sophia, Princess *of* Mecklenburgh Strelitz, *September,* 8. 1761 — *and* both *were* Crowned *September,* 22nd 1761. —

"How much more interesting is it to have A KING WHO'S GOING TO DO THE MOST HORRIBLE THINGS, AND IS THE OTHER, AND YET WE LOVE HIM?"

won Broadway.com's Audience Choice award—three of them, actually.

Groff was happy to steal some of Brian's choices: the king's extreme stillness onstage, the little shoulder wag he does toward the end of "You'll Be Back." But he also started to play with what the song and its reprises could be. "The great thing about the song is that it's bullet-proof," he says. "It's always hilarious. Literally anyone could walk onstage and get laughs. You can mess with it and you still won't mess up the whole train."

Everybody assumed that Groff's involvement in the show—the reign of King George the Third the Second, as they called him—would last for six weeks. Then he would go back to *Looking*, and the show would go

---

"A SHOW LIKE THIS COMES ALONG ONCE IN A GENERATION. To be a small part of that is why I went into performing in the first place. It's such rare air that we're breathing."

---

uptown with somebody new: King George the Third the Third. But a few weeks after his reign began, HBO unex-pectedly canceled *Looking*. And it left Groff with a dilemma: Make a yearlong commitment to play the king—"a cameo, essentially," in his words—or resume his climb through TV and film?

What looked like a hard call from the outside really wasn't. It was "a no-brainer," he says. "A show like this comes along once in a generation. To be a small part of that is why I went into performing in the first place. It's such rare air that we're breathing."

Eight times a week, Groff spends his nine minutes onstage—funny, seductive, scary, haughty, perplexed. Because he treats the songs as a relationship with the audience, his performance naturally varies to match whatever energy the crowd feeds him. After the curtain call, you can find him offstage right and up a flight of stairs, in the suite of dressing rooms that he shares with Lin. During tech, he devised a plan to replace his door with a beaded curtain he had found online.

"We're making it our little nest up there," he says. "It's gonna get real personal."

I KNOW HIM

[1] *BAHAHAHA.* King George showed up again!

This surprised me, just as it surprised me when the Piragua Guy showed up for his reprise in *In The Heights*, one of the last songs we added for that show. But sometimes a character just will not be denied.

To be honest, his reappearance here was probably inspired by the anecdote wherein King George says of Washington's resignation: "If he does that, he will be the greatest man in the world." I love that.

[2] I'm just taking it as a given that everyone watched the John Adams miniseries on HBO. The scene between Adams and King George in that film is my favorite scene in the whole series.

King George enters.[1]

KING GEORGE: They say
George Washington's yielding his power and
    stepping away.
'Zat true?
I wasn't aware that was something a person
    could do.
I'm perplexed.
Are they gonna keep on replacing whoever's in
    charge?
If so, who's next?
There's nobody else in their country who looms
    quite as large . . .

A sentinel whispers in King George's ear.

What?

The sentinel whispers again.

John Adams?!
I know him.
That can't be.
That's that little guy who spoke to me[2]
All those years ago.
What was it? Eighty-five!
That poor man, they're gonna eat him alive!
Oceans rise.
Empires fall.
Next to Washington, they all look small
All alone
Watch them run.
They will tear each other into pieces.
Jesus Christ, this will be fun!

Da da da dat da da da da ya da
Da da da dat da ya daaaaa!

Hahahaha.
President John Adams.
Good luck.

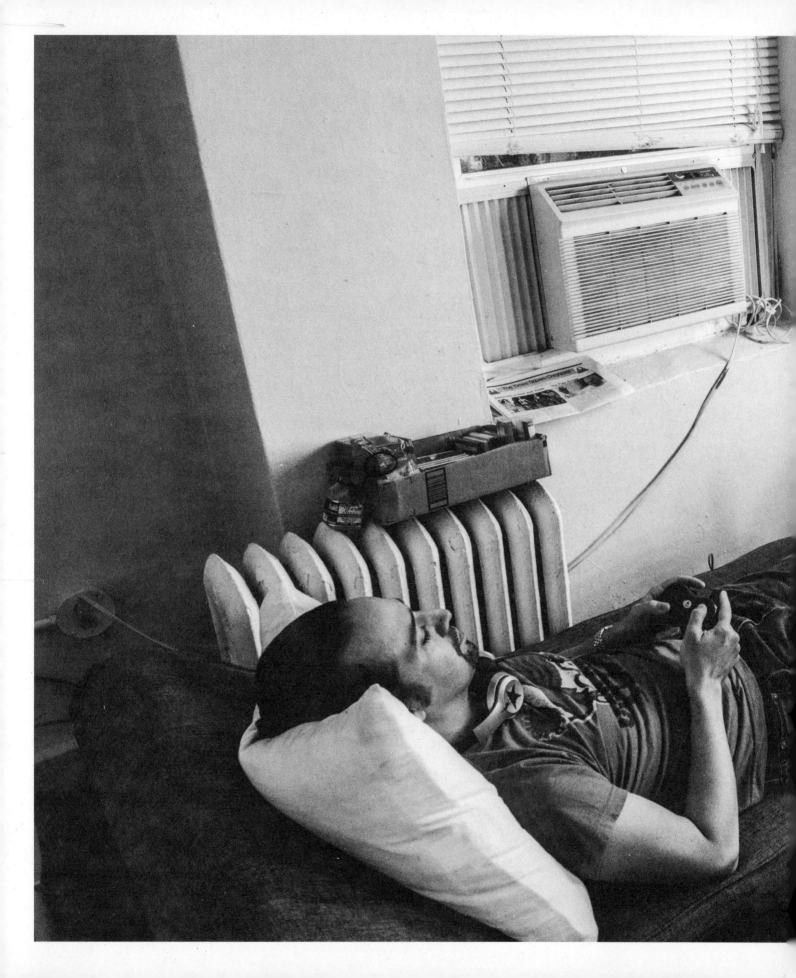

ON KILLING YOUR DARLINGS,

with Reference to

"THE ADAMS ADMINISTRATION,"

the SEDUCTIONS *of* BEN FRANKLIN,

AND SONGS ON THE CUTTING-ROOM FLOOR

WHILE THE *HAMILTON* COMPANY prepared for Broadway, Lin collected one last accolade from the show's downtown run: the Best Musical prize from the New York Drama Critics Circle. At 54 Below, a cabaret venue in Midtown, John Kander presented the award, saying such nice things that Lin cried on his way to the stage. He recovered sufficiently to tell the room full of critics, politely but firmly, that he

> *"Lin is unleashing the energy of crossing boundaries. He is saying, 'I can tell American history using popular song, I CAN MIX BROADWAY AND HIP-HOP. I CAN FLY HIGH AND FLY LOW.'"*

would not be following the advice that several of them had volunteered in their reviews: "I'm not going to cut 15 minutes."

Hamilton had been, and was destined to remain, torrential. "What you can feel is the overflowing generosity of somebody who has tapped into the well of his subject, and it just keeps giving more and more. And this does feel like *Angels*," says Oskar, whose work on Tony Kushner's seven-hour masterpiece *Angels in America* makes him an authority on volcanic literary hyperproduction. "You just feel like, *Oh my God, there's no bottom to this.* Lin is unleashing the energy of crossing boundaries. He

is saying, 'I can tell American history using popular song, I can mix Broadway and hip-hop. I can fly high and fly low.' It feels like it's unlimited. And that liberatory feeling spills out into the audience."

Even in its early incarnations, when the show was longer than it became, *Hamilton* never felt messy or scattershot. Lin was profusely productive—he needed to be, to write a score with four dozen songs, more than double the usual number—but he was also efficient. As Jeffrey points out, "Lin wrote exactly one opening number. He wrote exactly one 'I want' song for the protagonist. That is not often said. This show does not have 20 or 30 songs in the trash heap."

The few songs that *did* disappear help illustrate what Lin and the Cabinet were after, and how different *Hamilton* could have been. Sometimes Lin and Tommy rethought the tone of a particular moment. Lin made an early demo recording of a boozy Hamilton, Laurens, and Lafayette slinging filthy innuendo about Alexander's sexual conquests, but replaced it with the better-behaved "A Winter's Ball." He made another early demo of "Valley Forge," a spooky dirge-like song about the carnage of the Revolutionary War, but decided to drop all but a few of its lines, which he folded into the more propulsive

"Stay Alive." One of them is Washington's grim declaration, "We're gonna fly a lot of flags half-mast." (The public mourning for Washington once had a song of its own, but Lin felt that they could do without it, since Chris ends Washington's Farewell Address by singing the lights out.)

Sometimes, Lin dropped a song because he narrowed his cast of characters. He started to write a country-rock tune for Benjamin Franklin, in which the wily diplomat seduced rich French ladies to help the American cause. But Franklin was also seducing *Lin*, who realized that Franklin would run away with any show in which he appeared. Lin said *adieu* to Franklin, the French ladies, and the song.

The most common reason for putting a song aside was to keep the audience focused on the story that Lin and Tommy were trying to tell. In one cut song, "Let It Go," Eliza tried to get Alexander to stop being so belligerent to his enemies, even as Burr campaigned for and won the Senate seat held by her father. (A long, fruitless discussion among Lin and his Cabinet about how to speed up the song ended when Lac proposed that they skip Burr's campaign altogether, thereby saving precious minutes—and eliminating a song that shared a title with the monster hit from Disney's *Frozen*.) For a time, Burr sang a tearful reprise of "Dear Theodosia" to tell his daughter that her mother had died. The third "Cabinet Battle," the fierce fight over slavery, didn't shed new light on the characters—the point, after all, is that none of the Founding Fathers did anything to stop it—so the song had to go. That's not a lot of misfires for six years of writing. "It was a very direct ascent up the mountain," Jeffrey says.

Lin and his collaborators needed the creativity to generate thousands of ideas and the pragmatism to test them all—both of which are key Hamiltonian virtues. But the show only works because they possessed a quality that their subject lacked: self-restraint. Again and again they sacrificed little pleasures (a beautiful melody, a big laugh) in pursuit of an overarching goal.

"The Adams Administration" demonstrates Hamilton's lack of discipline and Lin and Tommy's abundance of it. Hamilton despised Washington's successor, John Adams, and the contempt was mutual. Adams insulted Hamilton's parentage, calling him "a bastard brat of a Scotch pedlar," and belittled his morals by declaring that Hamilton's ambitions were due to "a superabundance of secretions which he could not find whores enough to draw off."

Once Washington retired to Mt. Vernon, there was nobody around to quell Hamilton's destructive (and self-destructive) tendencies. In 1800, he unleashed a scathing 54-page pamphlet attacking Adams. Hamilton wreaked havoc on his own prospects and the Federalist Party that the two men led.

Lin's original version of the song included all of the lyrics printed on page 224, an explosion of pure fury, which must have been even more fun to deliver than it was to hear. But the song asked the audience to spend two minutes thinking about a character they never get to meet. For the final version, Lin cut all but his last two lines. Hamilton would have been wise to do the same.

The ADAMS ADMINISTRATION

—◆—

[1] When I cut the contents of Hamilton's angry pamphlet about Adams, I also cut Adams's insults, which had provoked Hamilton in the first place. At this point our show is moving very quickly, so I had to get in and out fast.

[2] Just begin with a burner of an opening sentence, as harsh as Burr's run-on sentences re: Hamilton.

[3] In a workshop reading, this was Hamilton talking smack about Abigail Adams's appearance—something the historical Hamilton never did, but par for the course in hip-hop insults. One look at the audience's cringing reaction and I cut it. *No one* messes with Abigail Adams. We just won't have it.

[4] This is actually my favorite nod to the musical *1776*, not the "Sit down" quote at the end.

[5] The wordplay in this is just so much fun. Nuisance/no sense, my level/malevolence. Hamilton's unhinged as hell here, which makes it fun to play. Alas, he's using all his best stuff against a character we never meet, so goodbye fun wordplay. You're doomed to a footnote in this book.

[6] A paraphrase of real-life Jefferson, who called Hamilton "an host within himself" in a letter to Madison about an unrelated beef.
  Also, one more thing: This was the site of one of my best typos of all time. You haven't lived til you've seen Daveed read: "As long as he can hold a pen, he's a *treat*!"

BURR: How does Hamilton the short-tempered
    protean creator of the coast guard
Founder of the New York Post
Ardently abuse his cab'net post
Destroy his reputation?
Welcome folks, to

BURR, COMPANY: The Adams administration!

BURR: Jefferson's the runner-up, which makes
him the vice president

JEFFERSON: Washington can't help you now,
no more mister nice president.

BURR: Adams fires Hamilton.
Privately calls him creole bastard in his taunts.[1]

JEFFERSON: Say what!

BURR: Hamilton publishes his response.

——————— *CUT LYRICS* ———————

HAMILTON: An open letter to the fat [2]
Arrogant
Anti-charismatic
National embarrassment
Known as President John Adams

BURR: Shit

HAMILTON: The man's irrational, he claims
    that I'm in league
With Britain in some vast, international intrigue.
Trick, please.
You wouldn't know what I'm doin',
You're always goin' berserk
But you never show up to work
Give my regards to Abigail [3]
Next time you write about my lack of moral compass
At least I'm doin' my job up in this rumpus

COMPANY: Oh!

HAMILTON: The line is behind me
I crossed it again
Well, the President lost it again
Aww, such a rough life
Better run to ya' wife
Yo, the boss is in Boston again
Lemme ask you a question: Who sits
At your desk when you're in Massachusetts?
They were calling you a dick back in
    'seventy-six [4]
And you haven't done anything new since!
You nuisance with no sense!
You will die of irrelevance!
Go ahead: You can call me the Devil
You aspire to my level,
You aspire to malevolence! [5]
Say hi to the Jeffersons!
And the spies all around me,
Maybe they can confirm
I don't care if I kill my career with this,
I am confining you to one term.

———————————————————

HAMILTON: Sit down, John, you fat mother—
[BLEEP]er.

*Hamilton drops a thick tome of paper on the
floor. The Company explodes.*

BURR: Hamilton is out of control.

MADISON: This is great! He's out of power. He
holds no office. And he just destroyed President
John Adams, the only other significant member
of his party.

JEFFERSON: Hamilton's a host unto himself.
As long as he can hold a pen, he's a threat. Let's
let him know what we know. [6]

XXVI

IN WHICH THE HERO

BLOWS UP HIS SPOT,

with the Assistance of

HOWELL BINKLEY'S LIGHTS

and OTHER FORMS of

INGENIOUS STAGECRAFT

WHEN LIN TOLD THE AUDIENCE AT the White House that Alexander Hamilton "embodies the word's ability to make a difference," he was thinking of all the good things that language can do.

Hamilton reminds us that the American Revolution was a writers' revolution, that the founders created the nation one paragraph at a time. But words can also wreak havoc. They also tear down. The heart of Act Two is a sequence of four songs that illustrate the destructive potential of language, and the perplexing fact that Alexander Hamilton never used words more devastatingly than when he used them against himself.

The sequence of songs—almost a play-within-a play—is shaped by Lin's historical compression. On December 15, 1792, three congressmen confronted Hamilton with what they thought was evidence that he had misused Treasury funds, only to discover that they had stumbled upon a very different offense: that he'd had a three-year affair with Maria Reynolds, and paid her husband to keep it clandestinely going. Those charges stayed private until 1797, when a journalist who was friendly with Jefferson leveled charges of improper financial speculation against Hamilton and Reynolds's husband. Feeling what he called a "desire to destroy this slander completely,"

Hamilton published a shockingly detailed pamphlet describing the whole affair, trying to salvage his professional integrity even at the expense of shaming his wife and children.

In Lin's compact version of the story, the three politicians who confront Hamilton in "We Know" are Jefferson, Madison, and Burr, and the decision to preempt their attack comes almost immediately after the meeting. Both acts of dramatic license make it easier for the audience to grasp the bewildering truth about America's first sex scandal: Hamilton made a conscious decision to write something that blew up his own life.

> "*. . . Alexander Hamilton NEVER USED WORDS MORE DEVAS-TATINGLY than when he used them against himself.*"

That decision was dramatic, but it wasn't necessarily theatrical: A man scratches parchment with a quill, somebody else flips through a pamphlet—where's the visual interest in that? Tommy's challenge, as he put it, was to find a vivid way to show "how a couple strokes of the pen can ricochet around the world and explode." He and his designers spent tech rehearsals at the Rodgers experimenting with new and more potent ways of depicting this crisis in Hamilton's life. It took cleverness to make

that play-within-a-play a theatrical climax of the show, but even more than that, it took extraordinary integration, many veteran artists working in harmony.

In "Hurricane," the second of the four songs, Lin depicts Hamilton looking all the way back to his childhood, trying to find some way out of his mess. A prior collaboration gave Tommy and Andy an idea for how to stage this introspection. In a production of *The Wiz*, they had dramatized a tornado by having a little model house get blown to pieces and scattered around. "Here it became not just the things that make up a house but the things he was made of," says Tommy. As Hamilton reflects on his past, figures from his life whirl around him: his mother, his friends, his enemies.

Howell Binkley gave the song an eerie dreamlike power. After 20 years as a professional lighting designer, and more than 40 shows on Broadway, he called *Hamilton* "the biggest challenge of my career in terms of storytelling." There are four dozen songs in the show, and many of them skip from one part of the story to another: It

required immense resourcefulness to generate hundreds of different looks. Luckily, as Tommy has found in his four collaborations with Howell, "he is incredibly fast."

In "Hurricane," Howell used purplish light at center stage and whirling instruments around the perimeter to make it seem as though Hamilton were in the eye of a swirling storm. Lin says the sensation of standing in the middle of these unsettling effects is a distilled version of how he feels throughout the show: "I am staying in my lane and doing what I'm supposed to do while everyone is doing what they do at the height of their abilities, and if I move to the left or right, I'll get hit with a desk."

When Hamilton has decided what to do, and the third song in the sequence begins, the action "needs to detonate, and it needs to be messy," according to Tommy. Bright white flares from six powerful lights—stronger instruments than Howell had downtown—fire the opening salvo. ("A nice sledgehammer effect," in the words of his associate designer, Ryan O'Gara.) Up to this point in the show, Nevin holds back on what his monster sound

ABOVE:
Tech at the Richard Rodgers Theatre—July 8, 2015.

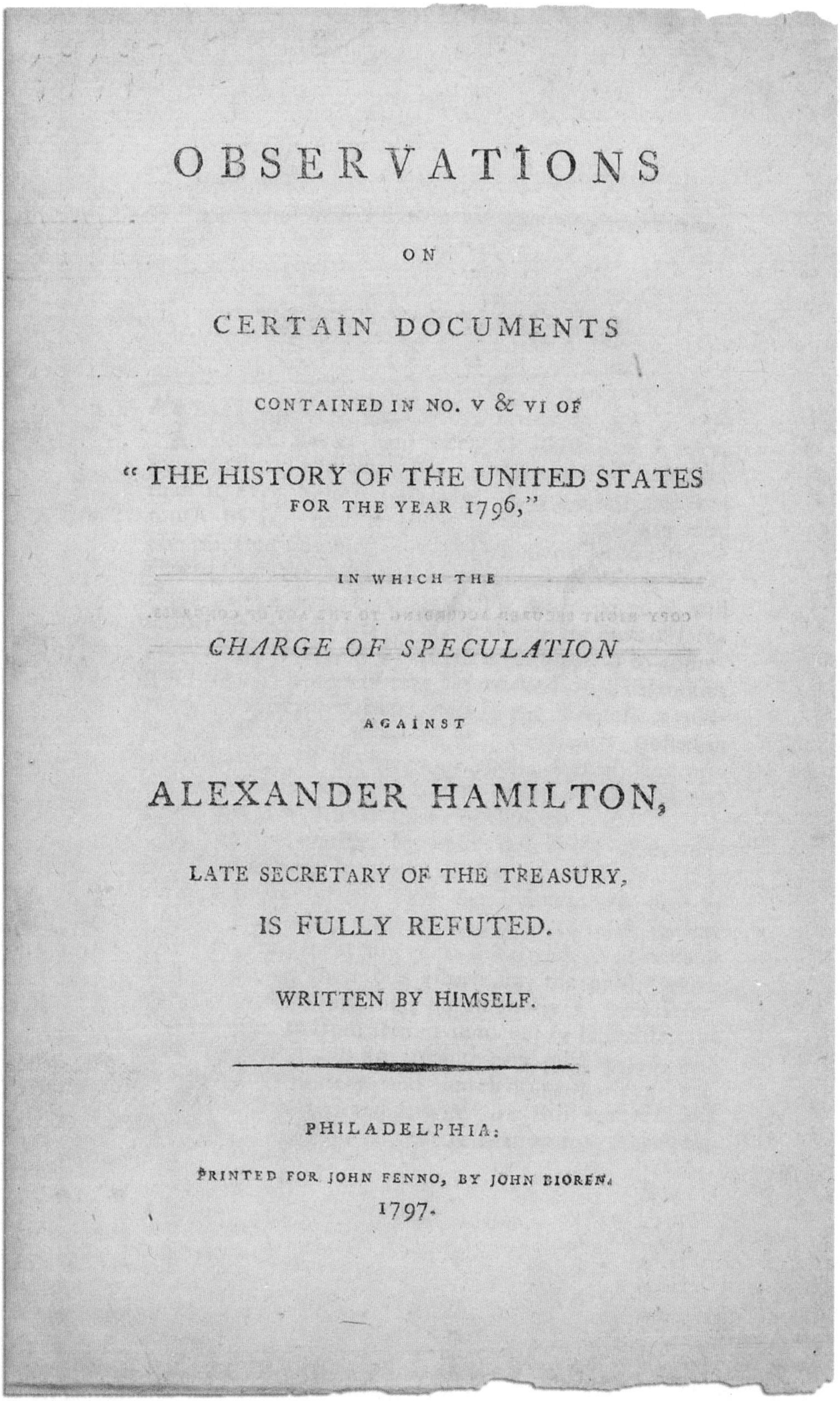

CHAPTER XXVI

OBSERVATIONS

ON

CERTAIN DOCUMENTS

CONTAINED IN NO. V & VI OF

" THE HISTORY OF THE UNITED STATES
FOR THE YEAR 1796,"

IN WHICH THE

CHARGE OF SPECULATION

AGAINST

ALEXANDER HAMILTON,

LATE SECRETARY OF THE TREASURY,

IS FULLY REFUTED.

WRITTEN BY HIMSELF.

———————

PHILADELPHIA:

PRINTED FOR JOHN FENNO, BY JOHN BIOREN.

1797.

THE REYNOLDS PAMPHLET

Alexander Hamilton's disastrous, self-destructive attempt to salvage his reputation.

system can do, saving its extremes for when he really needs them. "The Reynolds Pamphlet" is when he really needs them.

"The Earth does move there—Hamilton's whole world has moved," he says. You don't just hear the murky, snarly opening chords of the song: You feel them.

As the pamphlet circulates, and Howell's lights flash, and Nevin's speakers boom, the ensemble dancers erupt. "They just go buck wild and play," says associate choreographer Stephanie Klemons. Some of them spin a pamphlet in front of their faces as if it's the steering wheel of an out-of-control car. King George joins in the evil glee, taunting Hamilton to his face. Jefferson flings pamphlets like he's dealing a pack of cards, or tossing Benjamins in a P. Diddy video. He even hands a pamphlet to Lac in the orchestra pit. For a delirious few seconds, every kind of stage effect adds up to create the sense that with a few ill-advised strokes of his quill, Hamilton has put himself in a living nightmare.

Then, in a heartbeat, the stage grows still. "All that's left is the remains of that explosion, the rubble," says Nevin. Eliza steps into a pool of patterned moonlight to sing the last song in the sequence, "Burn."

Lin's lyrics convey Eliza's bewilderment, the shock that she must have felt at her betrayal. "Indeed my angelic Betsey, I would not for the world do any thing that would hazard your esteem," Hamilton had vowed during their courtship. "'Tis to me a jewel of inestimable price & I think you may rely I shall never make you blush." The staging contributes to her feeling of shame. When Pippa stands in the wings, waiting to enter, she can hear the fury and chaos of "The Reynolds Pamphlet," the laughing and jeering onstage and in the audience. "I like to imagine that's the feeling Eliza had when she read the pamphlet for the first time," she says. Paul Tazewell designed her gown to emphasize her innocence. "The very open neckline suggests a vulnerability and allows the audience access to her emotionally," he says.

"Pippa, that's a good look for you," Tommy told her one day during tech. "Moonlight. Tazewell gown. Now all you need is fire." She got it. The sequence of songs ends with Eliza taking revenge for what her husband had done, and what he had written. What retribution could be crueler or more fitting? She burned the letters he had written to her—she destroyed his words.

"*For a delirious few seconds, every kind of stage effect adds up to create the sense that with a few ill-advised strokes of his quill, HAMILTON HAD PUT HIM-SELF IN A LIVING NIGHTMARE.*"

ABOVE:
Tech at the Richard Rodgers. Top: The Cabinet. *Bottom:* Phillipa Soo and Tommy Kail.

WE KNOW

—•—

*Hamilton, in his study. Jefferson, Madison &
Burr enter.*

HAMILTON: Mr. Vice President.
Mr. Madison.
Senator Burr.
What is this?

JEFFERSON: We have the check stubs. From
separate accounts.

MADISON: Almost a thousand dollars, paid in
different amounts.

BURR: To a Mr. James Reynolds way back in
seventeen ninety-one.

HAMILTON: Is that what you have? Are you
done?

MADISON: You are uniquely situated by virtue
of your position—

JEFFERSON: Though "virtue" is not a word I'd
apply to this situation—

MADISON: To seek financial gain, to stray from
your sacred mission—

JEFFERSON: And the evidence suggests you've
engaged in speculation—

BURR: An immigrant embezzling our government funds—

JEFFERSON, MADISON: I can almost see the
headline, your career is done.

BURR: I hope you saved some money for your
daughter and sons.

BURR, JEFFERSON, MADISON: Ya best g'wan
run back where ya come from—[1]

HAMILTON: Ha! You don't even know what
you're asking me to confess.

JEFFERSON, MADISON, BURR: Confess.

HAMILTON: You have nothing. I don't have to
tell you anything at all.
Unless.

JEFFERSON, MADISON, BURR: Unless.[2]

HAMILTON: If I can prove that I never broke
the law,[3]
Do you promise not to tell another soul what
you saw?

BURR: No one else was in the room where it
happened.

HAMILTON: Is that a yes?

JEFFERSON, MADISON, BURR: Um, yes.

*Hamilton pulls a letter from his desk and
hands it to Burr. He begins to read:*

BURR: "Dear sir, I hope this letter finds you in
good health
And in a prosperous enough position to put
wealth
In the pockets of people like me, down on their
luck.
You see, it was my wife who you decided to—"

JEFFERSON: Whaaaat—

[1] The original line
here was a Lauryn Hill
quote, but I was told
that she does not allow
her work to be sampled
at all. I like the rewrite,
because by flipping into
Jamaican patois, it
becomes an ugly dig at
Hamilton's Caribbean
origins.

[2] This is a super-esoteric
reference to my favorite
podcast, *My Brother,
My Brother and Me.*
In this podcast, the
McElroy brothers—
Justin, Travis, and
Griffin—dispense
hilarious, often terrible
advice to listeners.
Often, one of them
will say "Unless,"
prompting the other
two to say "Unless...,"
and then they'll give
completely contradic-
ry, equally hilarious
advice. It seemed fitting
that Hamilton would
go full "Unless" right
before telling his
enemies one of his
biggest secrets. Thanks,
McElroys.

[3] Hamilton is self-
sabotaging by telling
his enemies way too
much. Note, too, that
the music under this
scene is the same as
James Reynolds's letter
in "Say No to This."

HAMILTON: She courted me.
Escorted me to bed and when she had me in a corner
That's when Reynolds extorted me
For a sordid fee.
I paid him quarterly.
I may have mortally wounded my prospects but my papers are orderly!

Hamilton begins pulling reams of paper out of his desk.

HAMILTON: As you can see I kept a record of every check in my checkered history.
Check it again against your list 'n see consistency.
I never spent a cent that wasn't mine
You sent the dogs after my scent, that's fine. [4]
Yes, I have reason for shame
But I have not committed treason and sullied my good name.
As you can see I have done nothing to provoke legal action.
Are my answers to your satisfaction?

[4] This section has some of my favorite internal rhyming in the show, beyond the spent/cent/sent/scent extravaganza. I dropped the music out under "consistency" because it puts a little highlight on it.

JEFFERSON: My God.

MADISON: Gentlemen, let's go.

HAMILTON: So?

JEFFERSON, MADISON: The people won't know what we know.

They exit.

HAMILTON: Burr!

Burr hangs back.

HAMILTON: How do I know you won't use this against me
The next time we go toe to toe?

BURR: Alexander, rumors only grow. And we both know what we know.

Burr exits.

HURRICANE[1]

— ◆ —

[1] The challenge with this song is such a strange one: a moment alone with Hamilton, wherein he thinks about his whole life and then comes to *the wrong conclusion* about what to do. He equates his success as a writer with success in general, and talks himself into writing "The Reynolds Pamphlet." This was only plausible to me if, in reviewing his life, we saw the cracks in the foundation of his mind.

[2] And here's the crack in the foundation: Here's the trauma to end all traumas. Surviving this must have felt like an even worse punishment than death.

HAMILTON: In the eye of a hurricane
There is quiet
For just a moment,
A yellow sky.

When I was seventeen a hurricane
Destroyed my town.
I didn't drown.
I couldn't seem to die.

I wrote my way out,
Wrote everything down far as I could see.
I wrote my way out.
I looked up and the town had its eyes on me.
They passed a plate around.
Total strangers
Moved to kindness by my story.
Raised enough for me to book passage on a ship
    that was New York bound . . .
I wrote my way out of hell.
I wrote my way to revolution.

I was louder than the crack in the bell.
I wrote Eliza love letters until she fell.
I wrote about the Constitution and defended it
    well.
And in the face of ignorance and resistance,
I wrote financial systems into existence.
And when my prayers to God were met with
    indifference,
I picked up a pen, I wrote my own deliverance.

In the eye of a hurricane
There is quiet
For just a moment,

A yellow sky.

I was twelve when my mother died.
She was holding me.
We were sick and she was holding me.
I couldn't seem to die.[2]

BURR:
Wait for it, [3]
Wait for it,
Wait for it . . .

**ENSEMBLE,
BURR:**
Wait for it,
Wait for it,
Wait for it . . .

HAMILTON:
I'll write my
way out . . .

Write ev'rything
Down, far as
I can see . . .

I'll write my
way out . . .
Overwhelm
them
with honesty.

Wait for it,
Wait for it,
Wait for it
Wait . . .

**ELIZA,
ANGELICA,
MARIA,
WASHINGTON:**
History has its
eyes on you. [4]

HAMILTON: This is the eye of the hurricane,
this is the only way I can protect my legacy.

COMPANY: Wait for it,
Wait for it,
Wait for it . . . Wait . . .

HAMILTON: The Reynolds Pamphlet.

[3] And here's Burr,
singing his theme, but
now it's in anticipation
of Hamilton's
self-sabotage.

[4] And here's Team
Hamilton and Maria
Reynolds, those who
will be most affected by
this thing he's writing,
trying to remind him of
the ramifications of
what he's about to do.
They're voices in
Hamilton's head as well,
but they're drowned out.

The
REYNOLDS PAMPHLET[1]

— ◆ —

Hamilton writes The Reynolds Pamphlet.

COMPANY: The Reynolds Pamphlet.

JEFFERSON, MADISON, ANGELICA: Have you read this?

BURR, JEFFERSON, MADISON: Alexander Hamilton had a torrid affair.
And he wrote it down right there.

MADISON: Highlights!

HAMILTON, JEFFERSON:
"The charge against me is a connection with one James Reynolds! For purposes of improper speculation. My real crime is an amorous connection with his wife For a considerable time with his knowing consent."[2]

JAMES REYNOLDS: James Reynolds!

BURR:
"My real crime is an amorous connection with his wife . . . "

COMPANY: Oooooh!

MADISON, BURR, JEFFERSON: Damn!

HAMILTON, JEFFERSON, MADISON: "I had frequent meetings with her. Most of them at my own house."

BURR: At his own house!

MADISON: At his own house!

DEEP VOICE: Damn!

HAMILTON, JEFFERSON: "Mrs. Hamilton with our children being absent on a visit to her father."

MADISON, BURR: No . . .

COMPANY: Boooo!

MADISON, BURR: Have you read this?

JEFFERSON: Well, he's never gon' be president now.[3]

MADISON, BURR: Never gon' be president now.

JEFFERSON: He's never gon' be president now.

MADISON, BURR: Never gon' be president now.

JEFFERSON: He's never gon' be president now.

MADISON, BURR: Never gon' be president now.

JEFFERSON: That's one less thing to worry about.

JEFFERSON, MADISON, BURR: That's one less thing to worry about!

Angelica enters with suitcases.

ANGELICA: I came as soon as I heard.

JEFFERSON: What?!

HAMILTON: Angelica—

[1] The beat for "The Reynolds Pamphlet" is actually a reprise of an earlier cut tune called "No John Trumbull." It's super contemporary and totally different from anything we've heard, and I love that the music that accompanies the nation's first sex scandal sounds *so* contemporary and crazy.

[2] This is all drawn from the actual "Reynolds Pamphlet," with some language updated—I took out "with his privity and connivance" and put in "with his knowing consent."

[3] What a joy it has been to see this line pop up during presidential election season. It's just catchy and bitchy enough to be the National Gaffe Theme Song.

COMPANY: All the way from London?! Damn.

HAMILTON: Angelica, thank God.
Someone who understands what I'm struggling here to do.

ANGELICA: I'm not here for you.

ENSEMBLE: Oooooh!

ANGELICA: I know my sister like I know my own mind, [4]
You will never find anyone as trusting or as kind.
I love my sister more than anything in this life,
I will choose her happiness over mine every time.
Put what we had aside.
I'm standing at her side.
You could never be satisfied.
God, I hope you're satisfied.

JEFFERSON, MADISON, BURR: Well, he's never gon' be president now.

JEFFERSON, MADISON, BURR: Never gon' be president now.

Well, He's never gon' be president now.

That's one less thing to worry about.

ENSEMBLE:
Never gon' be president now.

Never gon' be president now.

Never gon' be president now.

That's one less thing to worry about.

[4] This was originally part of a longer tune titled "Congratulations." It came between "The Reynolds Pamphlet" and "Burn," but we realized that the audience desperately wanted to see Eliza's reaction, so I folded the best parts of it into the "The Reynolds Pamphlet." I love how different it is from everything else in this section. It contributes to the feeling that the world is crashing, pathos within celebration within schadenfreude.

JEFFERSON, MADISON:
Hey! [5]
At least he was
Honest with our money!

Hey!
At least he was
Honest with our money!

HAMILTON:
Hey!
At least I was
Honest with our money!

Hey!
At least he was
Honest with our money!

WOMEN:
Well, he's never gon'
be President now.

Well, he's never gon'
be President now.

Well, he's never gon'
be President now.

That's one less thing
to worry about.

MEN:
Well, he's never gon'
be President now.

Well, he's never gon'
be President now.

Well, he's never gon'
be President now.

Well, he's never gon'
be President now.

[5] Here's where King George gets in on the fun onstage. A late addition by Tommy and Andy that kicks the deliriousness up to 11.

FULL COMPANY: That's one less thing to
worry about!
The Reynolds Pamphlet.

JEFFERSON, MADISON, BURR: Have you
read this?
Did you ever see somebody ruin their own life?

**COMPANY (EXCEPT HAMILTON,
ELIZA):** His poor wife.

BURN

— ❖ —

[1] Eliza's response is lost to time—those letters were burned after Hamilton's death. This gave me enormous freedom, but also gave me a dramatic action. What if Eliza's reaction is to erase her reaction from memory? Writing this song is the first time I introduced the theme of "narrative" for Eliza—which I then promptly went back and threaded into "That Would Be Enough" and the finale of the show.

[2] Chernow found a letter from Angelica to Eliza that says pretty much this.

Eliza sits with a lantern and a stack of letters.[1]

ELIZA: I saved every letter you wrote me.
From the moment I read them
I knew you were mine.
You said you were mine.
I thought you were mine.

Do you know what Angelica said
When we saw your first letter arrive?
She said,

"Be careful with that one, love.
He will do what it takes to survive."

You and your words flooded my senses.
Your sentences left me defenseless.
You built me palaces out of paragraphs,
You built cathedrals.
I'm re-reading the letters you wrote me.
I'm searching and scanning for answers
In every line,
For some kind of sign,
And when you were mine
The world seemed to

Burn.
Burn.

You published the letters she wrote you.
You told the whole world how you brought
    this girl into our bed.
In clearing your name, you have ruined
    our lives.

Do you know what Angelica said
When she read what you'd done?
She said,
"You have married an Icarus.
He has flown too close to the sun."[2]

You and your words, obsessed with your legacy
Your sentences border on senseless
And you are paranoid in every paragraph
How they perceive you?

You, you, you . . .

I'm erasing myself from the narrative.
Let future historians wonder
How Eliza reacted when you broke her heart.
You have torn it all apart.
I am watching it
Burn.
Watching it burn.
The world has no right to my heart.
The world has no place in our bed.
They don't get to know what I said.
I'm burning the memories,
Burning the letters that might have
    redeemed you.
You forfeit all rights to my heart.
You forfeit the place in our bed.
You'll sleep in your office instead,
With only the memories
Of when you were mine.

I hope that you burn.

GIVING AN ACCOUNT OF A HURRICANE,

with a Notable Appearance by

PRESIDENT OBAMA

and the Remarkable Rise of

ANTHONY RAMOS

THE HURRICANE HIT ON A HOT MONDAY in July. On the morning of *Hamilton*'s first Broadway preview, *The New York Times* ran a front-page story about the show. This followed two other *Times* stories over the previous weekend, and a photo spread of the cast in the new issue of *Cosmopolitan*, to say nothing of the dozens of stories in countless publications in the preceding few weeks.

All afternoon, eager theatergoers flooded the sidewalk outside the theater to enter the "Ham4Ham" lottery: a chance to win a $10 seat in the front row for that night's performance. By the time the winning names were drawn, 697 people had entered. The crowd stretched most of the way to Eighth Avenue, and nearly shut down 46th Street.

For all the commotion outside the Rodgers, inside it felt like another day on the job. The contrast was weird, considering the buzz from the star-studded downtown run and the fact that six of the 21 actors were a few hours away from making their Broadway debuts. "I've never worked on a show where the stakes were so high and the temperature was so low," marveled Nevin Steinberg.

That was largely because of the show's director. In rehearsal that afternoon, as Andy ran the cast through the curtain call, Tommy kept up a stream of banter and in-jokes so everybody stayed loose. Directing, he believes, isn't just giving notes to an actor after a scene. It's the tone you set at every moment: "It's what you say in a two-minute elevator ride." Before leaving his apartment that morning, he had thought about wearing a special outfit for *Hamilton*'s first night on Broadway but reverted to the usual untucked shirt and jeans.

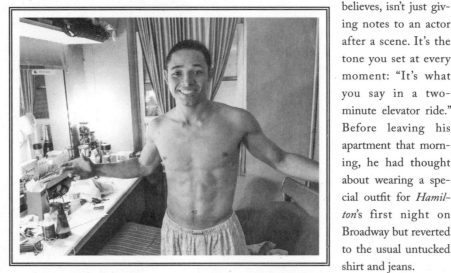

"This is what they're used to," he says, meaning the cast and production team. He wants to keep them calm. Of course, it's also what *he* is used to. He needs to keep calm, too.

A few days earlier, Jeffrey had offered a prediction of what would happen at the first preview. It wasn't verbal, it was a gesture: He put his arms together, raised them skyward, then flared them apart, like a geyser going off. The prediction was also a goal. For just as directors steer actors and choreographers guide dancers, Broadway producers harness the public. They turn a show into an event, a phenomenon—or at least they try to. Sander Jacobs, who joined Jeffrey as a general partner on *Hamilton*, as he had been on *In the Heights*, had a good vantage point to watch him do it. Two decades earlier, he had been an investor in *The Phantom of the Opera*, a monumental hit that became the longest-running show of the time. As *Hamilton* barreled toward its first Broadway performance on July 13, he thought: *I have never seen a reception like this.*

At half past seven on that hot Monday night, the lobby staff pulled open the doors of the Richard Rodgers, and the hurricane swept in.

"Oh look!" cried a tall man in a suit. "They've got the trinkets!"

They did indeed have the trinkets. The audience crowded the merchandise counters so thickly that the ushers had to scream at them to keep moving.

The theatergoers who attend first previews tend to be boisterous. "They're the people who have the date circled in blood on their calendars," Tommy told the cast. But the reaction that night surprised even him. The audience screamed when Lac's curly hair appeared at the conductor's stand. They screamed again when the house lights dimmed, and screamed some more when Leslie sauntered onstage to begin the opening number. When Lin made his first entrance, the roar stopped the song for 18 seconds.

The show felt like it lasted six hours that night. After the cuts during rehearsals, it was tighter, sharper, and a few minutes shorter than it had been at the Public, but the peaks and valleys of the audience's reaction still made it an ordeal for the cast. When it ended, they

congregated onstage as if they'd just survived something. Jasmine was crying; Renée looked dazed. A career in noisy rap clubs hadn't prepared Daveed for what he'd been through: "I heard 'H—' and then nothing. My computer overloaded." He had spent the first three numbers wondering if he would be able to finish the

"When I was singing, 'I'm not throwing away my shot,' I COULD'VE EXPLODED—I felt like a bomb inside me just went off that day."

show. Pippa said she was so scared during the opening song that "I was drinking my own tears."

The next day (and every other day throughout previews), Tommy held a company meeting in the empty theater. Rookies and veterans alike talked about the overwhelming energy they had felt the night before. The most emotional response came from Anthony Ramos.

"Nobody's ever done that before," he said, gesturing toward the stage. "We gotta rise up. We gotta fuckin' do it." He got a little choked up. "I don't know about y'all, but it's been a long to road to get here. A long road."

At 24, Anthony is the youngest person in the cast. You might expect his more experienced castmates to scoff at what he said. In fact, they were moved: Groff would later call this "the day Anthony had everybody in tears."

ABOVE:
Tommy Kail and the company at the Richard Rodgers Theatre.

Anthony hadn't spent as much time getting to Broadway as other people, but his road might have been the hardest.

Anthony grew up in a housing project in Bushwick, a rough part of Brooklyn, where he played baseball and sang with his friends. In high school, he auditioned for the school talent show, realizing only after he had been chosen to play the lead that he had actually tried out for the school *musical*. He liked it enough to want to keep performing, but paying for training was out of the question. When he got into the American Musical and Dramatic Academy, Sara Steinweiss, a staff member at his high school—"an angel in my life," Anthony says—got him an interview with the Jerry Seinfeld Scholarship Program. "I actually said, 'All I need is one shot. All I need is someone to believe in me. And I won't let you down. My grades are not a reflection of who I am.'" He got the scholarship.

"SEE I NEVER THOUGHT I'D LIVE PAST TWENTY . . . *That's how a lot of people in my neighborhood think. A lot of them didn't live past 21.*"

After AMDA, he pieced together gigs, went to open auditions, and struggled: When Lin and Tommy called him back again and again but decided not to cast him for a tour of *In the Heights*, he was crushed. Three years later, he still didn't have an agent or manager. But a casting agent who saw him audition for a different show suggested that he try out for *Hamilton*.

"In the final callback, I was doing 'My Shot,' and I wasn't acting," Anthony says. "When I was singing, 'I'm not throwing away my shot,' I could've exploded—I felt like a bomb inside me just went off that day."

He learned that he had been cast as John Laurens and Philip Hamilton, two fortunate sons who died tragically young in gunfights. Anthony can relate to that. When he first heard Lin rap, "See I never thought I'd live past twenty," it reminded him of home. "That's how a lot of people in my neighborhood think. A lot of them didn't live past 21." Tommy watched Anthony imbue both of his characters with "an awareness of the randomness of who gets out and who doesn't. He's seen a lot of things that he wishes he hadn't seen."

Anthony's mix of gentleness and persistence lends

force to "Blow Us All Away" and "Stay Alive," a pair of songs that routinely wreck the audience. Philip challenges one of his father's critics to a duel, even though he doesn't know how to fight, and doesn't want to. "I've fought for things in life," Anthony says. "I learned how to grind and hustle, but I was never a kid who was ready to fight all the time, you know what I'm saying?"

His preparation for those scenes is pretty simple: He imagines how he would feel in that situation. He thinks of how scared he would be to look around and see no way out. It's easy to do.

◆

FOUR DAYS AFTER ANTHONY SPOKE AT the company meeting, the hurricane hit again, but stronger. On the afternoon of Saturday, July 18, the block was barricaded at both ends. When the house lights dimmed, President Obama walked into the theater. Everybody cheered; dozens of cameras flashed.

At intermission, the fire curtain rolled down, dividing the audience from the stage. The company assembled on the set and the president walked out to greet them.

"It's really good!" Obama said. "Sometimes it takes a while until people know something is good. Here, people know."

After a big group photo, Obama said hello to Lin's dad and kissed Lin's mom on the cheek. He beamed when he looked up and saw Rocco Landesman, who had run the National Endowment for the Arts in Obama's first term.

"You're not running out the clock," said Rocco.

"No, man. I've got things to do," the president replied. Then, loud enough for the whole company to hear, he said: "I've got to take my shot."

On his way offstage, the president shook hands with Lin and said, "I'm proud of you, man." (In a gesture of self-restraint, Lin had stuck to the performance calendar they had announced before learning that President Obama was coming, the one that said Javier Muñoz would play Hamilton that afternoon.)

Before disappearing into the wings, President Obama veered a half-step out of his way so he could grab one more hand.

"You're really gifted," he told Anthony Ramos.

PREVIOUS PAGE:
A #Ham4Ham performance by Lin-Manuel Miranda and Jonathan Groff.

BLOW US ALL AWAY[1]

◆

Philip Hamilton enters, now nineteen years old.

PHILIP: Meet the latest graduate of King's
    College!
I prob'ly shouldn't brag but dag I amaze
    and astonish!
The scholars say I got the same virtuosity
    and brains as my pops!
The ladies say my brain's not where the
    resemblance stops!
I'm only nineteen but my mind is older,
Gotta be my own man, like my father
    but bolder.
I shoulder his legacy with pride,
I used to hear him say
That someday
I would—

ENSEMBLE: Blow us all away.

*Philip approaches two young women, Martha
& Dolly.*

PHILIP: Ladies, I'm lookin' for a Mr. George
    Eacker.
Made a speech last week, our Fourth of July
    speaker.
He disparaged my father's legacy in front of
    a crowd.
I can't have that, I'm making my father proud.

MARTHA: I saw him just up Broadway a couple
    of blocks.
He was goin' to see a play.

PHILIP: Well, I'll go visit his box.

DOLLY: God, you're a fox.

PHILIP: And y'all look pretty good in ya frocks.
How 'bout when I get back, we all strip down to
    our socks?[2]

BOTH: OK!

Philip struts.

RECORDING: Blo- blo- blo-

COMPANY: Blow us all away!

*The theater. George Eacker with a friend in
the balcony. Philip enters behind him.[3]*

PHILIP: George!

GEORGE: Shh.

PHILIP: George!

GEORGE: Shh! I'm tryin' to watch the show!

PHILIP: Ya shoulda watched your mouth before
you talked about my father though!

GEORGE: I didn't say anything that wasn't true.
You father's a scoundrel, and so, it seems,
    are you.

ENSEMBLE: Ooooooooooh!

PHILIP: It's like that?

GEORGE: Yeah, I don't fool around.
I'm not your little schoolboy friends.

PHILIP: See you on the dueling ground.
That is, unless you wanna step outside and
    go now.

[1] This song was originally called "Ya Boy Is Killin' Em"—a hip-hop-inspired title that felt too on the nose. The beat was the same, though. This is the brightest, happiest music in the show—happy flutes and rock basslines—but all slightly dissonant. I'm trying to ratchet up tension and contrast for what will follow.

[2] I always thought of this scene as the talk between Salt-N-Pepa in the song "Shoop:" *"And he's coming this way Oooohhh!"*

[3] The name of the play George Eacker was watching: *The West Indian.* Given Hamilton's origin in the West Indies, it's too good not to mention.

GEORGE: I know where to find you, piss off.
I'm watchin' this show now.

The scene shifts. Hamilton enters.

PHILIP: Pops, if you had only heard the shit he
    said about you
I doubt you would have let it slide and I was not
    about to—

HAMILTON: Slow down.

PHILIP: I came to ask you for advice: This is
    my very first duel.
They don't exactly cover this subject in boarding
    school.

HAMILTON: Did your friends attempt to
negotiate a peace?

PHILIP: He refused to apologize, we had to let
the peace talks cease.

HAMILTON: Where is this happening?

PHILIP: Across the river, in Jersey.

HAMILTON, PHILIP: Everything is legal in
New Jersey . . .

HAMILTON: Alright. So this is what you're
    gonna do.
Stand there like a man until Eacker is in front
    of you.
When the time comes, fire your weapon in the
    air.
This will put an end to the whole affair. 4

PHILIP: But what if he decides to shoot? Then
I'm a goner.

HAMILTON: No. He'll follow suit if he's truly a
    man of honor.
To take someone's life, that is something you
    can't shake.

4 This was an actual
technique in dueling
called the "delope." It
allowed for everyone to
show up and prove they
were men, and go home
alive.

5 To go back to Philip's
nine-year-old rap here is
almost cruel of me, but
God it's effective.

Philip, your mother can't take another
    heartbreak.

PHILIP: Father—

HAMILTON: Promise me. You don't want this
Young man's blood on your conscience.

PHILIP: Okay, I promise.

HAMILTON: Come back home when you're
    done.
Take my guns. Be smart. Make me proud, son.

Hamilton hands his guns to Philip and exits.

PHILIP: My name is Philip
I am a poet 5
And I'm a little nervous, but I can't show it.
I'm sorry, I'm a Hamilton with pride.
You talk about my father, I cannot let it slide.

Philip & George face off.

PHILIP: Mr. Eacker! How was the rest of your
show?

GEORGE: I'd rather skip the pleasantries.
Let's go.
Grab your pistol.

PHILIP: Confer with your men.
The duel will commence after we count to ten.

ENSEMBLE: Count to ten!

PHILIP: Look 'im in the eye, aim no higher.
Summon all the courage you require.
Then slowly and clearly aim your gun towards
    the sky—

MEN: One two three four

ENSEMBLE: Five six seven—

Eacker fires early. Philip goes down.

STAY ALIVE

(REPRISE)

———— ◆ ————

The scene changes, as Philip's body is pulled away. We segue to a doctor's house. Hamilton bursts in.[1]

**ENSEMBLE
WOMEN:**
Stay alive . . .

                                HAMILTON:
Stay alive . . .   Where's my son?

DOCTOR: Mr. Hamilton, come in.
They brought him in a half an hour ago.
He lost a lot of blood on the way over.

**ENSEMBLE
WOMEN:**   **HAMILTON:**
Stay alive . . .   Is he alive?

DOCTOR: Yes. But you have to understand
The bullet entered just above his hip and lodged
      in his right arm.

HAMILTON: Can I see him please?

DOCTOR: I'm doing ev'rything I can but the
wound was already infected when he arrived—

They enter the room. Philip is in agony on the table.

HAMILTON: Philip.

PHILIP: Pa.

Hamilton rushes over to his bedside and kisses his forehead.

[1] As a new father, this is the hardest scene to play every night. Not even what's about to follow, but the frenzy of not knowing.

PHILIP: I did exactly as you said, Pa.
I held my head up high.

HAMILTON:
I know, I know. Shh.   **PHILIP:**
I know, I know.   High.
Shh. I know you did
ev'rything just right.
                         Even before we got to ten—
Shh.
                         I was aiming for the sky.
I know, I know. Shh.
I know, I know.
I know,   I was aiming for the sky.

Save your strength
and
Stay alive . . .

ENSEMBLE MEN:
Stay alive . . .

Eliza enters.

ELIZA: No!

HAMILTON: Eliza.

ELIZA:
Is he breathing? Is he going to survive this?

ENSEMBLE MEN:
Stay alive . . .

ELIZA: Who did this, Alexander, did you know?

PHILIP: Mom, I'm so sorry for forgetting what you taught me.

ELIZA: My son—

PHILIP: We played piano.

ELIZA: I taught you piano.

PHILIP: You would put your hands on mine.

ELIZA: You changed the melody every time.[2]

PHILIP: Ha. I would always change the line.

ELIZA: Shh. I know, I know.

PHILIP: I would always change the line.

ELIZA: I know, I know.

Eliza sings with Philip.

ELIZA:
Un deux trois
quatre
Cinq six sept huit
neuf.

PHILIP:
Un deux trois quatre

Cinq six sept huit
neuf.

Good.

Un deux trois quatre
Cinq six sept   Un deux trois . . .
Huit neuf.
Sept huit neuf–
Sept huit . . .

Philip dies. The music takes over.

[2] This is why I never got good at piano—I was always changing the written melodies. This is tough to get through every night.

A   GRIEVING   CHAPTER :

ON LOSSES
BEYOND WORDS

THERE ARE NEARLY 24,000 WORDS IN *HAMILTON*. THAT IS A lot of words. It is more than than an audience hears in a performance of *The Merchant of Venice, Richard II*, or T*he Taming of the Shrew*. It is significantly more than in *Macbeth*. Alexander Hamilton speaks, sings, and raps more words in the course of a show than King Lear does.

Hamlet dwarfs *Hamilton*—it dwarfs pretty much everything—but there's a revealing similarity between them. Shakespeare's longest play leaves its audience in the dark about some basic and seemingly crucial facts. It's not as if the Bard forgot, in the course of all those words, to tell us whether Hamlet was crazy or only pretending: He *wanted* us to wonder. He forces us to work on a puzzle that has no definite answer. And this mysteriousness is one reason why we find the play irresistible.

Hamilton is riddled with question marks. The first act begins with a question, and so does the second. The entire relationship between Hamilton and Burr is based on a mutual and explicit lack of comprehension: "I will never understand you," says Hamilton, and Burr wonders, "What is it like in his shoes?"

"Actors cried while singing it, the production team cried while listening to it, Andy couldn't bear to choreograph it."

Again and again, Lin distinguishes characters by what they wish they knew. "What'd I miss?" asks Jefferson in the song that introduces him. "Would that be enough?" asks Eliza in the song that defines her. "Why do you write like you're running out of time?" asks everybody in a song that marvels at Hamilton's drive, and all but declares that there's no way to explain it. *Hamilton*, like *Hamlet*, gives an audience the chance to watch a bunch of conspicuously intelligent and well-spoken characters fill the stage with *words words words*, only to discover, again and again, the limits to what they can comprehend.

CHAPTER XXVIII

The idea that some things lie beyond even the most articulate expression is the subject of "It's Quiet Uptown." Lin wrote the song in part to solve a problem. A workshop in January 2014 had ended with "Burn." At a notes session in the Public's conference room afterwards, everybody laughed at how he seemed to have written himself into a corner: How would an audience believe a reconciliation between Alexander and Eliza after hearing her sing "I hope you burn"?

Even more daunting than patching up their marriage, Lin would need to dramatize their grief over their son Philip's death. Unlike the boyish camaraderie that he could recall for "The Story Tonight" or the relentlessness that he depicted in "Non-Stop," the overwhelming sorrow of losing a child is something he had never felt firsthand. "I can't know what this is," he remembers feeling.

"The song is loss, and then it's being able to forgive the loss . . . There's some kind of magic in that, too."

He sequestered himself in a quiet corner of the Public, composing music, scribbling verses, occasionally wandering the halls. The staff got used to seeing him pacing in his slippers. One day he realized that his inability to grasp the enormity of Alexander and Eliza's loss wasn't a barrier to writing the song, it *was* the song.

"Once I got the line, 'There are moments that the words don't reach,' I had the song," he says. He wrote it in a day.

The power of "It's Quiet Uptown" was intact from its first day: Actors cried while singing it, the production team cried while listening to it, Andy couldn't bear to choreograph it, not with his daughter, Sofia, fighting cancer, and getting sick on the way to school, and the whole family hoping the next round of chemotherapy would work.

The most affecting part of the song, curiously enough, always tended to be its one consoling moment: Alexander and Eliza's reconciliation, which turns out to be more convincing than anyone dreamed possible that day in the conference room.

Lin credits Lac's orchestration with the moment's beauty. The music moves down, down, down for much of the song, creating what Lin calls a "hypnotizing" effect. Then, a moment before the reconciliation, the band plays Lac's quick, bright upward flourish. (If you want to be technical about it, they play the song's root chord with an added ninth tone—the sound of yearning, of seeking release.) When the full company sings the word "Forgiveness"—men higher than the women, voices blending to form the song's root chord—you don't need to understand a word of English, or a bit of music theory, to grasp that Alexander and Eliza have found their way home.

"The song is loss, and then it's being able to forgive the loss," says Lin. "There's some kind of magic in that, too."

THE MYSTERY OF WHAT LIES BEYOND WORDS, THE UNFATHOMABLE action of grief, are things that everyone associated with *Hamilton* reckoned with, and not just because the show explores them. On November 16, 2014, Oskar and Laurie Eustis's beloved son, Jack, died. He was 16 years old.

The shock of the news, the enormity of the loss, left family, friends, colleagues, and the *Hamilton* company devastated and bewildered. Everyone thought, first, of what could be done to help the Eustis family, to ease even slightly the pain they were feeling. Everyone thought, second, about a cruel coincidence of the schedule. Dance rehearsals were set to begin the very next day, which meant that Oskar and Laurie were about to spend half a year or more in the world of a show that pivots on the loss of a child. "It's Quiet Uptown" had been wrecking people who *weren't* grappling with the death of an only son. What would it do to people who were?

Two weeks later, the full company assembled for the first sing-through of the show. The actors stood at music stands. Lac presided at the piano. Tommy, Andy, Jeffrey, Jill, and a few members of the Public staff were situating themselves in folding chairs when

---

"The mystery of what lies beyond words, the unfathomable action of grief, are things that everyone associated with Hamilton *reckoned with, and not just because the show explores them."*

Oskar and Laurie walked in. Only a few of the people in the room had seen them since Jack's death, so there were greetings, hugs, condolences. Hearing "It's Quiet Uptown" for the first time since their unimaginable loss was bound to be wrenching. It *was* wrenching, for everyone. When the sing-through ended, we offered words of consolation that were heartfelt but inadequate before a grief larger than anyone could comprehend.

There was one thing that the *Hamilton* company didn't know that day. When Lin had learned of Jack's death, he had sent an email to Oskar and Laurie expressing his deepest condolences. He also sent the demo recording of "It's Quiet Uptown."

"If art can help us grieve, can help us mourn, then lean on it," he wrote. If they preferred to delete the song, he would understand.

Oskar and Laurie did lean on it. In the rehearsal studio that afternoon, nobody knew that "It's Quiet Uptown" was the only song they had listened to in their first week of mourning. They had listened to it every day.

IT'S QUIET UPTOWN

ANGELICA: There are moments that the words
    don't reach.
There is suffering too terrible to name.
You hold your child as tight as you can
And push away the unimaginable.
The moments when you're in so deep
It feels easier to just swim down.

ANGELICA, ENSEMBLE: The Hamiltons move
    uptown
And learn to live with the unimaginable.

HAMILTON: I spend hours in the garden.
I walk alone to the store.
And it's quiet uptown.
I never liked the quiet before.
I take the children to church on Sunday.
A sign of the cross at the door.
And I pray.
That never used to happen before.

ANGELICA, WOMEN: If you see him in the
    street, walking by himself, talking to
    himself.
Have pity.

HAMILTON: Philip, you would like it uptown.
It's quiet uptown.

ANGELICA, WOMEN: He is working through
the unimaginable.

ALL MEN (EXCEPT HAMILTON): His hair
has gone grey. He passes every day. They say he
walks the length of the city.

HAMILTON: You knock me out, I fall apart.

**COMPANY (EXCEPT HAMILTON AND
ELIZA):** Can you imagine?

Eliza enters.

HAMILTON: Look at where we are.
Look at where we started.
I know I don't deserve you, Eliza.
But hear me out. That would be enough.

If I could spare his life
If I could trade his life for mine,
He'd be standing here right now
And you would smile, and that would be enough.
I don't pretend to know
The challenges we're facing.
I know there's no replacing what we've lost and
    you need time.
But I'm not afraid.
I know who I married.
Just let me stay here by your side,
That would be enough.

**COMPANY (EXCEPT HAMILTON AND
ELIZA):** If you see him in the street, walking by
her side, talking by her side, have pity.

HAMILTON: Eliza, do you like it uptown? It's
quiet uptown.

**COMPANY (EXCEPT HAMILTON AND
ELIZA):** He is trying to do the unimaginable.
See them walking in the park, long after dark,
    taking in the sights of the city.

HAMILTON: Look around, look around, Eliza.

**COMPANY (EXCEPT HAMILTON AND
ELIZA):** They are trying to do the unimaginable.

ANGELICA: There are moments that the words
    don't reach.
There is a grace too powerful to name.

We push away what we can never understand,
We push away the unimaginable.

Hamilton & Eliza stand side by side.

ANGELICA: They are standing in the garden,
Alexander by Eliza's side.
She takes his hand.

Eliza takes Hamilton's hand.

ELIZA: It's quiet uptown.

Hamilton shatters.

**COMPANY (EXCEPT HAMILTON AND
ELIZA):** Forgiveness. Can you imagine?

Forgiveness. Can you imagine?
If you see him in the street, walking by her side,
    talking by her side, have pity.
They are going through the unimaginable.

XXIX

CONTAINING A DIALOGUE ON

AMBITION

AND SOME TOPICAL COMMENTS,

from

DAVID BROOKS *&* CHRISTOPHER HAYES

---

*I*T SOUNDS LIKE SOMETHING LIN COOKED up for dramatic purposes, but it really happened this way.

In 1800, Thomas Jefferson ran for president with Aaron Burr as his de facto running mate. It was "de facto," because the screwy electoral system of the era didn't allow candidates to run as a ticket. Jefferson anticipated that he would win the most electoral votes, and Burr would come in second, which would make them president and vice president, respectively.

Instead, the two men tied, and Burr, discovering that he'd like to be president after all, declined to step aside. The Federalists who controlled the House of Representatives now got to pick the winner. Just as Lin dramatizes, they sought Hamilton's advice about which man to elevate: Jefferson, whom Hamilton had called "an Atheist in Religion and a Fanatic in politics," or Burr, the embodiment of "a daring and unprincipled ambition"?

"Politically, if I were Hamilton, and I have a choice between a guy who doesn't really believe anything and a guy who believes the opposite of what I believe, the smart thing is to go with the guy who doesn't believe anything," says David Brooks, the best-selling author and *New York Times* columnist.

"You can talk to that guy. You can work him over," agrees Chris Hayes, the host of MSNBC's *All In with Chris Hayes.*

"It's not going to be *that* bad," says Brooks, and they both laugh.

Hayes is among the country's leading liberals and Brooks is among its leading conservatives: Both of them have a special relationship to *Hamilton.* Brooks had seen an early performance at the Public, and written a glowing column that lifted the show off the arts pages and into the political conversation. Hayes has known Lin since they were teenagers, when they did plays together at Hunter College High School. (Hayes remembers Lin as "just this classic fricking generative compulsive genius who makes stuff, presents it to the world, makes more stuff, and is constantly full of schemes and projects." They are good friends.)

"But, of course, Hamilton was not just a political officeholder," continues Brooks. "He was a believer in virtue. He had an ethical system."

"I find that really resonates for me," says Hayes. "My grandfather was a right-wing conservative Catholic, someone who went to Mass every day, and hated, *hated* communism. But I still feel like I'm his inheritor, because he really believed in something. As a reporter I often feel closer to people who feel strongly about things on the opposite side from me than people who don't care. So that section of the show is super-believable. I would have voted for Jefferson."

I had invited Hayes and Brooks to see *Hamilton* again during its Broadway previews, then share a dinner, in hopes that they could unravel a mystery. In 1800, enough politicians took their cues from Alexander Hamilton that he might have swayed the outcome of a presidential election. But look around Capitol Hill today: Where are the Hamilton devotees in government now?

"My view is that Hamiltonians existed until Teddy Roosevelt," says Brooks. "Hamilton used limited but energetic government to create mobility, but after Roosevelt, the debate became big government versus small government, so the Hamilton tradition got caught cross-ways."

Neither party has room for him now, Brooks believes. Republicans have become allergic to government, and can't see what Hamilton saw: that government can let more people into the system, and help capitalism solve the structural problems it is facing. But Democrats balk at embracing somebody whose programs would create more opportunity for gifted upstarts at the expense of creating more misery for the people who can't excel.

"Hamilton said that if we have to make life harder for people who can't hack it, we're going to do that," says Brooks. "The goal is greatness."

"The goal is greatness, but he says that as someone who is a world-historical genius," says Hayes. "I have a certain deep affection for the brilliant outer-borough striver, but I also recognize the limitations of that structure. My visceral emotional reaction is in favor of that system, but my intellectual bearings are that that's not a way to run a society."

"I would have thought it's the other way around," I say. "Your head would say, 'Strive, that's how you get greatness,' and your heart would say, 'But a lot of people will be left behind.'"

"My heart is with the outer-borough strivers because that's the world I lived in, and so did Lin," says Hayes. "He is from Inwood. I am from the Bronx. We bonded over two things: We both loved theater, and we took the express bus together. We were both sort of outsiders. Everything about that play we just saw is about an outer-borough striver, and I get it in *my goddamn blood cells*. When I saw it for the first time, I told him, 'You have managed to channel something in history that is our shared experience of this world, where we were getting on that bus every day, and we put our armor on, and said *we're gonna slay*.' I didn't think of it in those terms then. I thought of it as going to Manhattan and being very lucky. But that metabolism as an outer-borough striver is so central to who I am, and who Lin is, and how we grew up. And that play is a masterpiece of its expression."

"That resonates for me," says Brooks. "I was raised by my grandfather, who grew up on the Lower East Side, and then in the Bronx. His father came from Russia. He would say, 'You want to make it in the city.' That meant Manhattan—Midtown, the Upper East Side. In college, I had pictures of Madison Avenue in my dorm room. Now it seems pathetic, but that was the dream, that was Mecca—to make it in the city."

The real conflict in *Hamilton*, Brooks and Hayes agree, lies deeper than political disputes of the past or present. "More than anything, the show is about Hamilton and Burr, and their styles of ambition," says Hayes. "How do you get to the top, and what's the most American way to do that?"

"Are you the operator or the crusader?" asks Brooks. "Every single person walks out of the theater thinking about Hamilton and saying, 'I want to have *that* kind of ambition.'"

"Right," says Hayes.

"Which is sort of deeply American. And that's why the show is universal. Because everyone wonders, *Are my dreams big enough? Am I really making the most out of my life?*"

	Thomas Jefferson of Virginia	Aaron Burr of New York	John Adams of Massachusetts	Charles Cotesworth Pinckney of South Carolina	John Jay of New York
New Hampshire			6	6	
Massachusetts			16	16	
Rhode Island			4	3	1
Connecticut			9	9	
Vermont			4	4	
New York	12	12			
New Jersey			7	7	
Pennsylvania	8	8	7	7	
Delaware			3	3	
Maryland	5	5	5	5	
Virginia	21	21			
Kentucky	4	4			
North Carolina	8	8	4	4	
Tennessee	3	3			
South Carolina	8	8			
Georgia	4	4			
	73	73	65	64	1

ABOVE:
Tally of electoral votes for the presidential election of 1800.

The ELECTION OF 1800

—◆—

COMPANY: The election of eighteen hundred.

Jefferson & Madison enter.

JEFFERSON: Can we get back to politics?[1]

MADISON: Please?

[1] There are so many emotional extremes in this show—it's great when you find the line that does the job just so. This is one of those lines.

JEFFERSON: Yo. Ev'ry action has an equal,
    opposite reaction.
John Adams shat the bed. I love the guy,
    but he's in traction.
Poor Alexander Hamilton? He is missing
    in action.
So now I'm facing—

JEFFERSON, MADISON: Aaron Burr!

JEFFERSON: With his own faction.

MADISON: He's very attractive in the North.
New Yorkers like his chances.

[2] And now Burr's initial advice to Hamilton is our nation's first campaign slogan, in our telling. It's fun to play with how familiar Burr is in his shamelessness here. You can *feel* the audience relaxing, as if to say, "Now *this* looks like our era."

JEFFERSON: He's not very forthcoming on any
particular stances.

MADISON: Ask him a question: It glances off,
he obfuscates, he dances.

JEFFERSON: And they say I'm a francophile:
At least they know I know where France is!

MADISON: Thomas, that's the problem, see,
they see Burr as a less extreme you.

JEFFERSON: Ha!

MADISON: You need to change course, a key
endorsement might redeem you.

JEFFERSON: Who did you have in mind?

MADISON: Don't laugh.

JEFFERSON: Who is it?

MADISON: You used to work on the same staff.

JEFFERSON: Whaaaat.

MADISON: It might be nice. It might be nice.
To get Hamilton on your side.

JEFFERSON, MADISON: It might be nice.
    It might be nice.
To get Hamilton on your side.

Burr campaigns in earnest.

BURR:	ENSEMBLE:
Talk less!	
	Burr!
Smile more!	
	Burr!
Don't let 'em know what you're against or what you're for![2]	
	Burr!
Shake hands with him!	
	Burr!
Charm her!	
	Burr!
It's eighteen hundred, ladies, tell your husbands: Vote for—Burr!	Burr!

CHAPTER XXIX

MALE VOTER: I don't like Adams.

FEMALE VOTER: Well, he's gonna lose, that's just defeatist.

ANOTHER MALE VOTER: And Jefferson—

TWO MEN: In love with France!

ANOTHER FEMALE VOTER: Yea, he's so elitist!

TWO WOMEN: I like that Aaron Burr!

A WOMAN: I can't believe we're here with him!

A MAN: He seems approachable?

ANOTHER MALE VOTER: Like you could grab a beer with him! [3]

ENSEMBLE: Dear Mr. Hamilton: Your fellow Fed'ralists would like to know how you'll be voting.

HAMILTON: It's quiet uptown.

ENSEMBLE: Dear Mr. Hamilton: John Adams doesn't stand a chance so who are you promoting?

HAMILTON:
It's quiet uptown.

MEN	WOMEN:
Jefferson or Burr?	Jefferson or Burr?
We know it's lose-lose	We know it's lose-lose.
Jefferson or Burr?	Jefferson or Burr?
But if you had to choose.	But if you had to choose.

EVEN MORE

VOTERS:	MEN	
Dear Mr. Hamilton:	Jefferson or Burr?	
		WOMEN:
		Jefferson or Burr?

John Adams doesn't stand a chance so who are you promoting?	We know it's lose-lose	We know it's lose-lose
	Jefferson or Burr?	Jefferson or Burr?
But if you had to choose.	But if you had to choose.	But if you had to choose.

Burr appears.

HAMILTON: Well, if it isn't Aaron Burr. Sir!

BURR: Alexander!

HAMILTON: You've created quite a stir, sir!

BURR: I'm going door to door!

HAMILTON: You're openly campaigning?

BURR: Sure!

HAMILTON: That's new.

BURR: Honestly, it's kind of draining.

HAMILTON: Burr—

BURR: Sir!

HAMILTON: Is there anything you wouldn't do?

BURR: No. I'm chasing what I want. And you know what?

HAMILTON: What?

BURR: I learned that from you. [4]

ENSEMBLE: If you had to choose
If you had to choose

MADISON: It's a tie!

[3] For a bizarre period in our contemporary history, this actually mattered to voters.

[4] And Burr's transformation is complete. He has thrown caution to the wind. It's fun playing Hamilton's reaction to this every night: This never happened, historically, but what would he have made of it?

ENSEMBLE: If you had to choose
If you had to choose

JEFFERSON: It's up to the delegates!

ENSEMBLE: If you had to choose
If you had to choose

JEFFERSON, MADISON: It's up to Hamilton!

VOTERS:	MADISON,	ENSEMBLE:
If you had to choose,	ENSEMBLE:	
If you had to choose,	Jefferson or Burr?	
If you had to		Jefferson or Burr?
choose,	Choose,	Choose,
choose,	choose,	choose,
choose!	choose!	choose!

5 This used to read, "And if you were to ask me who I'd prefer—don't vote Burr." I changed it because I thought "prefer" might tip my hand to the decision, so I ended the line with a word that didn't rhyme with either last name.

Hamilton steps forward.

HAMILTON: Yo.

ENSEMBLE: Oh!

HAMILTON: The people are asking to hear my voice.

ENSEMBLE: Oh!

HAMILTON: For the country is facing a difficult choice.

ENSEMBLE: Oh!

HAMILTON: And if you were to ask me who I'd promote—5

ENSEMBLE: Oh!

HAMILTON: Jefferson has my vote.

JEFFERSON, MADISON, ENSEMBLE: Oh!

HAMILTON: I have never agreed with Jefferson once.

JEFFERSON, MADISON, ENSEMBLE: Oh!

HAMILTON: We have fought on like seventy-five diff'rent fronts.

JEFFERSON, MADISON, ENSEMBLE: Oh!

HAMILTON: But when all is said and all is done. Jefferson has beliefs. Burr has none.

ENSEMBLE: Oooooooooooooh.

Madison & Jefferson exchange a glance, as the company hurries away.

MADISON, JEFFERSON: Well, I'll be damned. Well, I'll be damned.

MADISON: Hamilton's on your side.

ENSEMBLE: Well, I'll be damned. Well, I'll be damned.

JEFFERSON: And?

MADISON: You won in a landslide.

Burr enters.

BURR: Congrats on a race well-run. I did give you a fight.

JEFFERSON: Uh-huh.

BURR: I look forward to our partnership.

JEFFERSON: Our partnership?

BURR: As your vice president.

JEFFERSON: Ha. Yeah, right.

You hear this guy? Man openly campaigns against me, talkin' 'bout, "I look forward to our partnership."

MADISON: It's crazy that the guy who comes in second becomes vice president.

JEFFERSON: Yeah, you know what? We can change that. You know why?

MADISON: Why?

JEFFERSON: Cuz I'm the President. Burr, when you see Hamilton, thank him for the endorsement.

Jefferson exits with Madison. Burr is alone.

XXX

FURTHER THOUGHTS ON

AMBITION

as It Pertains to

THE PLAYWRIGHT *and*

THE ENIGMATIC BURR

L IN THE ACTOR STOOD STILL, BUT Lin the Writer kept moving. One afternoon in July, he was holding a position on the walkway above the stage, hands on the railing. Howell Binkley needed to see him standing up there to adjust a lighting look. As Lin waited, he got an idea: a more compelling way for Burr to introduce Hamilton's pamphlet about John Adams.

Lin called to Leslie, who was standing in his own pool of light downstage right, and proposed the new line. Leslie tried it a couple of times and liked it. Lac popped his head out of the orchestra pit, and Lin explained it again. Lac liked it too. The change was formally incorporated just as Howell finished his cue.

"Lin, you can relax," somebody shouted from the audience.

"No," he said, "I can't."

Even after previews began, and President Obama came through, work on the show continued. The company rehearsed in the afternoons and performed at night. Those were long days for the actors, especially for the one trying to finish revising the script. As other items got crossed off the to-do list and the company drew nearer and nearer to press performances (the traditional deadline for making changes to a show), Lin had one more big puzzle to finish: how to dramatize the final confrontation between Hamilton and Burr.

"The white whale," Tommy calls their duel: elusive, monstrous, unknowable. It was the last part of the show that clicked into place.

Lin and Tommy had known from the start that for any treatment of the duel to be dramatically satisfying, Burr had to seem like a worthy adversary. That meant they needed to understand Burr and his motivations, which

---

"Leslie's VERY SMOOTH, but he's CAPABLE OF REAL FEROCITY."

---

was no easy task. Before history labeled him a villain, he was an enigma, a man who puzzled even his associates. "He is a grave, silent, strange sort of animal, insomuch that we know not what to make of him," wrote one contemporary. Actually, that was written by Aaron Burr, describing himself in the third person.

The aspect of Burr's persona that seemed most difficult to convey had come the most easily: his strange magnetism. Onstage and off, Leslie was soft-spoken, self-contained, charismatic. Even his dressing room was perfectly appointed. But Lin could see something beneath the savoir faire of the actor who castmates had nicknamed "Silky": "Leslie's very smooth, but he's capable of real ferocity," he says.

Leslie says he spent his early adulthood driving away the impulse to lose his cool; his serenity only *seemed* effortless. The two years he had spent mastering Lin's songs and Andy's choreography had also been spent learning how to unleash his anger onstage—and to enjoy it. In pre-Broadway rehearsals, Tommy worked with him on sharpening and simplifying what he did, finding small gestures that would have a large impact. This required plenty of trust between actor and director. "You have to hope you're not whittling it to nothing, or turning the volume down to a whisper for the whole show," Leslie says.

"I feel like I HAVE BEEN BURR IN MY LIFE as many times AS I HAVE BEEN HAMILTON."

In fact, when Leslie began performing at the Rodgers, his depiction of Burr deepened and grew. He started to seem like Michael Corleone: a man whose power is intimidating precisely because it is held in check, one who doesn't need to raise his voice to convey the emotions churning within. The wider the contrast between Lin's volubility and Leslie's restraint became, the more excited Lin got about finding ways to exploit its power.

In real life, the fatal animosity between Hamilton and Burr revealed itself in a series of letters in the summer of 1804. Burr, furious about a life of personal insults and political opposition, demanded that Hamilton explain the report that he had made a "despicable" reference to him at

a recent dinner. Lin set Burr's peremptory challenge and Hamilton's condescending replies to music in "Your Obedient Servant." In the downtown version of the song, he and Leslie had sniped at each other in a quick waltz tempo, a musical counterpart to the bizarre formality of vitriolic letters that ended with "Your obedient servant." Lin rewrote the song for Broadway. He cut Burr's tempo in half, he made room for silence. At the Rodgers, Leslie delivered his side of the exchange at a writing desk, still as a cobra.

Burr looked and sounded ready to kill, but he didn't seem like a cliché villain of melodrama. In the show, as in real life, Hamilton really had insulted him, giving him legitimate grounds for fury. Leslie won praise for humanizing Burr, and was gracious about sharing it. "Lin got inside his head first," he says. "He saw Burr with love and compassion first."

Lin's identification with Burr mystified some people close to the show. His depiction of Hamilton's killer was more generous than virtually any other writer's. Even Gore Vidal's novel about Burr, which takes a remarkably friendly view of its hero's schemes, finds room to call him "a monster," "a labyrinth," "the slyest trickster of our time," and a man who "makes even a trip to the barber seem like a plot to overthrow the state." At various points during the development of *Hamilton*, people wondered if Lin might be overshooting the mark, and making Burr *too* sympathetic.

Lin hinted at an explanation in a profile for *The New Yorker*, when he told Rebecca Mead that he identified with Hamilton but had "equal affinity" with his killer: "I feel like I have been Burr in my life as many times as I have been Hamilton. I think we've all had moments where we've seen friends and colleagues zoom past us, either to success, or to marriage, or to home-ownership, while we lingered where we were—broke, single, jobless. And you tell yourself, 'Wait for it.'"

You don't expect to hear that kind of frustration from somebody who won a Tony at 28—an artist regarded as a valued collaborator by Stephen Sondheim, an esteemed fellow craftsman by John Kander, a respected fellow MC by Black Thought and Talib Kweli, a happy husband and father.

"Why do you identify with Burr so much?"

The question (asked over coffee, a few weeks before Broadway opening night) takes Lin back to his school days. "Hunter is a very 'Whadju get?' place," he says. He looks into my mug as if it were a freshly graded paper. *"Whadju get? Whadju get?"* He remembers when a friend

---

ABOVE:
Illustration of the duel between Alexander Hamilton and Aaron Burr.

264

1. The parties will leave town tomorrow morning about five oClock, and meet at the place agreed on. The party arriving first shall wait for the other

2. The weapons shall be pistols not exceeding eleven inches in the barrel. The distance ten paces.

3. The choice of positions to be determined by lot.

4. The parties having taken their positions one of the seconds to be determined by lot (after having ascertained that both parties are ready) shall loudly and distinctly give the word "present" ~~and fire~~"— If one of the parties fires, and the other hath not fired, the opposite, word shall say one, two, three, fire, and he shall then fire or lose his shot. a snap or flash is a fire

Monday.
11 July 1804.

started taking high-school-level math classes when they were still in middle school—something Lin couldn't do, no matter how hard he tried.

"But after *Hamilton*, you can retire the Burr perspective, right?"

"No!" he says. "It's not like a jacket I can take off." He is smiling but he is serious.

"Yeah, but *you wrote* Hamilton. I've read your press."

"I have so much to do!"

High-octane strivers don't operate in a vacuum: There are all those *other* high-octane strivers around. Until the country has enough brass rings for everybody to grab (and maybe even then), being Alexander Hamilton, the all-American overachiever, also means being Aaron Burr: restless, watchful, unsatisfied.

"So you're still going to write like you're running out of time?"

"Because I am."

ABOVE:
Arrangements for the Hamilton/Burr duel—July 11, 1804.

YOUR OBEDIENT SERVANT

BURR: How does Hamilton,
An arrogant,
Immigrant, orphan,
Bastard, whoreson
Somehow endorse
Thomas Jefferson, his enemy,
A man he's despised since the beginning,
Just to keep me from winning?
I wanna be in the room where it happens—[1]

BURR, COMPANY: The room where it happens.
The room where it happens.

BURR: You've kept me from—

BURR, COMPANY: The room where it happens.

BURR: For the last time.

Burr begins to write a letter.

[1] Sometimes there's a perfect reprise so quickly. Burr should be happy—he's ascended to the second-highest office in the land. But it's an empty victory. Jefferson has just made clear that while Burr may be vice president, Jefferson trusts him about as far as he can throw him. "The Room Where It Happens" is the only thing to evoke here.

[2] Originally, my lyrics for these letters were super historically accurate, but I could feel us losing the audience. I figured, if they can't speak plainly here, then when?

Dear Alexander:

I am slow to anger,[2]
But I toe the line
As I reckon with the
        effects
Of your life on mine.
I look back on where
        I've failed,
And in every place
        I checked,
The only common thread
        has been your
        disrespect.
Now you call me
        "amoral,"
A "dangerous disgrace,"
If you've got something
        to say,
Name a time and place,
Face to face.

I have the honor to be
Your Obedient Servant,
A dot Burr.

CHAPTER XXX

Hamilton writes a letter in response.

HAMILTON: Mr. Vice President,
I am not the reason no one trusts you.
No one knows what you believe.
I will not equivocate on my opinion,
I have always worn it on my sleeve.
Even if I said what you think I said,
You would need to cite a more specific grievance.
Here's an itemized list of thirty years of disagreements.[3]

BURR: Sweet Jesus.

HAMILTON: Hey, I have not been shy
I am just a guy in the public eye
Tryin' to do my best for our republic.
I don't wanna fight.
But I won't apologize for doing what's right.

I have the honor to be Your Obedient Servant,
A dot Ham.

BURR: Careful how you proceed, good man.
Intemperate indeed, good man.
Answer for the accusations I lay at your feet or prepare to bleed, good man.

HAMILTON: Burr, your grievance is legitimate.
I stand by what I said, every bit of it. [4]
You stand only for yourself.

It's what you do.
I can't apologize because it's true.

BURR: Then stand, Alexander.
Weehawken. Dawn.
Guns. Drawn.

HAMILTON: You're on.

BURR, HAMILTON: I have the honor to be your obedient servant,

HAMILTON: A dot Ham.

BURR: A dot Burr.

[3] This is my *Parks & Recreation* homage—such a Leslie Knope thing to do.

[4] This is a fun one to play, because Hamilton understands the consequences of not apologizing, yet refuses to back down. That allows me to calibrate the degrees of stubbornness, anger, and regret differently every night. Playing contradictions is fun.

In the musical of my life after I'm long gone, my wife Vanessa is going to be the one who steps forward as the hero. Vanessa is not particularly fond of musicals—she only likes good ones. She is not effusive in her praise, or boastful. But when I looked up from that Chernow book and said "I think this is a hip-hop musical," she didn't laugh, or roll her eyes. She just said, "That sounds cool." And that was all I needed to get started. As I fell in love with the idea of a love triangle between Eliza, Alexander, and Angelica, she said, "Can you have Angelica rap? That would be cool."

I am someone who is so averse to travel that I wrote a whole musical about not wanting to leave my block in Washington Heights. It was Vanessa who booked us trips and time away from New York. "You don't get any writing done here because life keeps popping up." Thanks to her, *Hamilton* was written in Mexico, Spain, Nevis, Sagaponack, St. Croix, Puerto Rico, The Dominican Republic—long trips where Vanessa would take me there and then leave me alone to write while she explored. She is my first audience, and she's a tough audience, so I know if I impress her I've cleared the highest possible bar. She'll come home from work and say, "Your king tune was stuck in my head all day—that's probably a good sign." This started out as a note trying to explain how my wife really *is* the 'best of wives and best of women,' but I'm trying to get at something more important—this show simply doesn't exist without Vanessa. It's a love letter *to* her.

BEST OF WIVES *and* BEST OF WOMEN[1]

———————◆———————

Hamilton is writing. Eliza enters.

ELIZA: Alexander come back to sleep.

HAMILTON: I have an early meeting out of town.

ELIZA: It's still dark outside.

HAMILTON: I know. I just need to write something down.

ELIZA: Why do you write like you're running out of time?

HAMILTON: Shhh.

ELIZA: Come back to bed. That would be enough.

HAMILTON: I'll be back before you know I'm gone.

ELIZA: Come back to sleep.

HAMILTON: This meeting's at dawn.

ELIZA: Well, I'm going back to sleep.

Hamilton kisses Eliza's hand.

HAMILTON: Hey. Best of wives and best of women.[2]

[2] I wept the whole time I wrote this scene—again, I can't tell you how many times my wife has woken up to me writing. She is the sleepiest.

XXXI

HOW THE
DUEL WAS FOUGHT,

---

and REWRITTEN, and FOUGHT AGAIN,

AS THE CLOCK RAN OUT

TWO BULLETS FLEW. THAT MUCH IS clear. One made a harmless journey through a cedar tree 12 feet off the ground. The other opened a hole two inches wide in the abdomen of Alexander Hamilton. Every other important aspect of his duel with Aaron Burr is a murky matter of speculation. Who shot first? Who aimed where? Why?

In script meetings throughout the show's development, brisk conversations about the best way to stage this or that scene would slow and sometimes halt when those few seconds in Weehawken came up. Then the room would begin to sound like a history seminar, as people compared diverging accounts, weighed evidence, and began a lot of sentences with, "Or, *maybe* . . ."

Lin and his collaborators could draw on two eyewitness accounts to the duel—accounts that don't agree. Nathaniel Pendleton, Hamilton's second for the duel, said Hamilton only pulled the trigger reflexively after being struck. That is why, on the boat ride back to New York, the stricken Hamilton warned people to be careful with his gun: He thought it was still loaded. But Burr's second, William P. Van Ness, said that Hamilton clearly fired first, and *of course* he aimed at Burr—he just missed. If that is true, then Hamilton got what he had coming at the hands of a deadlier rival.

Lin decided to ignore both these accounts, and listen to Hamilton himself. In a letter to be opened after his death, he explained that he didn't want to fight Burr. He claimed to have a religious scruple against dueling, and was only going through with it because of a "public prejudice" in favor of the practice. If he refused, he would lose

his usefulness in future crises that were sure to threaten his beloved Union. He had to go to Weehawken, and he had to hold a loaded gun, but he didn't have to fire it at Aaron Burr.

But this only cracked open another, more vexing set of questions. How could Hamilton be so cavalier about his possible death? Was the duel an elaborate way to commit suicide, as some historians believe? He was grief-stricken over Philip's death, a tragedy that also drove his daughter Angelica mad. Or maybe he saw the duel as a way to secure his legacy—a final expression of what Lin called his "martyrdom death wish." Or maybe Hamilton was playing a badass game of chess, wagering that his death would take the dangerous Burr off the board forever.

Throughout 2013 and 2014, Lin's collaborators waited to learn which of these theories he would endorse. His decision would determine how they would depict that baffling morning in Weehawken, which was sure to be the climax of the night. When Lin finally made up his mind about the question, he picked an option that nobody expected: He wasn't going to answer it.

"It's not a whodunit to me, this story," he says. "I'm not interested in weighting pros and cons. And I don't think we really think that way as humans. I don't think we go, '*This, this, this,* and *this,* and so I'm going to fire into the air.' When you're in that adrenalized state, I think there's a lot of things at play."

Just before the run at the Public, Lin wrote lines for Hamilton that traced a thought as it "pinged around in his brain." Time would stop, and Hamilton would think about the prospect of imminent death. "I don't run or fire my gun

/ I let it be," he would say. And though he wouldn't explain his decision, he would announce it: "I've got to throw away my shot." The lines would rhyme, but there would be no music behind them. In other words, at the climax of the show, Lin veered away from hip-hop, and revived the old methods of verse drama, the same ones that Shakespeare used to give shape and order to jumbled thoughts.

Lin said that he was "very happy" with how it played Off-Broadway. Most people were. Oskar wasn't.

"Lin has a resistance to wrapping it up neatly, or explaining things, or closing it off. And I admire that," he says. "I told him at one point, 'You know, I have the same notes for you I have for Shakespeare.' He refuses to tell you." The problem, as Oskar saw it, is that a character who defined himself in Act One by his refusal to throw away his shot needed to tell the audience what changed in him that made him do the opposite when his life was on the line.

Once the show got on its feet at the Public, Lin and Tommy began having regular meetings with Oskar and Jeffrey to discuss script revisions. Jeffrey brought to the conversation his expertise with Broadway musicals, knowing how certain moments needed to pop for an audience of 1,300 people. Oskar brought his expertise as a dramaturg, his insistence that characters define themselves through their choices. He used those meetings to stay on Lin about the duel. Both of them used the same phrase to describe his dramaturgical technique: "pushing and pushing."

Oskar kept it up throughout the spring and into the summer, even after the Broadway run began. In late July, he tried one last approach. He asked Lin, "What if it's not a fait accompli at the top of the duel?" That is, what if Hamilton goes into the duel intending to throw away his shot, but still wrestling with the decision?

Lin perked up. "That to me is inherently more dramatic," he says.

A few days before the critics arrived, Lin rewrote a half dozen lines that changed the whole song. Statements turned into questions. Instead of merely reviewing his life, Hamilton now searched it for the answer to his newly stated dilemma: "Do I run or fire my gun or let it be?" Lin's performance changed along with the text. At the Public, he had sounded defiant when delivering his final line, "Raise a glass to freedom." Now he sounded vulnerable, unsure. When the bullet struck, people in the audience gasped.

"That's exactly what you want when you're producing *Romeo and Juliet*," Lin says. "Juliet, just wake up before he drinks the thing!' And we know what's gonna happen! We know they're both gonna die! But if it's a good production, you gasp anyway. And that's what we're after here. By Oskar pushing and pushing, he got us to a place where we get the audience gasping."

Of course, Hamilton is only half the duel. Burr, ever-inscrutable, presented his own puzzles. Did he go to Weehawken to scare Hamilton, or was he carried away by rage, or was he really a sociopath, seeking to murder a rival in

cold blood? Just as Lin decided to leave some of Hamilton's motivation unexplained, Leslie made no ultimate decision about Burr. In fact, Leslie isn't sure, from night to night, which version of Hamilton's killer is going to show up. "If I'm not shocked by the way the show ends, I'm not happy," he says. "I want the thing to feel off the *rails*. And *alive*."

After six years of writing and rewriting, and staging and restaging—a process that ended mere days before time ran out—Hamilton and Burr's duel remains mysterious even to the actors performing it.

ABOVE:
Replicas of Alexander Hamilton's dueling pistols, as used in Hamilton.

The WORLD WAS WIDE ENOUGH[1]

— ◆ —

[1] Much later in life, Burr read Laurence Sterne's novel *Tristram Shandy*. The book has a scene wherein somebody catches an annoying fly but decides not to kill it, saying, "This world surely is wide enough to hold both thee and me." Burr reportedly said, "Had I read Sterne more and Voltaire less, I should have known the world was wide enough for Hamilton and me." If he was joking, it was a wicked joke. But sometimes the jokes we choose to tell are the ones in which we reveal ourselves. The notion of the world being wide enough for all of us is a heartbreaker, because it's true. So I took out Sterne and Voltaire and kept the heartbreaker.

[2] This is historically true. It also requires the actor playing Hamilton to wear glasses on and off throughout the show, so the detail doesn't come out of nowhere at the duel. The number of times I've misplaced my glasses offstage....

MALE COMPANY: One two three four

FULL COMPANY (EXCEPT HAMILTON AND BURR): Five six seven eight nine—

BURR: There are ten things you need to know.

COMPANY: Number one!

BURR: We rowed across the Hudson at dawn.
My friend William P. Van Ness signed on
    as my—

BURR AND COMPANY: Number two!

BURR: Hamilton arrived with his crew:
Nathaniel Pendleton and a doctor that he knew.

COMPANY: Number three!

BURR: I watched Hamilton examine the terrain.
I wish I could tell you what was happ'ning in
    his brain.
This man has poisoned my political pursuits!

COMPANY: Most disputes die and no one
shoots! Number four!

BURR: Hamilton drew first position.
Looking, to the world, like a man on a mission.
This is a soldier with a marksman's ability.
The doctor turned around so he could have
    deniability.

COMPANY: Five!

BURR: Now I didn't know this at the time, but
we were—

BURR, PHILIP:	**HAMILTON:**
Near the same spot your son died, is that why—	Near the same spot my son died, is that why—

COMPANY: Six!

BURR: He examined his gun with such rigor?
I watched as he methodically fiddled with the
    trigger.

COMPANY: Seven!

BURR: Confession time? Here's what I got.
My fellow soldiers'll tell you I'm a terrible shot.

COMPANY: Number eight!

BURR, HAMILTON, MEN: Your last chance to
    negotiate.
Send in your seconds see if they can set the
    record straight.

Pendleton & Van Ness meet in the middle to speak, but it is Burr & Hamilton we see, staring at each other across the way.

BURR: They won't teach you this in your
    classes,
But look it up, Hamilton was wearing his
    glasses.[2]
Why? If not to take deadly aim?
It's him or me, the world will never be the same.
I had only one thought before the slaughter:

This man will not make an orphan of my
   daughter.

COMPANY: Number nine.

BURR: Look him in the eye, aim no higher.
Summon all the courage you require.
Then count:

COMPANY: One two three four five six seven
   eight nine
Number ten paces! Fire—

***Burr fires a shot. Before Hamilton is hit, the
action freezes.***

HAMILTON: I imagine death so much it feels
   more like a memory. [3]
Is this is where it gets me, on my feet, several
   feet ahead of me?
I see it coming, do I run or fire my gun or
   let it be?
There is no beat, no melody.
Burr, my first friend, my enemy,
May be the last face I ever see?
If I throw away my shot, is this how you
   remember me?
What if this bullet is my legacy?

Legacy. What is a legacy?
It's planting seeds in a garden you never get
   to see.
I wrote some notes at the beginning of a song
   someone will sing for me.
America, you great unfinished symphony,
You sent for me.
You let me make a difference.
A place where even orphan immigrants can
   leave their fingerprints and rise up.
I'm running out of time, I'm running and my
   time's up.
Wise up. Eyes up.
I catch a glimpse of the other side.

Laurens leads a soldiers' chorus on the other
   side.
My son is on the other side.
He's with my mother on the other side.
Washington is watching from the other side.

Teach me how to say goodbye.

Rise up, rise up, rise up,
Eliza

My love, take your time.
I'll see you on the other side.

Hamilton raises his pistol.

HAMILTON: Raise a glass to freedom . . .

BURR, COMPANY: He aims his pistol at the sky.

BURR: Wait!

Burr fires a shot. Hamilton goes down.

BURR: I strike him, right between his ribs.
I walk towards him, but I am ushered away.
They row him back across the Hudson.
I get a drink.

COMPANY:
Aaaah
Aaaah
Aaaah

BURR: I hear wailing in the streets.

COMPANY:
Aaaah
Aaaah
Aaaah

BURR: Somebody tells me, "You better hide."

[3] Sometimes Tommy Kail just calls 'em right. At the end of 2014, we were making our final push in rehearsal before starting tech at the Public, and I still hadn't written Hamilton's side of the duel. He looked at me and said, "I feel like it's going to be a New Year's Baby." Which meant he thought that the answer would come to me on my only day off. Well, cut to January 1, 2015. My infant son is asleep on my chest, my wife asleep, our dog between us on the bed. And as I lay there with only the sound of Sebastian's breathing, I realize that silence is the one thing we haven't done. The whole show. It's been, to borrow from Act One, non-stop. I place Sebastian back in the bed and walk the dog, beginning to put together this final soliloquy.

COMPANY:
Aaaah
Aaaah
Aaaah

BURR: They say

BURR, ANGELICA: Angelica and Eliza—

BURR: Were both at his side when he died.
Death doesn't discriminate
Between the sinners and the saints,
It takes and it takes and it takes.
History obliterates.
In every picture it paints,
It paints me and all my mistakes.
When Alexander aimed

At the sky,
He may have been the first one to die,
But I'm the one who paid for it.

I survived, but I paid for it.

Now I'm the villain in your history.
I was too young and blind to see.

I should've known.
I should've known
The world was wide enough for both
     Hamilton and me.
The world was wide enough for both
     Hamilton and me.

XXXII

WHAT IS A LEGACY?

Or, a Sketch of

OPENING NIGHT,

AND WHAT CAME AFTER,

AND WHAT MIGHT COME NEXT

*L*IN COULDN'T SEE THE PEOPLE, BUT the people could see Lin.

He entered at the back of the stage and strode all the way to the front. "What's your name, man?" asked Leslie, and he replied, "*Alexander Hamilton.*" The audience roared. For 27 seconds he stood there, bombarded by a crowd he couldn't see. (Afterwards, he compared the sensation to death: the bright lights, the screaming, the void.) Finally he gave a slight nod to signal that they had better let him finish the song. It was August 6, 2015, and the opening night performance of *Hamilton* had begun.

The first time Lin performed that song publicly, there had been a few hundred people in front of him

at the White House, and he had only Lac by his side. Now there were 1,300 people in the audience, 20 other performers onstage, 10 musicians in the pit, and a dozen dressers and stage managers backstage. All of them turned the dial all the way up that night, trying to make it the best possible show for their families and the various VIPs. It wasn't the most technically precise performance, but it was the most impassioned: "The Room Where It Happens," which had grown into precisely the showstopper that Andy hoped it would be, got applause *before it ended.*

Nearly three hours later, Lin exited the way he had entered, disappearing upstage after the duel. But Hamilton's death doesn't end his story. The last song in the show captures the bitter historical truth that every one of Hamilton's enemies outlived him, and they did all they could to efface his memory. By ending with Hamilton's afterlife, not his death, the show asks us to think about what we leave behind when we're gone: It invites us to think about legacies.

Hamilton thought about them a lot. So does Lin. "I think we all dream—or it might be just me—that when we pass on, the people we love are going to keep us alive in some way, whether that's talking about us or keeping our picture up," he says. He thinks about his grandfather, who lived in a small town in Puerto Rico, occupying a position roughly equivalent to George Bailey's in *It's a Wonderful Life*. When he died, crowds of mourners filled the streets. ("Like the beginning of *Evita*," Lin says.) He thinks, too, about the legacy of his father, Luis, who has spent decades as a political consultant and activist, who has helped to get mayors elected, who was a constant presence around the show during its development. "My dad will shut down New York when he dies, or at least Latino New York, political New York," Lin says.

As the show depicts, there was widespread grief when Hamilton died, but it passed quickly, leaving his legacy to be protected by one person: Eliza. She lived for 50 years

"Her whole life was to have her husband's story be told, and we're about to open this big honking Broadway musical about him," he says. On opening night, standing under the Rodgers's marquee, he realized that if Eliza's struggle was the element of Hamilton's story that had inspired him the most, then the show itself was a part of her legacy. To borrow an image from his script, she had planted seeds in

after his death, and devoted them to maintaining his reputation, to publishing his papers, to reminding future generations of what he had achieved. Serving his legacy didn't just mean commemorating him, though: It also meant continuing his work. She crusaded against slavery, as Hamilton had. And this widow of an orphan helped to found the first private orphanage in New York. That's the real power of a legacy: We tell stories of people who are gone because like any powerful stories, they have the potential to inspire, and to change the world.

A new thought about legacies struck Lin on opening night, and several hundred people got to watch it happen. He presented that day's Ham4Ham show, the short performance that one or several company members (or surprise guests) give outside the theater to entertain people who had entered the lottery for front-row seats. In honor of opening night, he returned to the place where his *Hamilton* experience had started: He read the first few pages of Ron Chernow's book, an account of Eliza's lonely struggle on behalf of Alexander's legacy. He had read these passages dozens of times. But that day, he started to cry.

a garden that she didn't get to see, and one of them turned out to be *Hamilton*.

"Is the ghost of Alexander Hamilton nonplussed that a Nuyorican kid has written a giant musical about his life? Probably!" says Lin. "He's gonna go, '*What's a Nuyorican?*'"

———————— • ————————

A CARAVAN OF DOUBLE-DECKER BUSES was ferrying the audience across town and down the West Side Highway when the reviews went online. The consensus was that *Hamilton* had grown more polished and more powerful in its uptown incarnation, that it was "radical," "stunning in its audaciousness," "vibrantly democratic," and "audaciously ambitious." Somehow it really did live up to its mountainous hype. Nobody seemed to mind that it wasn't 15 minutes shorter than it had been at the Public.

The buses deposited everybody at Chelsea Piers, a sports and fitness complex along the Hudson River. For Jeffrey, the choice of Pier 60, the hangar-sized party space, had been instinctive: He has been throwing

ABOVE:
Opening night curtain call—August 6, 2015.

"The critical consensus was that Hamilton *had GROWN MORE POLISHED AND MORE POWERFUL IN ITS UPTOWN INCARNATION . . . Somehow it really did live up to its mountainous hype."*

opening-night parties there since *Rent* back in 1996. But since he thinks that *Hamilton* is the best show he has produced, he was motivated to make this the best opening-night party he has thrown. It meant, among other things, that only one band would do. The Roots, the best live act in hip-hop, tore the place up.

"One love, one game, one desire," rapped Black Thought. "One flame, one bonfire, let it burn higher."

At the end of hourlong set, he looked over the dancing crowd, several hundred strong. "Where's my man? Lin-Manuel Miranda."

Lin was standing directly in front the stage, wearing a dark suit, his hair in a ponytail: Travolta in *Pulp Fiction*, but Puerto Rican. Hands pushed him onto the stage. For the third time that day, he turned to face an audience. He looked delighted. Also alarmed. Black Thought handed him a mic, Questlove lay down a beat, and Lin's freestyling instincts kicked in.

"I worked for seven years, these are the fruits," he rapped. "I'm standing onstage with the fucking Roots!" Everybody screamed.

Rapping alongside giants of hip-hop was only the most visible sign of how radically Lin's life had changed. "This puts my dreams to shame," he said of the whole experience in a laudatory segment on *60 Minutes*, the existence of which underscores the point he was making. Thanks to *Hamilton*, the word "genius" started popping up in front of his name before he was named a MacArthur "genius" fellow. Extraordinarily eminent people started inviting him to do things, to go places, to write this, to say that. Performing seven shows a week can be a grind, he says, but it also grants him seven pockets of peace in his hurricane of a life.

Many of his castmates can tell similar stories. For all the subtle, long-aborning things that will change because of *Hamilton*, the revolution in some of their lives has been immediate and profound. By opening night, Pippa, Leslie, Renée, Daveed, and the rest were becoming stars. People wanted to know about the clothes they wore, where they ate, the kind of music they listened to. They appeared on magazine covers, they went to stadiums to sing the national anthem.

"I get to be in rooms I have no business being in," Anthony says. He can't put into words how this feels. He mimes his forehead blowing up.

———◆———

A VOICE ON THE P.A. SYSTEM INVITED everybody to move onto the long platform that runs along the edge of Pier 60, facing the Hudson. A thousand people streamed out into the dark.

Considering the story that brought everybody together that night, walking out there felt like a pilgrimage. If you had been standing on this exact spot in the early hours of July 11, 1804, you would have seen Alexander Hamilton being rowed from a Manhattan pier (downstream, on your left) to the dueling grounds of Weehawken (upstream, on your right). In fact, if you had waved to him, he might have waved back, for we know that he was looking at New York on that journey. One of his last observations before Burr shot him was to reflect on his city and how much it had grown, and his great hopes for the people who would find their way there, as he had.

The crowd out there on this night was a happy jumble of celebrities, producers, spouses, press, and friends. Lin and Tommy were laughing about something, or everything. Andy stood behind his wife, Elly, hugging her and beaming: They had learned that the chemo had worked, and that their daughter, Sofia, was going to be fine.

A few people pointed out something unusual about this opening-night crowd: Lots and lots of parents of *Hamilton* cast members had come to celebrate what their children had made. Lin's mother and father came from Upper Manhattan, and Anthony's came from Brooklyn. Jasmine's father came from Manhattan and her mother from upstate. Neil's parents drove down from Buffalo. Those were just the New Yorkers.

Stephanie's parents came from New Jersey. So did Oak's mom. Pippa's parents came from Chicago, as did Austin's. Carleigh's mother came up from Delray Beach, Florida, and Ephraim's came from West Palm Beach, and Ariana's came from Raleigh, North Carolina. Leslie's parents came up from Philly; Sasha's from Macon, Georgia. Renée's father came from Detroit and her mother from Houston. Daveed's mother came from Northern California, Andrew's came from Southern, and Voltaire's came from Bakersfield, which is in-between. Chris's mother came from his hometown, Cairo, Illinois, and Alysha's from hers, Dallas, and Seth's from his, in Ohio.

Plot those places on a map, and you'd see that the company drew on extraordinarily talented performers who hailed from all over America. They worked insanely hard to get to opening night. And the parents who came to cheer them on sacrificed God-knows-what to make it possible for them to have a career in the first place. Every performance of *Hamilton* features 21 performers giving 21 performances, and each one is a legacy in its own right. No wonder it was such a good party.

All those mothers and fathers would have one more story to tell when they got home: Jeffrey had ordered up fireworks. In a final flurry of creativity, Lin had put together a playlist to go with them. He mixed up all sorts of styles, but he put special emphasis on New York anthems of every variety: old ones like Frank Sinatra's rendition of "New York, New York," new ones like Jay Z and Alicia Keys's "Empire State of Mind," even a very new one, "The Schuyler Sisters." It sounded right at home in that company.

The music started. The show began. Everybody cheered and lots of people sang along. The sky flashed and the river turned colors. It looked like the Fourth of July.

WHO LIVES, WHO DIES, WHO TELLS YOUR STORY?

—◆—

WASHINGTON: Let me tell you what I wish I'd
known
When I was young and dreamed of glory.
You have no control:

WASHINGTON, COMPANY: Who lives,
Who dies,
Who tells your story?

BURR: President Jefferson:

JEFFERSON: I'll give him this: His financial
system is a work of genius . . . I couldn't
undo it if I tried.
And I tried.

WASHINGTON, COMPANY: Who lives,
Who dies,
Who tells your story?

BURR: President Madison:

MADISON: He took our country from bankruptcy
to prosperity. I hate to admit it, but he doesn't get
enough credit for all the credit he gave us.

WASHINGTON, COMPANY: Who lives,
Who dies,
Who tells your story?

ANGELICA: Every other Founding Father story
gets told.
Every other Founding Father gets to grow old.

BURR: And when you're gone, who remembers
your name?
Who keeps your flame?

BURR, MEN:	**ANGELICA, WOMEN:**
Who tells your story?	Who tells your story?
Who tells your story?	Your story?

Eliza enters.

WOMEN: Eliza.[1]

ELIZA: I put myself back in the narrative.

WOMEN: Eliza.

ELIZA: I stop wasting time on tears.
I live another fifty years.
It's not enough.

COMPANY: Eliza.

ELIZA: I interview every soldier who fought by
your side.

MULLIGAN, LAFAYETTE, LAURENS: She
tells our story.

ELIZA: I try to make sense of your thousands of
pages of writings.[2]
You really do write like you're running out of—

ELIZA, COMPANY: Time.

ELIZA: I rely on—

ELIZA, ANGELICA: Angelica.

ELIZA: While she's alive—

ELIZA, ANGELICA: We tell your story.

ELIZA: She is buried in Trinity Church, [3]

ELIZA, ANGELICA: Near you.

ELIZA: When I needed her most, she was right on—

ELIZA, COMPANY: Time.

ELIZA: And I'm still not through.
I ask myself, "What would you do if you had more—

ELIZA, COMPANY: Time?"

ELIZA: The Lord, in his kindness,
He gives me what you always wanted.
He gives me more—

ELIZA, COMPANY (EXCEPT HAMILTON):
Time.

ELIZA: I raise funds in D.C. for the
Washington Monument.

WASHINGTON: She tells my story.

ELIZA: I speak out against slavery.
You could have done so much more if you
only had—

ELIZA, COMPANY: Time.

ELIZA: And when my time is up, have I
done enough?

	COMPANY (EXCEPT
ELIZA:	**HAMILTON):**
Will they tell our story?	Will they tell your story?

ELIZA: Oh. Can I show you what I'm proudest of?

COMPANY (EXCEPT HAMILTON):
The orphanage.

ELIZA: I establish the first private orphanage in
New York City. [4]

COMPANY (EXCEPT HAMILTON):
The orphanage.

ELIZA: I help to raise hundreds of children.
I get to see them growing up.

COMPANY (EXCEPT HAMILTON):
The orphanage.

ELIZA: In their eyes I see you, Alexander.
I see you every—

ELIZA, COMPANY (EXCEPT HAMILTON):
Time

ELIZA: And when my time is up?
Have I done enough?

| **ELIZA:** | **COMPANY:** |
| Will they tell my story? | Will they tell your story? |

Hamilton enters.

ELIZA: Oh, I can't wait to see you again.
It's only a matter of—

ELIZA, COMPANY: Time.

Eliza sees Hamilton. He takes her hand and leads her to the edge of the stage.

COMPANY:	**COMPANY:**
Will they tell your story?	
	Time . . .
Who lives, who dies,	
who tells your story? [5]	
	Time . . .
Will they tell your story?	
	Time . . .
Who lives, who dies—	

FULL COMPANY: Who tells your story?

THE END.

[3] This fact kills me. It's the line that made me cry the hardest in the writing of it—Angelica, near Alexander but not with him, for eternity.

[4] If this were a work of fiction, any screenwriting teacher would say, "Take it out, it's too on the nose." But Eliza's true legacy is in the futures of those children. She was the director of this orphanage for 27 years. The orphanage still exists in the form of the Graham Windham organization.

[5] Again, I'm so grateful that these words showed up for Washington to say way back in Act One. I knew they'd come in handy when we needed them.

EPILOGUE

THE BLACK FIRST PRESIDENT EXITED; the first black president appeared. On November 2, 2015, Chris Jackson and his castmates stood gaping offstage left as Barack Obama entered from stage right. The president (the real one, not the one Chris plays in the show) smiled and waved, waiting for the entrance applause to end.

"What'd I miss?" he said.

It would have blown the powder clear off George Washington's wig to imagine a half-Kenyan man becoming president. Yet there was Obama, his 43rd successor, raising funds to help elect his 44th. Democratic Party officials had arranged a special performance of *Hamilton*, guessing that donors would pay generously to see the hottest show in New York. They guessed right. It meant that six years after Lin had gotten a boost from his association with the White House, the White House was, improbably, getting a boost from Lin. Obama teased the audience about it: "You write a check and you listen to some boring politician talking—now that's commitment," he said. "Coming to this show—you don't get special props for this."

Obama rallied the troops that night by reviewing his legacy. This touched off another bout of historical vertigo. Didn't we just watch a president sum up his legacy, when Chris sang Washington's Farewell Address at the end of "One Last Time"? Past and present seemed to be tumbling together—a shimmery double exposure.

But the president had an aim beyond "reviewing the incidents of my administration," as Lin had said onstage about 45 minutes earlier. Obama wanted to make an argument about change, and how it comes to America. To do so, he turned to *Hamilton* again and again for illustration. "Part of what's so powerful about this performance is it reminds us of the vital, crazy, kinetic energy that's at the heart of America—that people who have a vision and a set of ideals can transform the world," he said. "Every single step of progress that we've made has been based on this notion that people can come together, and ideas can move like electricity through them, and a world can change."

This is a community organizer's vision of progress, one that Obama has advanced since before he became president. In the 2004 speech that made him a national figure overnight, he insisted that in spite of our outward differences, "there's not a black America and white America and Latino America and Asian America—there's the United States of America." One measure of America's health, then, is how warmly it embraces the diverse souls who live here. Obama found this spirit in *Hamilton* as well: "The idea of America that was represented here was more than just numbers, more than just statistics. It's about who we are, who's seen, who's recognized, whose histories are affirmed."

In spite of all the similarities between his worldview and the show's, Obama didn't try to claim it for a single political party. It is, he said, "the only thing Dick Cheney and I agree on." What's really striking, though, is the fact that Obama could locate so many parallels to his ideas in a historical drama. *Hamilton* depicts events that happened a long time ago; its ideas are, by definition, old. Why, then, do so many people greet them as bold and revelatory when Obama says them? For that matter, why do so many different kinds of people leave a performance of *Hamilton* feeling newly connected to their country?

Unless Lin made the whole thing up—and nobody has said that he did—it suggests that however innovative Obama's speeches and Lin's show might seem, they are, in fact, traditional. They don't reinvent the American character, they *renew* it. They remind us of something we forgot, something that fell as far out of sight as the posthumously neglected Alexander Hamilton, who spent his life defending one idea above all: "the necessity of *Union* to the respectability and happiness of this Country." Obama's speeches and Lin's show resonate so powerfully with their audiences because they find eloquent ways to revive Hamilton's revolution, the one that spurred Americans to see themselves and each other as fellow citizens in a sprawling, polyglot young republic. It's the change in thought and feeling that makes all the other changes possible.

The Obama presidency will end in January 2017, but the show that shares so much of its spirit will keep running.

At the Rodgers that night, the president all but anointed *Hamilton* as a keeper of the flame. His "primary message," he said, was to remind people of the need to keep hoping and to work together, but "this performance undoubtedly described it better than I ever could." The most important affinity that *Hamilton* will carry into its future isn't a specific message, though, political or otherwise: It's an underlying belief in stories, and their power to change the world.

Good community organizer that he is, the president knows that stories can be an engine for empathy, and a way to show people what they share. It's why he introduced himself, in that first big speech in 2004, by telling his own story. In the years to come, some of the many, many kids who are going to see and even perform *Hamilton* will be newly inspired to tell *their* stories too. Every time they do, the newly kaleidoscopic America will understand itself a little more.

"I can do that," they'll say. And if they're like Alexander Hamilton, they'll add, "And I can do it *better*."

LIN-MANUEL MIRANDA *(Book, Music, and Lyrics/Alexander Hamilton)* is the Tony and Grammy award–winning composer-lyricist-star of Broadway's *In the Heights*—winner of four 2008 Tony Awards including Best Musical, Best Orchestrations, and Best Choreography with Miranda receiving the award for Best Score. Additionally, he is the co-composer and co-lyricist of Broadway's Tony-nominated *Bring It On: The Musical* and provided Spanish translations for the 2009 Broadway revival of *West Side Story*. Miranda, along with Tom Kitt, won the 2014 Creative Arts Emmy for Best Original Music and Lyrics for their work on the 67th Annual Tony Awards. In 2015, Miranda was named as a Fellow of the John D. and Catherine T. MacArthur Foundation. He lives with his family in New York City.

JEREMY McCARTER wrote cultural criticism for *New York* magazine and *Newsweek* before spending five years on the artistic staff of the Public Theater, where he created, directed, and produced the Public Forum series. He served on the jury of the Pulitzer Prize for Drama, and is writing a book about young American radicals during World War One. He lives with his family in Chicago.

The authors would like to thank: Candi Adams, Jason Bassett, Andy Blanken-buehler, John Buzzetti, Julie Bosman, Ron Chernow, Oskar Eustis, Kaitlin Fine, Jimmy Franco, Joanne Freeman, Ben Greenberg, Jennifer Joel, Tommy Kail, Stephanie Klemons, Alex Lacamoire, Derik Lee, Karen Leeds, Josh Lehrer, Tom McCann, Ginger Bartkoski Meagher, Luis Miranda, Riggs Morales, Vanessa Nadal, Lauren Nathan, Justin Nichols, Owen Panettieri, Jamie Raab, Sam Rudy, Jeffrey Seller, James Shapiro, Bill Sherman, Victoria Spencer, Nevin Steinberg, Ahmir Thompson, Tarik Trotter, Patrick Vassel, and Deanna Weiner

HAMILTON

Book, Music and Lyrics by

LIN-MANUEL MIRANDA

Inspired by the book Alexander Hamilton by
RON CHERNOW

This book was produced by

▢ **MELCHER MEDIA**

124 West 13th St., New York, NY 10011
www.melcher.com

President and CEO: Charles Melcher
Vice President and COO: Bonnie Eldon
Senior Editor/Producer: Lauren Nathan
Production Manager: Susan Lynch
Associate Digital Producer: Shannon Fanuko
Editorial Assistant: Victoria Spencer

Designed by Paul Kepple and Max Vandenberg
at Headcase Design

Melcher Media would like to thank: Chika Azuma,
Callie Barlow, Jess Bass, Kirk Caldwell, Karl Daum,
Barbara Gogan, Mary Hart, Betsy Hillman, Luke Jarvis,
Paul Kepple, Weronika Jurkiewicz, John Morgan, Vita
Newstetter, Kate Osba, Nola Romano, Julia Sourikoff,
Saif Tase, Zoe Valella, Max Vandenberg, Lee Wilcox,
Michelle Wolfe, and Megan Worman